Dissolution

The Soviet Bloc and After
Series Editor: Gail Lapidus

℘

Making and Breaking Democratic Transitions:
The Comparative Politics of Russia's Regions
By Vladimir Gel'man, Sergei Ryzhenkov, and Michael Brie
with Vladimir Avdonin, Boris Ovchinnikov, and Igor Semenov

Russian Strategic Modernization: Past and Future
By Nikolai Sokov, foreword by Benjamin S. Lambeth

Dissolution

Sovereignty and the Breakup of the Soviet Union

EDWARD W. WALKER

ROWMAN & LITTLEFIELD PUBLISHERS, INC.
Lanham • Boulder • New York • Oxford

BERKELEY PUBLIC POLICY PRESS
*Institute of Governmental Studies, University of California
Berkeley, California*

ROWMAN & LITTLEFIELD PUBLISHERS, INC.

Published in the United States of America
by Rowman & Littlefield Publishers, Inc.
A Member of the Rowman & Littlefield Publishing Group
4501 Forbes Boulevard, Suite 200, Lanham, Maryland 20706
www.rowmanlittlefield.com

P.O. Box 317, Oxford OX2 9RU, United Kingdom

British Library Cataloguing in Publication Information Available

Library of Congress Cataloging-in-Publication Data

Walker, Edward W.
    Dissolution : sovereignty and the breakup of the Soviet Union / Edward
W. Walker.
        p. cm. − (The Soviet bloc and after)
Includes bibliographical references and index.
    ISBN 0-7425-2452-3 (cloth : alk. paper) − ISBN 0-7425-2453-1 (pbk. :
alk. paper)
    1. Soviet Union–Politics and government–1985-1991. 2. Sovereignty.
I. Title. II. Series.
    DK288 .W348 2003
    320.1'5'0947—dc21

                                                                        2002156611

Printed in the United States of America

♾ ™ The paper used in this publication meets the minimum requirements of American
National Standard for Information Sciences—Permanence of Paper for Printed Library
Materials, ANSI/NISO Z39.48-1992.

This book is dedicated to the memory of my father, Peter Cuyler Walker.

Contents

Acknowledgments

This is a story that took too long in the telling. It began in 1997 as a paper for a joint research project, "Challenges to Sovereignty from Above and Below: Europe East and West after the Cold War," which was cosponsored by UC Berkeley's Center for Slavic and East European Studies and the Center for German and West European Studies. The bulk of the manuscript was completed while on leave from Berkeley in the 1997–98 academic year as a National Fellow at the Hoover Institution on War, Revolution, and Peace at Stanford University. I worked on it, more off than on, in the following years, filling in holes and making revisions after presenting chapters at various workshops and conferences. I am very appreciative of the patience that my colleagues, and even more my family, have shown for what must have seemed to be a perpetual "work-in-progress."

The book would not have been possible without support from the Hoover Institution, the Berkeley Program in Soviet and Post-Soviet Studies, and Berkeley's Institute of Slavic, East European, and Eurasian Studies. The Berkeley Public Policy Press of the Institute of Governmental Studies helped prepare the manuscript for publication. I am also very grateful for comments on earlier drafts from Victoria E. Bonnell, George W. Breslauer, Keith Darden, M. Steven Fish, John B. Dunlop, Stephen E. Hanson, Andrew C. Janos, Gail W. Lapidus, Yuri Slezkine, Ronald G. Suny, and Lucan Way. Jerry Lubenow of the Institute of Governmental Studies provided helpful editorial guidance, as did Susan

McEachern at Rowman & Littlefield. Maria Wolf was a careful and always co-operative copyeditor. Jan Plamper, a UC Berkeley Ph.D. candidate in history, was a diligent and insightful research assistant for the historical chapter.

The person to whom I am the most indebted for help, however, is Laura Henry, a Berkeley Ph.D. candidate in political science who was an outstanding research assistant as well as a constant source of encouragement and, on occasion, of firm reminders that I needed to transform a work-in-progress into a completed manuscript.

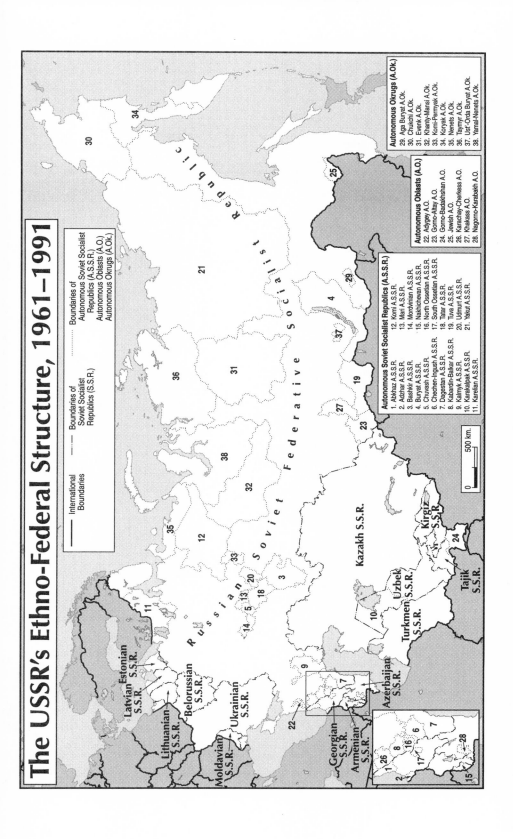

The USSR's Ethno-Federal Structure, 1961–1991

International Boundaries

--- Boundaries of Soviet Socialist Republics (S.S.R.)

.... Boundaries of Autonomous Soviet Socialist Republics (A.S.S.R.) Autonomous Oblasts (A.O.) Autonomous Okrugs (A.Ok.)

Autonomous Soviet Socialist Republics (A.S.S.R.)
1. Abkhaz A.S.S.R.
2. Adzhar A.S.S.R.
3. Bashkir A.S.S.R.
4. Buryat A.S.S.R.
5. Chuvash A.S.S.R.
6. Chechen-Ingush A.S.S.R.
7. Dagestan A.S.S.R.
8. Kabardin-Balkar A.S.S.R.
9. Kalmyk A.S.S.R.
10. Karakalpak A.S.S.R.
11. Karelian A.S.S.R.
12. Komi A.S.S.R.
13. Mari A.S.S.R.
14. Mordvinian A.S.S.R.
15. Nakhichevan A.S.S.R.
16. North Ossetian A.S.S.R.
17. South Ossetian A.S.S.R.
18. Tatar A.S.S.R.
19. Tuva A.S.S.R.
20. Udmurt A.S.S.R.
21. Yakut A.S.S.R.

Autonomous Oblasts (A.O.)
22. Adygey A.O.
23. Gorno-Altay A.O.
24. Gorno-Badakhstan A.O.
25. Jewish A.O.
26. Karachay-Cherkess A.O.
27. Khakass A.O.
28. Nagorno-Karabakh A.O.

Autonomous Okrugs (A.Ok.)
29. Aga Buryat A.Ok.
30. Chukchi A.Ok.
31. Evenk A.Ok.
32. Khanty-Mansi A.Ok.
33. Komi-Permyak A.Ok.
34. Koryak A.Ok.
35. Nenets A.Ok.
36. Taymyr A.Ok.
37. Ust'-Orda Buryat A.Ok.
38. Yamal-Nenets A.Ok.

0   500 km.

Russian Soviet Federative Socialist Republic

Latvian S.S.R.
Estonian S.S.R.
Lithuanian S.S.R.
Belorussian S.S.R.
Ukrainian S.S.R.
Moldavian S.S.R.
Georgian S.S.R.
Armenian S.S.R.
Azerbaijan S.S.R.
Kazakh S.S.R.
Uzbek S.S.R.
Turkmen S.S.R.
Kirgiz S.S.R.
Tajik S.S.R.

Chapter 1

Introduction

> As soon as the word "sovereignty" resounded in the air, the clock of history once again began ticking and all attempts to stop it were doomed. The last hour of the Soviet Empire was chiming. (Boris Yeltsin, *The Struggle for Russia*, 1996)

"Sovereignty" killed the Soviet Union. By "Soviet Union" I do not mean Soviet socialism as a regime type—that died from other causes. Rather I mean the Soviet Union as a territorial state. Nor am I suggesting that the attainment of "sovereignty" by the USSR's fifteen union republics caused the Soviet Union to fragment, which, depending on one's understanding of the term "sovereignty," would be a tautology. Instead, my claim is that, for reasons that I will set forth in what follows, the *concept* of "sovereignty," more than any other competitor such as "democracy," "liberty," or "markets," was used with great effect by the anti-union opposition in the union republics to challenge the authority of the USSR's central government. The political efficacy of the term helps explain both the fact of the USSR's dissolution and, even more clearly, its character—why, that is, the Soviet Union fragmented into fifteen, rather than five, or fifty, successor states.

The explanation for this outcome is less obvious than might be assumed. In the first place, one cannot look at a map of ethno-linguistic or religious groups in the Soviet Union and determine why the USSR broke up into fifteen successor states or deduce their borders. The USSR was a highly heterogeneous coun-

tautology (tauto Greek for I same) saying the same thing twice in different words.

heterogeneous: diverse in character

try, with 126 officially recognized "nationalities" (in Soviet parlance) in 1989, the year of the last Soviet census.[1] There were in addition numerous other ethnolinguistic groups, including some that were relatively large, that for various reasons were not afforded the status of a "nationality" by Soviet ethnographers.[2] Given this extensive diversity, it was inevitable that only a minority of the USSR's ethnic groups had their "own" eponymous administrative units in the Soviet federal system.[3] In March 1985, when Gorbachev came to power in Moscow, the USSR's federal hierarchy included the fifteen Soviet socialist republics (SSRs or "union republics") as well as thirty-eight ethnically defined "autonomies"—twenty autonomous Soviet socialist republics (ASSRs), eight autonomous oblasts (AOs), and ten autonomous districts (okrugs)—for a total of fifty-three ethnically defined territorial units.[4]

oblast - russian division or unit.

Why some nationalities were afforded administrative recognition while others were not, and why a particular "national territorial formation" had the status of union republic, autonomous republic, autonomous oblast, or okrug, was, like the designation of "nationality" itself, to a certain extent arbitrary.[5] Neither size of population nor territory was determinative—in many cases, lower-level units had more people and more land than units higher up the federal hierarchy.[6] Nor were higher-level units necessarily more homogeneous than those lower down the administrative ladder.[7]

There was another, even more counterintuitive aspect to the way the USSR broke apart. Contrary to popular assumptions, it had little to do with the distribution of nationalist or separatist aspirations. In certain cases, such as Estonia, Latvia, Lithuania, and Georgia, nationalist and separatist sentiments at both elite and popular levels were indeed widespread and deeply felt by the end of the Gorbachev era. In others, however, these sentiments were shared by a decided minority, as evidenced most clearly in the Gorbachev-sponsored referendum of 17 March 1991 on the preservation of the union, which was held a mere nine months before the USSR passed into history. Although six union republics—Azerbaijan, Estonia, Latvia, Moldavia (Moldova), Lithuania, and Georgia—announced an official boycott,[8] overall turnout elsewhere was high, and of those voting, 76.4 percent expressed their support for the union, with large majorities voting "yes" in Belorussia (Belarus), the five Central Asian republics, Russia, and Ukraine. Moreover, in the Central Asian republics, and to a lesser extent in Belarus, political elites were overwhelmingly in favor of preserving the union. Even in Russia, as we will see, it is far from clear that Yeltsin, let alone a majority of the republic's political elite, wanted the union completely destroyed. In this sense, rather than "winning" their independence, it would perhaps be closer to the truth to say that Kazakhstan, Kyrgyzstan, Turkmenistan, Uzbekistan, Tajikistan, and Belarus, and arguably even Russia and Ukraine, had independence forced upon them.[9]

The outcome of the Soviet disintegration for the autonomies, on the other hand, was the mirror image of that of the union republics. Whereas *all* of the union republics would receive international recognition as independent states in late 1991, *none* of the autonomies would do so, again despite great variation in demand for independence. Indeed, the separatist aspirations of many Chechens, Abkhaz, Ossetians in South Ossetia, and Armenians in Karabakh were such that they would take up arms in pursuit of independence. But despite victories on the battlefield and de facto political control of their territories, in no case would a subnational government located within the former union republics attain formal independence under international law. Clearly, the intensity of ethno-nationalist aspirations alone explains neither the fact nor the character of the USSR's dissolution.

Why, then, did the fifteen union republics, and only the fifteen union republics, become legally independent after the Soviet collapse? And why did the fragmentation occur precisely along the internal borders separating the union republics? An essential part of the answers to these questions, I will argue, is to be found in the institutions and mythologies of Soviet federalism, and particularly in the supposedly "sovereign" status of the fifteen ethnically defined union republics.

While this book is not explicitly comparative, powerful evidence of the role played by the institutions and norms of Soviet federalism in the breakup is suggested by comparative inference.[10] There were a total of eight countries in Eastern Europe that abandoned communism at more or less the same time as the Soviet Union—Albania, Bulgaria, Czechoslovakia, the German Democratic Republic (GDR), Hungary, Poland, Romania, and Yugoslavia. Of these, only two—Czechoslovakia and Yugoslavia—fractured. Both were ethnic federations, and both were in large measure modeled on the Soviet federal system, including the claim that their constituent units were "sovereign." The Yugoslav constitution described the federation's six constituent republics as "states" whose statehood reflected the "sovereignty" of their people, while the Czechoslovak constitution described the Czech and Slovak republics as "sovereign states."[11] In contrast, *all* of the nonfederal states—Albania, Bulgaria, the German Democratic Republic, Hungary, Poland, and Romania—remained intact (the GDR was absorbed in toto by the Federal Republic of Germany). Only in one case have any first-level (i.e., republics rather than autonomies) federal units remained formally united—the republics of Serbia and Montenegro remain part of a unified state, but it is yet unclear whether this common state will long survive.[12] Of the twenty-three first-level federal units of the former USSR, Czechoslovakia, and Yugoslavia,[13] then, only two are not fully independent today. And in each case, the internationally recognized borders of the region's twenty-two new states[14] are precisely the internal borders of the preexisting federations, despite the fact that many of those borders are ahistorical, arbitrary, and contested. Moreover, in not a single case to date has fragmentation gone beyond first-level federal units. The two former autonomies of Serbia (Kosovo and Vojvodina) have, like those in the former Soviet Union, remained legally a part of their "host" republic, despite the NATO air campaign of 1999 that forced the Yugoslav military to withdraw from Kosovo.[15] Like the Abkhaz, Chechens, Karabakh Armenians, South Ossetians, and Transdniestrians in the former Soviet Union, the Kosovars achieved a victory on the battlefield but failed to win international recognition for their republic as an independent state.

To some, the explanation for the breakup of the socialist federations is to be found in the rise of ethno-nationalist and separatist aspirations among the titular nationalities of the union republics. Numerous factors are adduced to account for these aspirations—the sheer extent of ethnic diversity in the region; historical legacies of interethnic resentment or enmity; modernization and the emergence of self-conscious national intelligentsias among minority peoples; regional disparities in wealth and income; economic distress in general and conflicts over shrinking national economies; the regional distribution effects of painful and disruptive economic reforms; incentives for political elites in democratizing polities to seek popular support by "playing the ethnic card"; and "contagion" effects whereby national mobilization in one area promotes increased national consciousness and mobilization in others.

But these factors alone cannot fully explain why these three states, the USSR, Czechoslovakia, and Yugoslavia, and only these three states, broke apart, for the obvious reason that the states that did not fragment shared many of these same characteristics and confronted similar problems. Romania, Hungary, and Bulgaria had significant minority populations; in all cases, the transition from central planning to a market economy proved extremely painful; in all cases, there were regional disparities in wealth and income; in all cases, political elites, both central and local, had incentives to mobilize public support by identifying some ethnic enemy; and contagion effects would have spread indiscriminately, not just to federations. The one property that clearly distinguished the USSR, Czechoslovakia, and Yugoslavia was a federal system in which constituent units were defined ethnically and were said to be "sovereign," and which was legitimated by "Leninist" norms of socialist federalism. At the least, it seems clear that the institutions of Soviet ethno-federalism and nationality policy served as an efficient lubricant of fragmentation.

In this sense, then, this book emphasizes the supply side, rather than the demand side, of the Soviet dissolution. It is not directed at explaining the emergence of ethno-nationalism or the dynamics of nationalist mobilization during perestroika in the union republics or the autonomies.[16] Neither does it attempt to explain why separatist aspirations emerged so quickly and grew so powerful in some union republics but not others, or in some autonomies but not others. Instead, I take the emergence of separatist aspirations and the variation in demand for granted and ask why, despite this variation, and despite a lack of evident popular or elite preference for the dissolution in a majority of union republics, all fifteen union republics, but none of the autonomies, become independent.

How did Soviet-type federalism, nationality policy, and the sovereign status of the union republics contribute to the breakup? I will offer three principal answers. First, the institutions and normative claims of Soviet federalism empowered what I will call the antiunion opposition in the union republics as they demanded greater autonomy from "the center" and increasingly challenged the central leadership's authority. Second, that same institutional and normative legacy helped to limit the choices and influenced the preferences of Gorbachev and his allies as they devised what proved to be a catastrophic strategy for defending the territorial integrity of the Soviet state. And finally, the USSR's federal institutions provided the international community with a convenient legal and political formula for accommodating the Soviet dissolution that did not entail acceptance of unilateral secession from an internationally recognized state.

As we will see, the Soviet federal system and the status and legal rights of the union republics facilitated the emergence of the antiunion opposition in the union republics in some rather obvious, as well as some not so obvious, ways. They provided in the first place relatively clear (albeit sometimes contested) borders along which fragmentation could occur, although in this respect the union republics were no different than the autonomies. They also were responsible for the fact that ramified governmental structures—distinct legislatures, executive organs and ministerial bodies, and judicial systems—existed in the regions, structures that, once controlled by separatists, provided an organizational base for challenging the center. But again, in this they were no different from the autonomies. What leaders of the antiunion opposition in the union republics had that separatists in the autonomies did not was the ability to appeal to the formal rights and powers supposedly "guaranteed" the union republics by the Soviet constitution and federal law. And they could insist on these rights under cover of a term, "sovereignty," that had been legitimated by Lenin and was central to the regime's legitimizing claims about the normative superiority of Soviet-style federalism.

Indeed, one of the distinctive features of the Gorbachev reforms was that preexisting organizations (e.g., the hierarchy of soviets) and legal norms (e.g., the constitutional right of "freedom of speech, press, assembly, meetings, street processions, and demonstrations") that had previously either lacked authority or meaning became genuine and meaningful, albeit gradually and often as a result of a prolonged struggle with Soviet authorities.[17] While these organizations and rights had various functions under the old regime—above all, legitimation of Party rule and obfuscation of the regime's dictatorial quality—in many cases they are more accurately described as latent or noninstitutionalized institutions. The transformation of these previously formal institutions into real institutions that actually constrained behavior during the Gorbachev era was sometimes the result of deliberate policies by the reformist leadership in Moscow. But in other instances, it was the result of efforts by political actors who advocated radical reforms that went farther than Gorbachev and his allies could accept. They would accordingly be referred to as "legal boomerangs" by Soviet analysts at the time.

The legal boomerang that would prove the greatest threat to the USSR's territorial integrity was the putative "sovereignty" of the union republics and their derivative right of secession. As we will see, the designation of the union republics as "sovereign" at the time of the USSR's establishment had been an entirely contingent phenomenon. It was entailed neither in socialism nor in Marxist doctrine, but resulted instead from decisions made in the heat of political battle. In practice, of course, it was an entirely fictional attribute of the union republics from the start. Political power was concentrated in the hands of the central organs of the Communist Party of the Soviet Union (CPSU), and a Soviet citizen who manifested "national deviationist tendencies," let alone publicly advocated secession, was subject to arrest. With Gorbachev's commitment to the rule of law, however, leaders of the antiunion opposition in the union republics quickly discovered that they could employ the term with great effect to pressure the center for greater autonomy and eventually full independence. In contrast, separatists in the autonomies would be severely handicapped by the fact that the autonomies were not "sovereign" under Soviet law and lacked a constitutional right of secession.

In fact, as we will see, the meaning of "sovereignty" as used in Soviet political discourse was entirely unclear. But ironically, the term's very ambiguity, and its consequent elasticity of meaning, actually enhanced its efficacy as a political weapon in the hands of the antiunion opposition. This confusion over the meaning of "sovereignty," it should be noted, is hardly unique to the USSR or successor states. In the West, the term has been central to a host of political/legal controversies, in the course of which it has been used in a great many ways. "Popular sovereignty," or the right of voters in territories seeking statehood to decide whether to enter as free or slave states, was a critical point of conflict in the period leading up to the U.S. Civil War. Indeed, it was only with the Union's victory in the Civil War that the issue of whether "state sovereignty" entailed an implied or natural right to secede was resolved in the negative. Even today, American constitutional theorists argue over the extent to which the supremacy clause in the Tenth Amendment and the interstate commerce clause reserve or fail to reserve specific powers for the states.[18] Likewise, indigenous peoples in the United States, Canada, Australia, and elsewhere continue to assert their "sovereign" (and frequently treaty-based) claims to territory, self-government, and traditional fishing and hunting rights, while in the U.S. case, the courts have had to decide whether the doctrine of "sovereign immunity" applies to institutions of self-government on Indian Territory (i.e., whether they have immunity from suits in U.S. courts by non–Native Americans). Beyond the legal field, normative theorists of democracy continue to debate the relationship between "popular sovereignty" and the rule of law—that is, who or what is or should be "sovereign": the people, the constitution, or the constitutional court? Similarly,

British scholars debate the advantages and disadvantages of British "parliamentary sovereignty," while comparative political scientists argue about the loss of "internal sovereignty" by states confronted by new forms of terrorism, the "anarchical" quality of the Internet and other technologies of mass communication, ethnic conflict, and secessionist movements. And finally, international relations theorists argue over the loss of "external sovereignty" or "Westphalian sovereignty" in the face of globalization and the growing tendency of states to pass authority "upwards" to international organizations such as the European Union.

Not surprisingly, then, the term has been plagued by persistent ambiguity and vagueness, and by frequent equivocation by its employers. It has also been the object of a vast volume of scholarly literature.[19] In the Soviet case, these inherent semantic problems became central to the political drama of perestroika, in no small part because the supposed "sovereignty" of the union republics was said by Soviet propagandists to be fundamental to Soviet-style federalism, with all its advantages over mere "bourgeois federalism." In fact, throughout virtually the entire Soviet period, the union republics were politically subordinate to the Party leadership in Moscow, and their legal status as "sovereign states" had no practical impact on the degree of autonomy Moscow was willing to afford them. Accordingly, as the term began to acquire political import in the Gorbachev era, it could be interpreted to mean almost anything or almost nothing. As we will see, this profound ambiguity helps explain why many of those who proved most ardent in asserting the "sovereignty" of the union republics—and particularly many of the champions of "sovereignty" for Russia—were equally passionate in their opposition to the dissolution of the Soviet Union.

Indeed, the term would be used in a great variety of ways in Soviet political discourse in the Gorbachev era. Few, if any, of these meanings were mutually exclusive—rather they constituted an escalating set of demands for greater freedom of action for particular governments, whether national or subnational. They therefore could be, and very often were, asserted simultaneously. These various meanings included the following, moving from the least to the most expansive:

Sovereignty as decentralization and greater autonomy. Here the argument was that genuine sovereignty entailed exclusive authority for subnational governments (e.g., the union republics, but also the autonomies vis-à-vis the union republics) in policy arenas such as education; language use in schools, government, and the workplace; environmental protection; the preservation of cultural and historical monuments; control of local media organs (television and radio stations, newspapers, journals, etc.); and control of cultural institutions (e.g., printing presses, theaters, opera houses, etc.).

Sovereignty as a right to positive affirmation of federal legislation. Sovereignty in this case denoted a right to the positive affirmation by subnational governments of all laws adopted by the center before such laws could become binding in its territory, regardless of whether those laws were consistent with the preexisting laws of the subnational government.

Sovereignty as a right to preemptive legislation. Sovereignty here meant that laws passed by subnational governments would take precedence over those of the center wherever there was a contradiction. For example, all-union laws would be binding across Soviet territory, but only to the extent that they did not conflict with the laws of subnational governments.

Sovereignty as fiscal autonomy. One component of what was broadly referred to as "economic sovereignty," fiscal autonomy entailed the right of subnational governments to determine their own budgets and to levy taxes independently of the center.

Sovereignty as a "single channel" tax system. Here the claim was that union republics had a right to determine tax rates and collect all taxes on their territory, with the federal government to receive a negotiated portion of tax revenue. The tax authorities themselves would be administratively controlled by subnational authorities, not federal organs in Moscow.[20]

Sovereignty as a property claim. In this case, "economic sovereignty" meant a claim to the ownership of land, mineral resources, internal and territorial waters, forests, and other natural resources on the part of subnational governments. In some cases, ownership claims were extended to virtually all state property within the republic, including all enterprises and state and collective farms, the principal exception being assets of military bases, which were normally understood as legitimately belonging to the federal government.

Other forms of "economic sovereignty." These included the right of subnational governments to enter directly (i.e., without requiring approval from federal authorities) into trade agreements with other subnational governments within the USSR; to enter into trade agreements with foreign governments; to determine the character and pace of local economic reform; and to issue their own currency and conduct an independent monetary policy.

Sovereignty as a right to negotiate bilateral power-sharing treaties with the federal government. The demand here was that the division of powers between subnational and national governments be negotiated through a series of bilateral treaties between the federal government and each republic individually, with each republic and the federal government treated as equal parties to the negotiations.

Sovereignty as a right to determine collectively powers delegated to the federal government. In this case, sovereignty was interpreted as entailing a right of the union republics, acting jointly and independently of the center, to agree collectively on all powers to be delegated to the federal government. The union republics would thus exercise their right as "sovereign states" to accede to a newly constituted union on a voluntary and equal basis, or alternatively to refuse to enter it. The new entity could have been either a federal "union in perpetuity" or a confederation in which the constituent units would retain a right of secession and/or opt-out provisions (as in the opt-out provisions in the European Union).

Sovereignty as a unilateral right to determine powers delegated to the federal government. Here each union republic acting separately would have a right to determine the extent of the powers that it would delegate to the federal center, irrespective of whether a treaty had been entered into on the "mutual delegation of powers" or of agreement with the other constituent units of the union.

Sovereignty as a right of secession in accordance with federal law. Traditional Soviet legal theory held that the union republics were sovereign by virtue of their formal right of secession. However, prior to perestroika no enacting legislation had been adopted that specified the procedures needed to effect secession. Gorbachev and other defenders of the union would assert that the union republics' sovereignty would be accommodated by such a law, which was eventually passed by the Soviet legislature in early 1990. However, the procedures provided for in the law for effecting secession proved so burdensome as to make secession all but impossible in practice. Nevertheless, some members of the antiunion opposition in the union republics would indicate a willingness to accept that a law that made secession difficult but practicable would have been compatible with union republic sovereignty.

Sovereignty as a unilateral right of secession. Here sovereignty was understood to mean that the constitutional right of secession could not be limited in any way by the federal government. The legislatures of the union republics, not the all-union legislature, would determine the procedures for declaring independence. Some republics would also insist that sovereignty meant the right to determine citizenship requirements unilaterally, which meant, inter alia, a right to decide who could vote in union republic referendums on independence.

Sovereignty as recognition of being a "subject of international law." In this meaning, "sovereignty" was said to entail recognition of a particular government as being a "subject of international law" with a right to bring claims before international courts against other "subjects of international law" (including, for example, the Soviet state), to membership in international organizations (e.g., the membership of Ukraine and Belorussia in the UN General Assembly), and to direct political and economic relations with other states (including possibly formal diplomatic relations) and international organizations without mediation by central authorities in Moscow.

Sovereignty as full independence under international law. Here sovereignty was simply a synonym for full independence under international law—only a government that was afforded diplomatic recognition by other states (and particularly major Western powers) and had a seat at the UN General Assembly was said to be truly sovereign.

Sovereignty as freedom of action for an independent state. Finally, the term was used on occasion to mean full freedom of action for formally independent states or as a norm of international behavior whereby states would agree not to interfere in the "internal affairs" of other states. Soviet foreign policy experts, for example, would sometimes complain about violations of Soviet sovereignty by Western powers when the latter criticized Moscow for violating human rights norms.

As we will see, the term's elasticity had the ironic effect of enhancing its effectiveness as a political slogan in the hands of the antiunion opposition. But the USSR's formal federal institutions, and the normative claims and myths that Soviet propagandists had developed to legitimate them, would constrain Gorbachev's choices in other ways as well. The existence of executive, legislative, and Communist Party organs at the union republic level meant that the jobs, authority, and power of particular individuals were dependent upon the USSR's federal structure. Those who occupied these offices, including many antinationalist, pro-CPSU conservatives as well as many Gorbachev allies, had an abiding interest in preserving that structure. Accordingly, there was never any question of Gorbachev simply doing away with the USSR's subnational governments—the use of force to *subdue* them was politically possible, but not their complete elimination. These interests largely account for why, even after the USSR's demise, there have been very few changes in administrative structure in the Soviet successor states.[21] For similar reasons, the internal borders that Gorbachev inherited were, and continue to be, very difficult to change. Indeed, from the start of perestroika virtually all political factions in Moscow agreed that the USSR's internal borders were sacrosanct, not because they were necessarily politically optimal or historically just, but because trying to redraw them would have opened up a Pandora's box of potentially violent border disputes.

There was another, perhaps even more important, way in which Soviet federalism and its normative mythologies would affect Gorbachev's response to the "nationality crisis." Like most of his colleagues, Gorbachev genuinely believed many of the regime's traditional normative claims about the success of "Leninist" federalism and Soviet policy in "solving the nationality question." These normative claims were manifold. Soviet federalism, it was said, accommodated both the internationalist spirit of the socialist movement as well as the right of nations to self-determination. It was responsible for a "flowering" (*rastsvet*) and "drawing together" (*sblizhenie*) of national cultures, and indeed was already leading to their gradual "merging" (*sliianie*) into a new, nonnational "Soviet" people (*Sovetskii narod*). Above all, it was responsible for the "friendship of peoples" (*druzhba narodov*) within the USSR, a friendship that allowed the great multinational Soviet state to devote its energies not to atavistic bickering between peoples but to the further perfection of socialism. In all these respects, Soviet ethnic federalism was said to be superior to the "bourgeois" forms of federalism found in countries like the United States that refused to recognize and accommodate national and racial minorities by affording them their own ethnoterritorial homelands.

It has become commonplace to argue that by the time Gorbachev came to power, the Soviet people and political elite no longer believed the regime's propaganda or took official ideology seriously. While in some respects this was true, the assertion vastly underestimates the extent to which Soviet ideology colored the worldview of both the Soviet people and its political elite. In fact, while many of the regime's claims about the USSR's rapid march toward a Communist utopia were viewed with deep cynicism, Soviet political culture and norms had, after some seventy years of Soviet power, been deeply internalized by the Soviet people. This was certainly true of Gorbachev. An idealist who doggedly attempted to preserve what he felt was valuable from the Soviet experience, Gorbachev took for granted, for example, that the regime had indeed "solved the nationality problem," and he was surprised and disturbed by the rise of what he viewed as parochial ethno-nationalism and the spread of interethnic conflict in the perestroika era. Despite the violence and intolerance that accompanied the "national awakenings" among the USSR's national minorities, he proved just as reluctant to give up on the fiction that the USSR was a "friendship of peoples" as he was to give up on the fiction that the Soviet people had voluntarily made a "socialist choice" in 1917. He was, however, also an advocate (albeit a sometimes less than enthusiastic one) of the rule of law, which meant that he was unwilling to ignore entirely the formal rights of the union republics and autonomies or to use massive force to suppress ethno-nationalist mobilization. As we will see, his belief in the regime's traditional normative claims and the ideals of perestroika help account for the hopelessly ineffective strategy he would adopt to preserve the Soviet state's territorial integrity—a strategy that required the leaderships of all fifteen union republics to ratify a new union treaty that, with each revised draft, would provide for an ever weaker and less coherent central government.

Finally, as discussed in chapter 6, the international community's reaction to the dissolution was powerfully influenced by the USSR's federal heritage, a reaction that would also help account for the form that the breakup would take. Foreign powers, including the American government, hoped that liberalization, democratization, and economic reform could be effected in the USSR without threatening the country's territorial integrity. Even the three Baltic republics, Estonia, Latvia, and Lithuania, which Western governments claimed had been illegally incorporated into the USSR, were encouraged to negotiate some kind of autonomy arrangement with Moscow that would fall short of full independence. To be sure, international public opinion was sympathetic to the demands for "self-determination" for the USSR's national minorities. And separatists were certainly encouraged by various nongovernmental organizations (NGOs), given succor by the apparent legitimation of the principle of the "self-determination of peoples" in international law, and encouraged by the reliance of Western governments on "self-determination" to justify their support for, inter alia, German unification. But foreign *governments,* if not foreign publics, were deeply fearful that any breakup of the Soviet Union would be accompanied by widespread violence, as proved the case in Yugoslavia. Unlike Yugoslavia, however, the USSR had thousands of nuclear warheads, huge stockpiles of chemical and biological weapons, and dozens of nuclear power stations. As a result, civil war or anarchy in the Soviet Union had far more terrifying implications than civil war in the Balkans. And finally, Western governments were concerned that open support for secession from the USSR would provoke a conservative backlash in Moscow on the one hand, or encourage secessionists in other parts of the world on the other.

Separatists in the union republics would therefore be surprised, and in many cases embittered, by the lack of support they would receive from Western governments, above all Washington. Territorial integrity and (to a lesser extent) noninterference in the internal affairs of other states, they discovered, in practice take priority over self-determination except in cases where the relationship is understood as clearly colonial—where, that is, the peoples of a particular territory are not full citizens of a metropole. Any changes in internationally recognized borders are acceptable only if they are effected through peaceful means and by agreement among legally recognized representatives of all states whose borders are involved. In addition, the Helsinki Accords of 1975 had not only committed the signatory states to recognition of the "inviolability" of existing borders in Europe, but obligated them to refrain from making any claims on the territory of other states, effectively ruling out even negotiated border changes.[22] Indeed, Western governments would refuse to recognize the independence even of the Baltic states until after the failed coup of August 1991, by which time the enfeebled Soviet state was on the verge of collapse. The other union republics would receive formal recognition only after the Soviet state was formally dissolved in December 1991. Western governments could then credibly claim that they were recognizing not unilateral secession but a political "dissolution" that had come about voluntarily and through peaceful means, a position they would take later in regard to Czechoslovakia and (considerably less credibly) Yugoslavia as well.

While international support for Gorbachev's effort to preserve the union would not save the USSR, the international community's bias in favor of territorial integrity would prove crucial to the territorial consolidation of the successor states. Secessionists in Abkhazia, Chechnya, Nagorno-Karabakh, South Ossetia, and Transdniestra (and more recently in Kosovo as well), would manage to exercise de facto "sovereignty" over their territory by force of arms. Not one, however, has been recognized as independent by any foreign government since the collapse of the Berlin Wall in 1989. To be sure, some of the region's new states remain whole in formal terms only, and it may be that some kind of negotiated settlement will eventually lead to the emergence of yet more states on the territory of the former Soviet Union. But the fact was that the autonomies were not the first-level units of the federation of which they were a part, however arbitrary their lower status might have been. And they accordingly lacked a legal right of secession. Foreign governments could therefore recognize the independence of the union republics, and only the union republics, as a convenient default solution to the otherwise intractable problem of which states to afford diplomatic recognition.

In short, the Soviet Union was like a peculiar kind of jigsaw puzzle. Its fifteen union republics made up the pieces of the puzzle, pieces that were held together by their arbitrary shape alone. Some of these fifteen pieces were in turn divided into subparts (the autonomies), but these subdivisions were only lightly etched in the cardboard. When the jigsaw puzzle was shaken by the rise of ethno-national separatism in some (but not all) of the union republics and autonomies, the puzzle fell apart along the lines of least resistance, which proved to be the borders of the union republics. But whereas severe shaking was enough to separate the first-level units, even violence would prove insufficient to rend asunder the successor states.

* * * * *

The book is organized as follows. In chapter 2, I briefly sketch the history of Soviet federalism and "nationality policy," stressing in particular their contingent character, the arbitrary aspects of the USSR's federal structure, and nature of the legitimizing mythologies of Soviet-style federalism and nationality policy. Chapter 3 traces the emergence of the antiunion opposition in the union republics beginning in late 1987, the importance of the term "sovereignty" (*suverenitet*) in the mobilization of the antiunion opposition, the ironic fact that the ambiguity of the term as used in Soviet political discourse actually enhanced its efficacy as a political weapon, the spread of the "parade of sovereignties" to those union republics where ethno-separatist sentiments were weak, and the international community's initial reaction to the "nationality crisis." In chapter 4, I describe the sovereignty campaigns of the autonomies, a phenomenon that served to deepen the USSR's already acute crisis of multiple sovereignty and complicated the efforts of the union republics to force the center to devolve more power as well as Gorbachev's efforts to cope with ethno-nationalism. Chapter 5 analyzes the intensifying struggle for power between Gorbachev and Yeltsin over the "sovereignty" of the RSFSR in 1989–early 1991, Gorbachev's attempts to save the union by convincing the republics to ratify a new "union treaty," and the continuing efforts of Western governments to support Gorbachev's struggle to keep the USSR together. Chapter 6 addresses the rush to independence in the union republics after the failed coup of August 1991, emphasizing in particular how confusion over the meaning of "sovereignty" contributed to similar confusion over the meaning of "independence" (*nezavisimost'*). It was then, in the final months leading up to the dissolution, that the role of the "fog of war" proved most important. I conclude in chapter 7 by returning to the broad themes addressed in the introduction, particularly the contingency, relative arbitrariness, and unintended quality of the outcome.

Notes

1. *National'nyi sostav naseleniia SSSR* 1991, 5–8. Twenty-two of the 126 nationalities had a population of over one million. The largest—ethnic Russians—totaled 145.2 million (only 50.8 percent of the total), while the second largest—the ethnic Ukrainians—totaled 44.2 million, more than the population of any country in Western Europe except France, West Germany, and Britain.

2. For example, the Mingrelians of western Georgia speak a Kartvelian language that is related to, but different from, Georgian (the two languages are mutually unintelligible). Mingrelian speakers were nevertheless classified as Georgians and had to identify themselves as such on their internal passports. Similarly, on the northern and southern slopes of the Caucasus mountain range, where numerous unique languages are spoken that in some cases are confined to single villages, linguistic minorities were frequently classified as part of a larger but distinct neighboring "nationality."

3. Arguably, the Soviet Union was not a true "federation." The term "federal," as Daniel J. Elazar has noted, comes from the Latin *foedus,* meaning "covenant," Daniel Elazar, *Exploring Federalism* (Tuscaloosa: University of Alabama Press, 1987), 5–6, and passim. Its etymology thus implies a voluntary, contract-based union in which contracting parties agree to a division of powers between a national (federal) government and subnational governments. In practice, few federations can credibly claim to have been formed purely as a result of a voluntary association of constituent units (the exceptions being the United States and Switzerland), and in this sense the USSR was not unusual, see Alfred Stepan, "Russian Federalism in Comparative Perspective," *Post-Soviet Affairs* 16, no. 2 (2000): 133–76. What was missing in the Soviet case was a rule of law in which constitutional provisions and other legal measures entrenched the powers of subnational governments. The powers of the USSR's constituent units were defined by the center, and they survived at the center's discretion. Regional executive and legislative organs were subordinated to institutions higher up the federal hierarchy and, most importantly, to the apparatus of the Communist Party of the Soviet Union (CPSU), which was itself a top-down organization in which ultimate authority rested with the Politburo (and under Stalin at least, with the general secretary himself). The USSR's subnational governments were thus part of an administrative hierarchy, not a hierarchy of autonomous governments with constitutionally entrenched powers. Like all administrative hierarchies, of course, each level of the hierarchy acquired over time an understanding of its prerogatives, an understanding that higher authorities were generally reluctant to violate without good cause. With these reservations in mind, I will continue to refer to the USSR, Czechoslovakia, and Yugoslavia as "federations."

4. There were in addition 120 nonethnically defined oblasts (districts) and seven krais, of which fifty-seven (including all seven krais) were located within the RSFSR. Only the five smallest republics—Armenia, Estonia, Latvia, Lithuania, and Moldavia (Moldova)—were not divided into administrative subunits. The constitution identified Moscow and Leningrad (St. Petersburg) as "federal cities" with an administrative status equal to that of the oblasts and krais.

5. The mainstream view in Western historiography today is that Soviet ethnographers generally did their best to use consistent ethnographic criteria in classifying minor-

ity peoples in the new Soviet state in the 1920s and 1930s. Likewise, the delineation of ethno-territorial units and their borders in the Soviet federal system was for the most part guided by a desire to match ethnicity and territory, particularly in the 1920s. In some cases, however, both national designations and administrative borders appear to have been influenced by political considerations, particularly for minorities with external national states (e.g., Germans, Poles, Bulgarians, Greeks, etc.) and in Central Asia. See Yuri Slezkine, "The USSR as a Communal Apartment, or How a Socialist State Promoted Ethnic Particularism," *Slavic Review* 53, no. 2 (Summer 1994): 414–52, and Terry Martin, *The Affirmative Action Empire: Nations and Nationalism in the Soviet Union, 1923–1939* (Ithaca, N.Y.: Cornell University Press, 2001). On Central Asia, see Olivier Roy, *The New Central Asia: The Creation of Nations* (New York: New York University Press, 2000), especially 66–68; but for an alternative view, see Adrienne Edgar, "Nationality Policy and National Identity: The Turkmen Soviet Socialist Republic, 1924–1929," *Journal of Central Asian Studies* 1, no. 2 (Spring-Summer 1997): 2–20. Regardless, there was an inevitable measure of arbitrariness in the classification of nationalities and the delineation of internal borders, as suggested by the fact that not only the number of ethno-territorial units (see chapter 2), but also the number of officially recognized nationalities changed over time. The 1979 census, for example, listed only 104 nationalities, a decrease from the 1959 and 1969 censuses and twenty-four fewer than in 1989. The decrease was intended to demonstrate the validity of the regime's claim that national identities were giving way to a common "Soviet" identity, while the increase in 1989 reflected the more accommodating nationality policy of the Gorbachev period and greater realism by that time about the resilience of national identities, Robert J. Kaiser, *The Geography of Nationalism in Russia and the USSR* (Princeton, N.J.: Princeton University Press, 1994).

6. For example, the Evenk Autonomous Okrug (770,000 sq. km.) was over twenty-five times the size of the Armenian SSR (29,800 sq. km.), while the enormous Yakut ASSR (3,103,200 sq. km.) was almost 18 times the size of the three Baltic republics combined (Estonia, 45,100 sq. km.; Latvia, 64,500 sq. km.; and Lithuania, 65,000 sq. km.). As for population, the Bashkir ASSR had 3.9 million residents in 1989, more than Lithuania (3.7 million), Turkmenistan (3.5 million), Armenia (3.3 million), Latvia (2.7 million), and Estonia (1.6 million). The population of the Tatar ASSR—3.6 million—was only slightly smaller than Bashkiria's.

7. The share of the titular nation in the union republics' population ranged from a high of 90 percent in Armenia to a low of 36 percent in Kazakhstan in 1989. In the autonomies, it was as high as 68 percent in Chuvashia and as low as 4 percent in the Jewish Autonomous Oblast. It is also worth noting that in some instances the majority of a titular people lived outside its national homeland. For example, only a minority of the USSR's 6.6 million Volga Tatars lived in the Tatar ASSR, while only some 10,000 of the USSR's 1.44 million Jews lived in the Jewish AO in the Russian Far East. Overall, the number of titulars living outside their national homeland totaled some 75 million, including 25.3 million Russians living beyond the borders of the RSFSR.

8. The six union republics that refused to participate were host to only 7.3 percent of the USSR's total population.

9. As we shall see, popular and elite attitudes toward the preservation of the union in Russia and Ukraine were more nuanced (see chapters 5–6). Suffice it to say at this point that the meaning of the 1 December 1991 referendum in Ukraine, in which 90 percent voted for "independence," was considerably more ambiguous than is generally assumed. As for Russia, there is no evidence of majority support for a full dissolution either before or after December 1991. Not only did a substantial majority of voters in Russia support

the preservation of the union in the March 1991 referendum, as noted previously, but polls taken after December 1991 consistently showed popular regret over the breakup. For example, three-quarters of respondents in a nationally representative poll taken in 1994 agreed with the statement, "It is a great misfortune that the Soviet Union no longer exists," while a similar number agreed that at least Belarus, Ukraine, and Kazakhstan should rejoin Russia in a common state, "Opinion Research Memorandum," Washington, D.C.: Office of Research, U.S. Information Agency, 3 August 1994.

10. For a comparative treatment of the breakup of the USSR, Czechoslovakia, and Yugoslavia that emphasizes the role of formal federal institutions, see Valerie Bunce, *Subversive Institutions: The Design and the Destruction of Socialism and the State* (New York: Cambridge University Press, 1999).

11. There were, however, some interesting differences in Soviet, Czechoslovak, and Yugoslav federal systems and nationality policies that warrant mention. In Yugoslavia, a formal distinction was made between "nations" and "nationalities," the latter being ethnic minorities that had a separate state outside of Yugoslavia, such as Albanians, Czechs, Hungarians, and Romanians. The largest of the nationalities—the Albanians and Hungarians—were given their "own" autonomous republics, Vojvodina and Kosovo, both within Serbia. The founding constitution of 1946 identified five founding "nations"— Croats, Macedonians, Montenegrins, Serbs, and Slovenes—but Muslims were added as a sixth in the constitution of 1963. Each of the Yugoslav constitutions described the six republics as "states" whose statehood reflected the "sovereignty" of their people, and the 1946 constitution afforded each republic a right of secession. However, the constitution of 1953 did not include a right of secession, while the constitutions of 1963 and 1974 afforded the right to the founding nations themselves. What this meant in practice became the subject of heated debate. Politically, power was concentrated initially, as in the USSR, in the hands of the central leadership of the Yugoslav Communist League (YCL), dominated at the time by Tito, but this began to change in the 1960s and early 1970s. In 1974, a new constitution was adopted that provided for significantly decentralized power, indeed to the point where the republics had an effective veto over most policies and legislation adopted by the federal center. There were other differences as well: the YCL after the late 1960s, unlike the CPSU, was a federation of republic party committees; federal authorities did not have the authority to transfer personnel between republics; Yugoslav citizens were not required to list their nationality on internal passports; choice of national affiliation was purely voluntary; and each individual had the option of listing "Yugoslav" as their national affiliation on census questionnaires and various official forms such as military enlistment papers, birth and marriage certificates, voter registration forms, and so on. See Susan L. Woodward, *Balkan Tragedy: Chaos and Dissolution after the Cold War* (Washington, D.C.: Brookings, 1995), 29–41; Sabrina Ramet, *Nationalism and Federalism in Yugoslavia, 1962–1991*, 2d ed. (Bloomington: Indiana University Press, 1992), 70–80; and Vojin Dimitrijevic, "The 1974 Constitution and the Constitutional Process as a Factor in the Collapse of Yugoslavia," in *Yugoslavia, the Former and the Future*, ed. Payam Akhavan and Robert Howse (Washington, D.C. and Geneva: Brookings and the United Nations Research Institute for Social Development, 1995), 45–74. As for Czechoslovakia, it was established in 1948 as a "unitary State of two fraternal nations possessing equal rights, the Czechs and the Slovaks." There were, however, some elements of asymmetry in the "unitary state," as the minority Slovaks but not the Czechs were allowed their own Communist Party and legislature (the Slovak National Council). At the time of the Prague Spring of 1968, Alexander Dubcek's reformist government drafted a new Federation Law that attempted to remove the asymmetry and establish a more genuine federation. The main outlines of the law survived the Soviet invasion in

August, and a federation was formally declared in October 1968. Little was done, however, to implement its provisions—for example, neither Slovakia nor the Czech Republic adopted their own constitutions, and in practice the Czech and Slovak parliaments remained extremely weak until after the collapse of the regime in 1989, Jan Rychlik, "From Autonomy to Federation," in *The End of Czechoslovakia,* ed. Jiri Musil (Budapest: Central European University Press, 1995), 193; and Petr Pithardt and Metta Spencer, "The Partition of Czechoslovakia," in *Separatism: Democracy and Disintegration,* ed. Metta Spencer (Lanham, Md.: Rowman & Littlefield, 1998), 185–204.

12. Interestingly, the constitution of rump Yugoslavia that was ratified in April 1992 after the international community recognized the independence of Slovenia, Croatia, Bosnia, and Macedonia specified that the remaining member-republics (Serbia and Montenegro) were only "sovereign in matters which under the present Constitution are not reserved to the jurisdiction of the Federal Republic of Yugoslavia" (Article 6). Neither did it afford member-republics a right of secession, while Article 3 specified that the international borders of the Federal Republic of Yugoslavia (FRY) were "inviolable." The international community thus faced a considerable dilemma in responding to Montenegro's moves to secede after Milo Djukanovic became Montenegro's president in 1997. On the one hand, for reasons discussed at length below, the international community is extremely reluctant to sanction secession if it is illegal under the law of the internationally recognized state in question. On the other hand, it has been difficult to argue that Montenegro should be treated differently than the other former Yugoslav republics on the basis of a 1992 constitution with very dubious democratic legitimacy. The dilemma for the international community is less acute in the case of Kosovo because it was not a full republic of the former Yugoslavia. Accordingly, foreign governments have made clear that they will refuse to recognize Kosovo's independence unless independence is negotiated with Serbia.

13. In addition to the fifteen union republics of the USSR, these included the Czech Republic and Slovakia, which made up Czechoslovakia, and the six Yugoslav republics of Bosnia, Croatia, Macedonia, Montenegro, Serbia, and Slovenia.

14. The constitution adopted for rump Yugoslavia in 1992 renamed the state the Federal Republic of Yugoslavia (FRY). While the FRY considered itself the legal successor of the Socialist Federal Republic of Yugoslavia, the U.S. government did not concur and thus referred to it formally as "the Republics of Serbia and Montenegro." The U.S. government accordingly treats it as a new state, and it is counted as such here.

15. Serbia eliminated the formal autonomy of Kosovo and Vojvodina under the terms of a Serbian constitution adopted under Slobodan Milosevic's national-Communist leadership in March 1989. Milosevic took the additional step of placing Kosovo under the direct rule of the Serbian government in 1990 (Ramet 1992, 76–78). In early January 2002, the Serbian parliament voted to restore Vojvodina's formal autonomy.

16. The most comprehensive study of nationalist mobilization during perestroika is Mark R. Beissinger, *Nationalist Mobilization and the Collapse of the Soviet State* (New York: Cambridge University Press, 2002). There are also many excellent studies of political mobilization in individual union republics, particularly the Baltic republics and Russia. See, for example, Alfred Erich Senn, *Lithuania Awakening* (Berkeley: University of California Press, 1990); Rasma Karklins, *Ethnopolitics and Transition to Democracy: The Collapse of the USSR and Latvia* (Baltimore: Johns Hopkins University Press, 1993); Anatol Leiven, *The Baltic Revolution: Estonia, Latvia, Lithuania, and the Path to Independence* (New Haven, Conn.: Yale University Press, 1993); John B. Dunlop, *The Rise of Russia and the Fall of the Soviet Empire* (Princeton, N.J.: Princeton University Press, 1993); M. Steven Fish, *Democracy from Scratch: Opposition and Regime in the New*

Russian Revolution (Princeton, N.J.: Princeton University Press, 1995); Andrew Wilson, *The Ukrainians: Unexpected Nation* (New Haven, Conn.: Yale University Press, 2000); Alfred Erich Senn, *Gorbachev's Failure in Lithuania* (New York: St. Martin's Press, 1995); Jane I. Dawson, *Eco-Nationalism: Anti-Nuclear Activism and National Identity in Russia, Lithuania, and Ukraine* (Durham, N.C.: Duke University Press, 1996); and Michael McFaul, *Russia's Unfinished Revolution: Political Change from Gorbachev to Putin* (Ithaca, N.Y.: Cornell University Press, 1991). For studies of the formation of national consciousness in the Soviet period that stress the role of Soviet ethno-federalism and nationality policy in reinforcing, and in some cases even creating de novo, national consciousness among the USSR's ethno-linguistic groups, see Ronald Grigor Suny, *The Revenge of the Past: Nationalism, Revolution, and the Collapse of the Soviet Union* (Stanford, Calif.: Stanford University Press, 1993); Slezkine 1994; Kaiser 1994; and Valerii A. Tishkov, *Ethnicity, Nationalism, and Conflict in and after the Soviet Union: The Mind Aflame* (Thousand Oaks, Calif.: Sage Publications, 1997).

17. In part, the practice of appealing to the rights and principles provided for in the Soviet constitution and Soviet law to promote liberalization predated the Gorbachev era. Most notably, after the signing of the Helsinki Accords of 1975, which committed the signatory states, including the USSR, to respect basic human rights, Soviet dissidents realized the tactical effectiveness of making reformist arguments by demanding that the authorities respect the rights that Soviet citizens were supposedly afforded under law but that were in practice ignored. The practice became far more widespread, however, after Gorbachev launched the liberalizing reforms of glasnost and *demokratizatsiia,* and it was embraced with particular enthusiasm, as we will see, by the antiunion opposition in the union republics.

18. To put the ambiguity of designating the USSR's union republics as "sovereign" states in some perspective, it is worth quoting the following passage from the Constitution of the Commonwealth of Massachusetts: "The people of this Commonwealth have the sole and exclusive right of governing themselves, as a *free, sovereign, and independent State:* and do, and forever shall, exercise and enjoy every power, jurisdiction, and right, which is not, or may not hereafter, be by them expressly delegated to the United States of America in Congress assembled" (Sec. 4) (emphasis added).

19. For analyses of the concept from different disciplinary perspectives, see Hurst Hannum, *Autonomy, Sovereignty, and Self-Determination: The Accommodation of Conflicting Rights* (Philadelphia: University of Pennsylvania Press, 1990); Stephen D. Krasner, *Sovereignty: Organized Hypocrisy* (Princeton, N.J.: Princeton University Press, 1999); Jens Bartelson, *A Genealogy of Sovereignty,* Cambridge Studies in International Relations, vol. 39 (Cambridge: Cambridge University Press, 1995); and Thomas J. Biersteker and Cynthia Weber, *State Sovereignty as a Social Construct* (New York: Cambridge University Press, 1996).

20. There was also consideration of various arrangements for putting tax authorities under the joint control of federal and union republic governments. For example, the head of the taxing authority might be nominated by the union republics and approved by the federal government. The notion was that the tax authorities would have had to abide by the laws of both the center and the union republics, assuming, of course, that those could be reconciled.

21. An exception was the division of Checheno-Ingushetia into the separate Chechen and Ingush Republics in early 1992. In other cases (e.g., Armenia and Georgia), an effort has been made to create new regional (the equivalent of oblast level) administrations where before there had been none. But in no case, despite a great deal of discussion about

the possibility in Russia in particular, have existing regional governments been abolished or substantially consolidated.

22. Provision 1 (a) (3) of the Helsinki Final Act of the Conference on Security and Cooperation in Europe, which was signed on 1 August 1975 by thirty-five states including the USSR and its East European allies, stated the following: "The participating States regard as inviolable all one another's frontiers as well as the frontiers of all States in Europe and therefore they will refrain now and in the future from assaulting these frontiers. Accordingly, they will also refrain from any demand for, or act of, seizure and usurpation of part or all of the territory of any participating State." Provision 1 (a) (4) then stated: "The participating States will respect the territorial integrity of each of the participating States," Thomas Buergenthal, ed., *Human Rights, International Law, and the Helsinki Accord* (New York: Allanheld, Osmund/Universe Books, 1977), 164–65.

Chapter 2

Sovereignty, Federalism, and Soviet Nationality Policy

> The union republic shall be a sovereign Soviet socialist state which has united with other Soviet republics in the Union of Soviet Socialist Republics. (Article 76 of the USSR Constitution, 1977)

From the establishment of the Union of Soviet Socialist Republics (USSR) in December 1922, Soviet legal theory held that the USSR's union republics, the constituent units of the Soviet federation, were "sovereign." Thus the second chapter of the first USSR constitution (1924) was entitled "The Sovereign Rights of the Union Republics and Union Citizenship."[1] Echoing the residual clause in the U.S. Constitution's Tenth Amendment, Article 3 asserted: "The sovereignty of the union republics shall only be restricted within the limits specified in this Constitution and solely in matters assigned to the competence of the Union. Except as so restricted, each union republic shall exercise its state power independently."[2] Article 4 followed by granting the union republics a right of secession, a right that would be included in the Soviet constitutions of 1936 and 1977 and that would distinguish the union republics from all other administrative units within the Soviet federal hierarchy.

Official Soviet reasoning about the putative "sovereignty" of the union republics emerged from the complicated history of the European socialist movement's position on "the national question" at the end of the nineteenth and early twentieth centuries and the particular interpretation of the principle of "national

21

self-determination" adopted by Lenin prior to the October Revolution. In principle, orthodox Marxists were committed to "proletarian internationalism." As Marx and Engels had written in the *Manifesto* in 1848, "The working men have no country." National identities were said to be legacies of the presocialist past while nationalism was a bourgeois ideology meant to divide the working class and deceive it into supporting the bourgeois state. Both, then, would gradually pass into history with socioeconomic modernization and the advent of socialism. In their later writings, however, Marx and Engels came to recognize the political potency of nationalism. They were particularly sympathetic to the Irish and Polish nationalist movements, which they felt were progressive forces at the time because of their contribution to the weakening of the British and Tsarist empires. Accordingly, in the "Proclamation on the Polish Question" drafted by Marx in 1865, Polish nationalists demanding autonomy and independence from Russia were supported on the grounds that they would help "to annihilate the growing influence of Russia in Europe." Marx went on to refer in the same sentence to "the right to self-determination which belongs to every nation."[3] Support for "the right of national self-determination" would become a standard part of the European socialist movements' program and was incorporated in the program of the Second International in 1896. Similarly, the Russian Socialist Democratic Labor Party (RSDLP) referred to "the right of nations (*natsii*) in the state to self-determination" in Article 9 of the program adopted at its famous 1903 Party Conference.[4]

In fact, this support was essentially pro forma, reflecting the opposition of Russia's Marxists to the treatment of minorities in the Tsarist "prison of nations," the global inequality of national groups, and imperialism generally, with little thought given either to what a "nation" was or to the means by which the principle of self-determination could be realized in practice. In the years leading up to World War I, however, Lenin became involved in a debate with West European socialists over the nationalist aspirations of ethnic minorities in the Austro-Hungarian, Tsarist, and Ottoman empires. On one side of this debate were the German socialists Rosa Luxembourg and Karl Kautsky, who took the orthodox Marxist position that minority cultures and nationalism were precapitalist anachronisms that were giving way to the pressures of assimilation within large capitalist states and that petty nationalist sentiments interfered with the solidarity of the international working class. On the other side were the Austrian socialists Otto Bauer and Karl Renner, who, well aware of the complexity of national identities and political aspirations in the multinational Austro-Hungarian empire, held that minority cultures were not only enduring but of value in their own right, even under socialism. They argued that nationalism was likely to intensify, not dissipate, with the spread and development of capitalism in the East, and socialists should therefore ally themselves with minority nationalists for both normative and pragmatic reasons. To be sure, Bauer and Renner conceded that larger states would be better able to coordinate and plan economic life under socialism and that national identities should not be entrenched by the rigid territorial borders implicit in territorial autonomy, thereby undermining proletarian internationalism. Instead, they advocated a form of "extraterritorial" national-cultural autonomy to deal with the national question in Eastern Europe, whereby elected representatives of national minorities would have autonomy over linguistic, educational, and cultural affairs for the members of that minority regardless of where they lived.

Initially, both Mensheviks and Bolsheviks tended to side with the orthodox position on the national question. When Lenin turned his full attention to the issue in 1912, however, he concluded that the Austrians were partly right—there was indeed a need for socialists to form alliances with anti-imperialist and anti-capitalist nationalists. He also agreed that nationalism was likely to intensify as capitalist relations of production took root in the East. But he was adamantly opposed to the adoption of federalist principles within the Russian socialist movement, as had already occurred with the Austro-Hungarian socialists, who were divided into a host of parties representing different national minorities.[5] Neither did he agree that cultural and linguistic diversity was of value in its own right or that minorities deserved institutional protections indefinitely under socialism.[6] Rather, socialist support for national liberation should depend upon the historical context and the opportunity to use, and benefit from, bourgeois nationalism in the struggle against capitalism.[7] Lenin was opposed to extraterritorial autonomy and, at least initially, to ethnic federalism. The former, he argued, would prevent the assimilation of minority cultures, which was a progressive and inevitable product of modernization, and would interfere with the international solidarity of the working class. The latter, in contrast, would undermine centralized state power, which had been one of capitalism's greatest achievements and would be needed under socialism above all to manage the planned economy. However, his views on ethnic federalism in the period leading up to the revolutions of 1917 were inconsistent, since he also indicated support for some form of territorial autonomy as a means to ensure democracy under "democratic centralism."[8] And in a letter written in 1914, he argued that the Bolsheviks should introduce a bill into the Duma "on the equality of nations and the definition of the rights of national minorities" that would provide for "the division of the country into autonomous and self-governing territorial units according—among other things—to nationality."[9] Whether these "autonomous and self-governing territorial units" would survive bourgeois capitalism and be preserved under a revolutionary socialist regime was left unclear.

In short, Lenin attempted to carve out a middle course between the orthodox position, with its neglect of the political potency of nationalism, and the Austrian position, with its excessive concessions to the "presocialist" aspirations of "bourgeois nationalists." His solution was to offer a unique interpretation of self-determination, an interpretation that he argued should be aggressively championed by socialism in the struggle against capitalism and imperialism.

Self-determination, he asserted, logically entailed a unilateral right of secession: "[Article 9 of the 1903 Party Platform] cannot be interpreted in any other way, but in the sense of political self-determination, that is, as the right to separation and creation of an independent government."[10] Once socialists had successfully seized power, national minorities would in effect be given a choice—either full independence or incorporation into a centralized socialist state, albeit one where some form of territorial autonomy in cultural affairs might be possible.

In late 1912, Lenin encouraged Stalin, who had recently joined Lenin in Cracow, to write an article summarizing his views on the national question, expressing in particular his opposition to the growing demands for the transformation of the Russian Social Democratic Party into a federation of parties representing different national minorities. The result was Stalin's best-known contribution to socialist thought, "Marxism and Self-Determination," which was published in early 1913 and would serve as the basis for what would become formal Soviet nationality policy. After reiterating the standard socialist commitment to self-determination, Stalin wrote:

> The right of self-determination means that a nation may arrange its life in the way it wishes. It has the right to arrange its life on the basis of autonomy. It has the right to enter into federal relations with other nations. It has the right to complete secession. *Nations are sovereign, and all nations are equal.*[11] (emphasis added)

In part, Lenin's advocacy of self-determination as necessarily entailing a unilateral right of secession resulted from his belief (like Marx and Engels before him) that an alliance between socialists and anti-imperialist forces could help to destroy the multinational Russian, Austro-Hungarian, Ottoman, and even British empires. Lenin also believed that socialist support for self-determination would facilitate an alliance between socialism and the subjugated peoples of the vast colonial territories of the Western powers. And finally, notwithstanding the arguments of many of his opponents, Lenin felt that the result would not be the establishment of "an idiotic system of petty states (*Kleinstaaterei*)." Rather, it would make secession and state proliferation *less* likely because minorities would be reassured by the sympathetic understanding of socialists, and as a result they would voluntarily chose to remain part of, or join, newly socialist states once the economic and political advantages of socialism became clear. As Lenin explained,

> We demand the freedom of self-determination, i.e., independence, i.e., the freedom of separation of oppressed nations, not because we dream of economic particularization, or of the ideal of small states, but on the contrary, because we desire major states, and a rapprochement, even a merging, of nations, but on a truly democratic basis, which is *unthinkable* without the freedom of secession.[12]

Lenin's support for self-determination and the right to secede deepened with the outbreak of World War I. As a member of the Zimmerwald opposition, he held that the Great War signaled the final crisis of finance capitalism and that socialists in the West should refuse to contribute to their nation's war effort and use the opportunity to press for the collapse of the now vulnerable imperialist powers. To this end, he became even more insistent that socialists should encourage minority peoples in Eastern Europe and the colonial peoples of the Third World to rise up against the imperialist powers in pursuit of national self-determination.

Lenin's program seemed to be vindicated by the 1917 February Revolution and the deepening anarchy that spread across the territory of what had been the Tsarist empire. The Provisional Government, it became clear, was even more vulnerable to the nationalist aspirations of minority peoples than the Tsarist state. Lenin castigated the Provisional Government for its vacillating and incoherent policies on the national question, criticizing in particular its unwillingness to recognize the independence of Finland and Ukraine. At a Party conference in May 1917, the RSDLP adopted a resolution drafted by Lenin that affirmed "the right of all of the nations forming part of Russia freely to secede and form independent states."[13] Immediately after the Bolsheviks' seizure of power in November 1917, the first formal document adopted by the new regime proclaimed its support for self-determination.[14] The following week, Lenin and Stalin signed the "Declaration of the Rights of the Peoples of Russia" on behalf of the newly formed "Commissariat of Nationalities" that reaffirmed the right of the "peoples of Russia to free self-determination, even to the point of separation and the formation of an independent state." The declaration guaranteed "equality and sovereignty (*suverennost'*) for all the peoples of Russia."[15] This was followed on 7 December 1917 by Lenin's appeal, "To All Muslim Toilers of Russia and the East," which called upon Muslims throughout Russia and Asia to rise up against their colonial oppressors and declare independence.

Having seized power in the Russian heartland, Lenin and his colleagues quickly began having second thoughts about affording the minority peoples of the former empire a blanket right of secession. On the one hand, the Bolsheviks' political weakness made it imperative that they prevent the non-Russian peoples from unifying in opposition to Soviet authority. On the other hand, they needed to defend the new regime and, as the "vanguard" of the working class, serve the "objective" interests of the proletariat by extending Soviet power wherever possible. This meant opposing the "bourgeois" governments that were declaring independence throughout the territory of the former empire. As Stalin bluntly put it that December, "The principle of self-determination must be subordinated to the principles of socialism."[16]

Doctrinally, this represented a major development. Both Lenin and Stalin (albeit with less enthusiasm in the latter case) had repeatedly asserted that the right of national self-determination would be extended to the bourgeoisie, explicitly rejecting the argument that it should be limited to the national proletariat. But both also recognized that the historical context had changed and that what was needed above all in the new circumstances was tactical flexibility. The new regime had to win the support of national minorities, or at least ensure their neutrality, by supporting self-determination and the right of secession in principle. At the same time it had to be free to establish Soviet power—by force if necessary—wherever doing so was in the "objective" interests of the working class. As Lenin explained in early 1918, "There is not a single Marxist who, without making a total break with the foundations of Marxism and Socialism, could deny that the interests of Socialism are above the interests of the right of nations to self-determination."[17]

To accommodate the new exigencies, a rapid and portentous decision was made by the new government in early 1918. Despite their unequivocal opposition to any form of federalism prior to the revolution, Lenin and his colleagues concluded that federalism would provide the new regime with the flexibility needed to deal most effectively with the "nationality problem." While rhetorical support for self-determination and the right to independence would continue, Russia's minorities would be offered a form of territorial autonomy within the newly established socialist state. As Lenin later explained, socialist federalism represented a compromise between "the national principle" and socialist internationalism, and as such was "the surest step towards the most lasting union of the various nationalities of Russia into a single, democratic, centralized, Soviet state."[18] In addition, Lenin and his colleagues remained hopeful that the Great War would lead to the collapse of imperialism, national liberation in the colonies, and socialist revolution in the West. Inducing the newly liberated nations to join the world's first socialist state (Soviet Russia) would be easier, it was felt, if they could do so as constituent units of a socialist federation. As Ronald Suny has put it, "Soviet Russia was conceived not as an ordinary national state but as the first stone in a future multinational socialist edifice."[19] Federalism would be the most effective mechanism for binding those stones together.

The new regime's commitment to federalism was first suggested in January 1918 during the Red Army's invasion of Ukraine. Even as a soviet government was being established in Ukraine by force, Moscow declared that it accepted "the supreme authority" of the Ukrainian Central Executive Committee of Soviets and called for "a federal union with Russia and complete unity in matters of internal and external policy."[20] Shortly thereafter, Soviet Russia was formally constituted as a federation—the Russian Soviet Federated Socialist Republic, or RSFSR. Article 11 of the RSFSR's 1918 constitution provided that "Soviets of regions with a distinct mode of living and national composition may unite in autonomous regional unions" and that these regional unions "shall enter the Russian Socialist Soviet Republic on a federal basis."[21] The structure of the new state's federal order was largely unspecified, however, and indeed in large part pro forma, as suggested by the fact that the constitution failed to specify a division of powers between federal and subnational governments.

The RSFSR was not the only state that emerged from the collapse of the Tsarist empire. In total, some thirteen governments declared independence within the empire's former territory.[22] Poland, Finland, Estonia, Latvia, and Lithuania won international recognition and managed to preserve their independence throughout the interwar period, in part because of protection for these fledgling states from first the Germans and later the victorious Allies.[23] In other regions, including Siberia, the Russian Far East, Ukraine, Belorussia, the Transcaucasus, and Central Asia, nationalists and socialists of various stripes took advantage of the chaos of the Civil War to establish autonomous governments and declare independence. Gradually, these governments were subordinated to Soviet power as their territories were occupied by the Red Army, thanks in large part to the hostility of minority peoples to the Whites, who were unabashed advocates of unitarism and Russian nationalism and whose armies acquired a reputation for ruthless treatment of non-Slavic peoples.

In most areas of the former empire, occupation by the Red Army meant incorporation into the RSFSR. In other cases, however, former nationalist governments had entered into direct contact with foreign powers and even won formal diplomatic recognition—Ukraine and Belorussia, for example, had been recognized by Germany, while Georgia, Armenia, and Azerbaijan had been recognized by most Western governments. The Bolsheviks were accordingly reluctant to undermine their claim that they respected the right to self-determination and secession by simply annexing these areas. Lenin also wanted support for the new Soviet state from "bourgeois nationalists" in Eastern Europe and the Third World. Open abandonment of the principle of self-determination and forcible incorporation of the fledgling "states" into the RSFSR would make any such support less likely. The Soviet regime therefore decided to recognize the formal independence of some of the "soviet" governments brought to power by the Red Army. Separate Soviet constitutions were accordingly adopted for Ukraine, Belorussia (Belarus), Azerbaijan, and Turkestan in 1921, and for Armenia, Georgia, and the "Peoples Republics" of Khorezm (Khiva) and Bokhara in 1922. At Moscow's insistence, and despite objections from the Georgians, the Transcaucasian Soviet Federated Socialist Republic was subsequently formed on 13 December 1922 through a union of Armenia, Azerbaijan, and Georgia.

As the occupation of Menshevik Georgia would later demonstrate, "bourgeois nationalists" were in practice denied the right to participate in the new political order despite Lenin's earlier promises that they, and not only Communists, would be afforded the right to exercise national self-determination.[24] As members of the newly renamed Bolshevik Party (RKP [b]), Communist leaders in these putatively independent states were in practice subject to the discipline of democratic centralism and thus ultimately subordinated to Moscow, a point made perfectly clear by a resolution adopted at the Communist Party's Eighth Congress in March 1918:

> All decisions of the Russian Communist Party and its leading organs are unconditionally binding on all elements of the Party, irrespective of their national composition. The Central Committees of the Lithuanian, Latvian, and Ukrainian Communists have the rights of regional committees of the Party and are completely subordinate to the Central Committee of the Russian Communist Party.[25]

As the Bolsheviks began to consolidate power in Russia, it became increasingly clear that the prospects for a decisive victory for socialism in Western Europe were bleak. As a result, militants in the Party began to argue that defending Soviet power against the aggressive designs of the imperialists and implementing the regime's political and economic program would be best served by forming a single state uniting the RSFSR, Ukraine, Belarus, and the Transcaucasian Federation. Stalin agreed, and at the same time he expressed his opposition to providing minority peoples with a right of secession in a future unified socialist state.[26] In August 1922, the Central Committee placed Stalin at the head of a special commission to draft a constitution for the new state. Stalin responded by proposing that Ukraine, Belarus, and the Transcaucasian republics be incorporated into the RSFSR with a status equal to the "autonomous areas" already incorporated in the RSFSR, such as Bashkortostan and Tatarstan. Stalin's so-called autonomization plan was vigorously opposed by the leaderships in many of the union republics, particularly Georgia. It was also rejected by Lenin, who by then was becoming increasingly concerned about "Great Russian chauvinism" and was arguing that a new union should be formed on the basis of formal equality between the RSFSR and the union's other constituent units.[27]

Relations between Stalin and Lenin were already deteriorating while Lenin's political strength was being weakened by his rapidly worsening health. Nevertheless, Stalin demurred. As a result, the Union of Socialist Soviet Republics (USSR) was established on 30 December 1922 on the basis of a "Union Treaty" adopted by the Central Executive Committee of the All-Russian Congress of Soviets (which by then included representatives from the non-Russian republics). A constitution for the new Union was promulgated on 6 July 1923 and ratified on 31 January 1924.

Consistent with Lenin's desires (the Bolshevik founder died on 21 January 1924), the 1924 constitution described the USSR as a "voluntary association of peoples with equal rights." There were four founding members—the RSFSR, the Ukrainian Soviet Socialist Republic (SSR), the Belorussian SSR, and the Transcaucasian SSR—although the constitution was amended to provide for the incorporation of Uzbekistan and Turkmenistan as union republics in 1925, and for the incorporation of Tajikistan in 1929.[28] Each republic was "assured of the right of free secession from the Union" (Article 4). While it was assumed that this right would never be exercised, Soviet legal theory held that the union republics were "sovereign" by virtue of their right to secede from the federation. And because "sovereignty" was an attribute of states, the union republics were ipso facto "states" (*gosudarstva*), which meant that they would be afforded many of the symbolic trappings and formal institutions of statehood, including their own constitutions, state flags and emblems, national anthems, state executive organs, and representation in all-union bodies such as the Council of Nationalities. They could also have their own "state language" and distinct cultural and scientific institutions, including separate academies of science (except for the RSFSR), state publishing houses, newspapers and journals, conservatories and art galleries, national theatres and film industries, symphonies, ballets, operas, and educational instruction in their titular language.[29] While the USSR's legislature was charged with adopting the fundamental principles that would guide the legislatures of the union republics in enacting their own legal codes, the criminal, civil, labor, family, and procedural codes actually enforced by the courts were particular to each republic.[30]

The 1924 constitution provided for a federal structure that consisted of a hierarchy of ethno-territorial units, including not only the union republics (formally SSRs), but also the "Autonomous Soviet Socialist Republics" (ASSRs, or *avtonomnye respubliki*), "autonomous oblasts" (*avtonomnye oblasti*), and (beginning in 1925) "national territories," or okrugs (*okruga*).[31] Unlike the union republics, however, the USSR's "autonomous formations" (the autonomous republics, autonomous oblasts, and national territories and soviets) had no constitutional right to secede. They were not, therefore, considered sovereign, and neither were they identified as states, which meant they were denied some of the trappings of statehood, including their own constitutions. Their lower status had many more concrete consequences, however, including lower levels of funding for cultural organizations and activities and titular language publications, less representation in all-union bodies, and fewer years of instruction in the titular language.

In general, Soviet nationality policies encouraged the development and entrenchment of a sense of territorial proprietorship by titular peoples in both the union republics and the autonomies, even in autonomies at the bottom of the federal hierarchy. With few exceptions, the union republics and autonomies were named after one or in some cases two nationalities (e.g., "the Ukrainian SSR," the "Tatar ASSR," etc.), a practice that reinforced the notion that each ethno-territorial unit somehow "belonged" to a particular people or peoples.[32] The regime also committed to what was in effect affirmative action for the eponymous peoples, called *korenizatsiia* (nativization), whereby individuals from the titular nation were afforded privileged access to jobs, university enrollment, and other advantages within their homelands.

To be sure, the Soviet system of ethnic federalism and *korenizatsiia* were intended in part to ensure the loyalty of local cadres and to provide them with a monopoly of local political resources.[33] But there was considerable plausibility to the official claim that the regime's nationality policy was also designed to promote a "flowering" (*rastsvet*) of national cultures through the promotion of minority languages and support for traditional culture, folklore, and crafts, even if some expressions of national culture were suspect because of their supposedly bourgeois flavor.[34] To this end, the regime provided national minorities with newspapers, journals, and books in their local vernaculars, educational opportunities in their own language, and support for cultural activities. Indeed, in many cases Soviet linguists and ethnographers in effect invented new identities for minority peoples by classifying particular languages and peoples as distinct where they might have been treated as dialects of a common language or regional variations of a single culture.[35] Tajiks, for example, had never really had a separate consciousness of themselves as a "Tajik" people and might have been labeled Persian or Iranian, while Karelians might well have been identified as Finns. The Turkic-speaking peoples of Central Asia, who lived in an area that had previously been referred to as "Turkestan," were divided into separate Kazakh, Kyrgyz, Uzbek, and Turkmen SSRs.[36] In the south Caucasus, Turkic-speaking Muslim peoples whom Russians had traditionally referred to, like most other Muslim peoples of the Tsarist empire, as "Tatars," became in effect the titular people of the Azerbaijan SSR but were only identified as "Azerbaijanis" by Soviet ethnographers beginning in 1937.[37] In other cases, written languages were created and sanitized national histories written for the first time in the Soviet period. As Stalin explained it (borrowing from Lenin), Soviet culture would be "national in form, socialist in content"—that is, Soviet citizens could use many languages and adhere to many national traditions, but the substance of their expression would have to be "socialist."

The introduction of internal passports in 1932, which Soviet citizens were issued at the age of sixteen and which required them to designate their nationality, was another powerful contributor to the entrenchment of national identities.[38] Only those nationalities that had been officially recognized could be listed in the passports, and individuals were not given an option to list "none," "mixed," or "Soviet." Moreover, while self-identification was permitted initially, by the time Stalin died each individual was required to designate the nationality of his or her parents, although children of mixed marriages could choose between the nationalities of their parents.[39]

Thus Soviet nationality policy was marked by a fundamental tension. On the one hand, the rigid system of national classification, the assignation of union republics and autonomies to particular peoples, *korenizatsiia* and the promotion of national languages, literary traditions, histories, and folklore, and the requirement that all citizens identify their nationality in their internal passport on the basis of ancestry reified and entrenched national identity. On the other hand,

Soviet Marxism was a decidedly internationalist ideology in which national identity was seen as an atavistic holdover from the past that, like the state itself, would eventually wither away under socialism and communism. The "flowering" (*rastsvet*) of national cultures was to be a temporary phenomenon, albeit one that might last for a considerable period. It would give way first to *sblizhenie* (drawing together) and then to the full-blown *sliianie* (merging) of cultures. The result would be the emergence of a nonnational "Soviet man," a cultural hybrid who would doubtless speak Russian but whose culture would be a synthesis of the cultural richness of all the peoples of the socialist world.

In practice, the commitment to a gradual and "dialectical" process of *rastsvet, sblizhenie,* and *sliianie* gave way to a more aggressive and voluntaristic approach to the sovietization of national minorities in the Stalin era, particularly in the 1930s. The titular elites in the union republics and autonomies were devastated by the purges, while the repression of all forms of "nationalist deviationism," which had begun in the early 1920s with a campaign against the high-ranking Tatar "national Communist," Sultan-Galiev, grew increasingly severe. A wholesale assault on religion and other "antisocialist" practices was launched in the 1930s. Power was increasingly centralized in Moscow, thanks to the full-scale nationalization of the means of production, forced industrialization, collectivization in agriculture, and the introduction of central planning for the national economy. Collectivization was particularly devastating for traditional rural cultures, most notably for the Soviet Union's nomadic peoples. Central planners also gave little thought to traditional patterns of production or interregional divisions of labor. The overweening objective of the regime in this period was to overcome backwardness, both the backwardness of the Soviet Union as a whole relative to advanced capitalist powers as well as the backwardness of USSR's minority peoples relative to the Russians.[40] To this end, central planners were even more inclined to treat the USSR as a single economic space, making investment decisions that frequently ignored local social, cultural, and environmental concerns. As a result, the economies of individual republics and autonomies became increasingly specialized, interdependent, and subject to the sometimes irrational whims of central authorities—the most notable example being the creation of an essentially monocultural economy in Uzbekistan that specialized in environmentally damaging cotton production. *Korenizatsiia* was pursued less aggressively as the regime complemented it with a policy of "circulation-of-cadres" designed to ensure that unionwide interests prevailed over "*mestnichestvo*" (literally "localism," but more broadly the privileging of local interests over all-union interests) and national loyalties.

At the same time, sovietization became difficult to distinguish from russification. The study of Russian, which was designated the language of "international communication," was made compulsory in all schools in the union republics and autonomies in a law adopted in March 1938, while the historiography of the period began to extol the "modernizing" impact of the Tsarist regime on "backward" minority nations, and Tsarist history was increasingly treated as the equivalent pre–Revolutionary Soviet history. Stalin's singling out of the Russians as "the first nation among equals" became even more explicit with the outbreak of "the Great Patriotic War" (World War II) when Stalin, himself a Georgian, enlisted the support of the Russian Orthodox Church in the campaign against the Germans and then explicitly thanked the Russian people at the conclusion of the war for leading the resistance to the invaders. Those years also witnessed the USSR's occupation and subsequent annexation of the Baltic republics, western Ukraine and Belorussia, and Bessarabia and Northern Bukovina in the wake of the Molotov-Ribbentrop Pact of 1939; the establishment of Soviet hegemony over Eastern Europe; the forced deportation of the Crimean Tatars, Volga Germans, Kalmyks, Chechens, Ingush, Meskhetian Turks, Balkars, Karachais, Digor Ossetians, and others from their homelands to remote areas of Siberia and Central Asia during the war (a great many of those deported died en route or soon after their arrival in their places of exile); as well as the arbitrary dissolution of the Kalmyk, Crimean Tatar, and Chechen-Ingush autonomous republics and the Karachai autonomous oblast, and the consolidation of the Karbardino-Balkarian autonomous republic into the Karbardin autonomous republic.

Despite this retreat from "Leninist" nationality policy, the basic institutions of Soviet federalism survived. Indeed, in the mid-1930s Stalin became even more explicit in arguing that national identity and ethnicity were resistant to change even under socialism, and, in what at one time might have been considered an ideological heresy, he claimed that there could be such a thing as a "socialist nation."[41] The regime continued to afford officially recognized minority cultures numerous institutional protections, including support for non-Russian newspapers, journals, and literature, cultural organizations, and educational opportunities in minority languages.[42]

The formal structure of Soviet federalism changed modestly with the adoption of the "Stalin" constitution of 1936. The previous year, Stalin had outlined three criteria for determining whether a particular national territory would be afforded union republic status: it would have to have an external border (on the grounds that the right of secession would be meaningless for any enclave); the titular minority would have to be a more or less "compact majority" within its territory; and it would have to have a population of at least one million.[43] This latter criterion, however, was not always adhered to—Estonia, for example, had a population of less than one million when it was incorporated into the USSR in 1940 as a union republic. Nevertheless, the guidelines were generally respected, and with the new constitution's adoption, the Transcaucasian SSR was dissolved and Armenia, Azerbaijan, and Georgia became full union republics. The former Kazakh and Kyrgyz ASSRs were raised to the status of union republics, bringing the number of union republics to eleven, to which were added the Karelo-Finnish, Moldavian, Latvian, Lithuanian, and Estonian SSRs in 1940 after their annexation in the wake of the Molotov-Ribbentrop Pact and the USSR's Winter War with Finland. With the demotion of the Karelo-Finnish SSR to the status of an autonomous republic in 1956, the number of union republics settled at fifteen, the same fifteen that would be identified in the Brezhnev constitution as union republics, and the same fifteen that would become, for better or worse, the fifteen Soviet successor states.

The Stalin constitution retained the union republics' right of secession (Article 17), while the union republics were again described as "sovereign" (Article 15) with a right to their own constitutions. The borders of the union republics could not be changed without their consent. An "upper house" of parliament, the Council of Nationalities, was formed and consisted of twenty-five deputies from each union republic, eleven deputies from each autonomous republic, five deputies from each autonomous oblast, and one deputy from each okrug (Article 35). On 1 February 1944, the union republics' formal powers were enhanced by a constitutional amendment (Article 18a) that granted them the right to enter into "direct relations with foreign states, to conclude agreements with them and to exchange diplomatic and consular representatives." Another amendment (Article 18b) adopted the same day provided that "Every union republic shall have its own republican military formations,"[44] although the center would have the right to define the "guiding fundamentals of the organization of the military formations of the union republics" (Article 14 [g] as amended).

While the powers of the autonomies had received scant attention in the USSR's first constitution, this changed with the new constitution of 1936. Each autonomous republic and autonomous oblast was specifically identified in the text, and each was described as being within, and thus subordinate to, a particular union republic. The powers of the autonomous oblasts were not specified, and the okrugs were not mentioned at all. The autonomous republics were to have their own constitutions, supreme soviets, and councils of ministers (Chapter VII). Only the union republics, however, had a right of secession, which meant that the autonomous republics were not sovereign and thus not quite "states." Their constitutions could not contradict those of the union republic of which they were a part (Article 92), just as the constitutions of the union republics could not contradict the USSR constitution. The autonomous republics were subject to the union republic's legal codes.[45] Article 14 (f) provided that the Union government had the right to approve the formation of new autonomous republics. This was later amended to include autonomous oblasts. While there was no provision specifically precluding the union republics from unilaterally eliminating an autonomous republic or autonomous oblast or from changing its borders, the fact that they were specifically identified as being part of particular union republics meant that they had some formal legal protection at the federal level. This was not true, however, for the autonomous okrugs.

In practice, of course, Stalin's rule was profoundly arbitrary—he could, and did, ignore or change the law as the spirit moved him. Certainly the right of secession of the union republics was a formal right only throughout the Stalin era (and after). The absence of enabling legislation made secession impossible even in legal terms. But more importantly, Stalin (and later the CPSU Politburo and, to a lesser extent, the Central Committee) exercised power from the center through the control of all Party and state organizations throughout the USSR, and the use of these and other organs of repression to prohibit open discussion, let alone realization, of secession. "Enemies of the people" were arrested for "national deviationism," spreading ethnic hatred, or promoting the breakup of the Soviet Union. Suggesting that a union republic consider exercising its formal right of secession was suicidal in the Stalin years and a prescription for instant arrest and incarceration in a labor camp or mental institution in later years. As a prosecutor explained to a Ukrainian nationalist being tried in 1961 for promoting Ukrainian secession, "Lukyanenko, you are a literate man, so why pretend to be a simple-minded dolt? You understand perfectly well that Article 17 of the Constitution [the right of secession] only exists for [the delusion of] the outside world."[46]

Nevertheless, the claim that the union republics were "sovereign states" became an axiom of Soviet federal theory and even had implications for Soviet foreign policy. At the Dumbarton Oaks conference, Stalin demanded of Roosevelt and Churchill that all of the USSR's sixteen union republics (which then included the Karelo-Finnish SSR) be afforded seats in the UN General Assembly. Despite the fact that it was well understood that the union republics' right of secession was fictitious, the West gave the Soviet claim a measure of international legitimacy when, in an effort to persuade Stalin to compromise over voting procedures for the Security Council, it was agreed at the Yalta Conference that the Ukrainian and Belorussian SSRs would be given seats in the General Assembly.[47] The United States and most other Western countries refused, however, to recognize the legality of the USSR's annexation of the three Baltic republics (Latvia, Lithuania, and Estonia), a position they would maintain throughout the remaining years of the USSR's existence.[48]

In the wake of Stalin's death in 1953, political repression abated. As part of his attack on Stalin's "personality cult," Khrushchev explicitly criticized the deceased dictator for having deported the USSR's "punished peoples," and he had them politically rehabilitated, with the notable exceptions of the Crimean Tatars and the Volga Germans.[49] He reestablished the Chechen-Ingush and Kalmyk ASSRs, and made the Kabardin ASSR once again the binational Karbardin-Balkar ASSR. Cultural policy was also relaxed as the regime adopted a less rigid understanding of "national deviationism," although Khrushchev sponsored a major reform of education that had the effect of increasing the use of Russian in the Soviet school system. Most importantly, personnel policies became more accommodating to regional elites, particularly after Khrushchev's ouster in 1964. While Khrushchev had generally adhered to the Stalin-era commitment to the "circulation-of-cadres," under Brezhnev a policy of "stability-in-cadres" was adopted, which meant that Party officials, particularly non-Russians, could expect to spend more of their careers in a single region. At the same time, the regime's commitment to *korenizatsiia* was intensified, while Party first secretaries at the union republic and regional level were given additional responsibilities and authority, becoming in effect the political "bosses" of their territories. Far from being mere "transmission belts" for implementing orders from the center, the first secretaries not only controlled access to scarce goods and privileges, but they could also, through their personal political connections and right to petition ministerial officials, central planners, and politicians in Moscow, influence investment and budget allocation decisions. Indeed, "crypto-politics" by subnational elites engaged in lobbying for funding frequently pitted republic elites against each other.[50] Regional Party organizations also consolidated their control of the "personnel weapon" through the institutionalization of the system of *nomenklatura* appointment, particularly after Stalin's death. At each level of the federal hierarchy, Party organizations possessed a list of *"nomenklatura"* positions (e.g., the managers of particular enterprises, directors of institutes, rectors of universities, etc.) along with a list of approved potential candidates (the so-called "members" of the *nomenklatura*) to fill those positions. When one of these positions became vacant, the local Party bureau, under the direction of its first secretary, would appoint a replacement from the list of pre-approved candidates. Regional and union republic first secretaries also benefited from Brezhnev's tolerance of official privilege, corruption, and "clan" politics. A Soviet critic writing in 1988 would describe the results of these policies as follows:

> In fact, one only has to call attention to the transformation of the "leaders" under Brezhnev: they lost their specializations, but they acquired territory. . . .
> The All-Union leaders of transportation, trade and industry endowed with super-rights disappeared, but in their place appeared province and republic leaders endowed not only with super-rights but with absolute power. . . . In their fiefdoms their rules, systems of relations, and laws of hierarchy flourished. In an atmosphere of unrestrained glorification of a top leader who was susceptible to flattery [i.e., Brezhnev], these lower ranking leaders did whatever they wanted, taking refuge behind inflated numbers and inflated achievements. Absolute rule, toadying, bribery and open extortion, flouting of the law, clannishness and nepotism, corruption and the embezzlement of state property came to life and thrived.[51]

While the center was generally willing to afford regional leaders considerable autonomy, it would not tolerate any overt challenges to the CPSU's authority or manifestations of political nationalism that could be construed as anti-union, anti-Soviet, antisocialist, or otherwise undesirable. Moscow would periodically launch public campaigns against *mestnichestvo* (localism). Indeed, union republic first secretaries were on occasion removed from office for being too aggressive in representing the "national" interests of their republics or for failing to repress nationalist sentiments with sufficient vigor.[52] In practice, the problem of *mestnichestvo* would tend to increase whenever the center tried to improve economic performance through decentralization. The most famous experiment in this regard came in 1957 with Khrushchev's "*sovnarkhozy*" reforms, whereby branch ministries in Moscow were briefly abolished and responsibility for the implementation of central plans was devolved to 105 "*sovnarkhozy,*" or regional economic councils (which were more or less coterminous with the USSR's oblasts and autonomies). In addition to various economic pathologies (e.g., the promotion of regional autarky), the attempts to decentralize economic decision-making authority would contribute to an increase in *mestnichestvo* as well as other "negative phenomena" (generally a euphemism for corruption). Moscow would then move to recentralize, a process that a Western economist would famously refer to as the Soviet "treadmill" of reforms.[53] Thus the *sovnarkhoz* reform was promptly abandoned after Khrushchev's ouster in 1964, and economic authority was once again concentrated in Moscow.

The renewed commitment to *korenizatsiia* in the Brezhnev era also had its limits. The informal practice was for the head of the KGB, the commander of the Soviet defense forces in the area, and the Party first secretary's deputy (the second secretary) to be from outside the area and a nontitular, and in most cases an ethnic Russian.[54] Although first secretaries were with few exceptions members of the titular nationality, many had completed at least part of their education, professional training, or early career outside the republic, most frequently in Moscow.[55] The appointment of a first secretary also had to be approved by organs higher up the Party hierarchy (i.e., the position would be on the higher organ's *nomenklatura*)—union republic first secretaries, for example, were on the *nomenklatura* of the Central Committee secretariat in Moscow.[56]

The general norms of cadre policy were not formal rules, and they were often disregarded by Moscow. For example, the first secretary of the Chechen-Ingush ASSR was never either a Chechen or an Ingush until the appointment of Doku Zavgaev in the Gorbachev era.[57] In Abkhazia, the titular Abkhaz were afforded an unusual degree of autonomy from the Georgian authorities in Tbilisi, despite the fact that the Abkhaz made up a very small proportion of the ASSR's population—17.8 percent in 1989. Relations between the Abkhaz and ethnic Georgians were strained, which led Moscow to place the first secretary of the Abkhaz ASSR on the *nomenklatura* of *both* the CPSU Central Committee and the Georgian Central Committee. As a result, the Abkhaz first secretary was relatively independent of the Party organization in Tbilisi. A similar arrangement prevailed in Karabakh, where relations between the majority Armenians and Azeris were even more strained. So, too, did the extent of *korenizatsiia* vary considerably, in some cases because of fears of *mestnichestvo* and in others because of a lack of qualified personnel. The non-Russian union republics with the highest percentage of titular elites were Georgia, Armenia, Azerbaijan, and (to a lesser extent) Ukraine and Belorussia. Those in the middle tier were the Baltic and the Central Asian republics, with the exception of Kazakhstan. Those with the lowest were Kazakhstan and Moldavia.[58] Similar variations existed among autonomies.

Despite problems of *mestnichestvo* and sporadic manifestations of "national deviationism" by a small number of active dissidents, the regime's claim that the "nationality problem" had been essentially solved became a frequently repeated, and widely believed, dogma, even if many ethnographers remained unconvinced. According to the 1961 Revised Party Program, the USSR had become an "all-peoples' state" (*obshchenarodnoe gosudarstvo*, sometimes translated as "state of all the people" or "state of the whole people") in which differences between nationalities were rapidly disappearing: "The borders between the union republics within the USSR," the Platform asserted, "are increasingly losing their former significance, since all the nations are equal, their life is organized on a single socialist foundation, the material and spiritual needs of each people are satisfied to the same extent, and they are united into one family by common vital interests and are advancing together toward a common goal—communism."[59] With internal borders "losing their former significance," the authorities considered transforming the USSR into a unitary state under a new constitution (sponsored by Khrushchev) on the grounds the USSR was now engaged in the "full-scale building of communism." Resistance to the plan from republic and regional elites, and recognition in Moscow that it might create very serious administrative problems, helped account for the long delay in drafting and ratifying the new constitution.

Indeed, when the "Brezhnev" constitution was finally adopted in 1977, opposition from regional elites to significant administrative redistricting meant that the existing federation structure was preserved. The constitution's preamble proclaimed that the USSR was "an all-people's state . . . in which a new historical community of people, the Soviet people, has been formed on the basis of the drawing together of all classes and social strata and the legal and actual equality of all nations and nationality and their fraternal friendship." The state was described as "a single union multinational state formed on the basis of the principle of socialist federalism as a result of the free self-determination of nations and the voluntary association of equal Soviet socialist republics" (Article 70). Moreover, the union republics were described for the first time as "sovereign Soviet socialist states" (Article 76),[60] while the Union was charged with protecting "the sovereign rights of the union republics."[61] Representation of the union republics in the Council of Nationalities was increased to thirty-two deputies for each union republic, from twenty-five in the 1936 constitution, while representation of the autonomies was unchanged—eleven deputies from each autonomous republic, five from each autonomous oblast, and one from each okrug. The 1944 amendment on the foreign policy of the union republics was reaffirmed—the union republics had the right to "enter into relations with foreign states, con-

clude treaties with them and exchange diplomatic representatives, and to participate in the activity of international organizations" (Article 80), although there
was no longer a provision allowing them to form their own military establish-
ments. Each union republic was afforded the right to "determine its division into
territories, regions, areas, and districts and decide other questions of administrative and territorial structure" (Article 79). Finally, they were once again granted
a formal right of secession, as provided for by the constitution's soon-to-be-
famous Article 72: "Every union republic shall retain the right of free secession
from the USSR."

The new constitution, like the 1936 version, had a separate chapter on the
powers and status of the autonomous republics (Chapter 10), although this time
the other autonomous areas did as well (Chapter 11). Again, the autonomous
republics and autonomous oblasts (but not the okrugs) were individually listed
and designated as part of a specific union republic. Article 84 provided that the
"territory of an autonomous republic may not be modified without its consent,"
although no such right was afforded the autonomous oblasts or okrugs, an omis-
sion that would later serve as the legal basis for Georgia's dissolution of the
South Ossetian autonomous oblast and Azerbaijan's dissolution of the Nagorno-
Karabakh autonomous oblast in the Gorbachev era.

When the Brezhnev constitution came into effect in late 1977, the USSR
was entering into the period that Gorbachev would later refer to as the "era of
stagnation" (*period zastoiia*). Brezhnev had suffered a serious heart attack in
1975 from which he never fully recovered, and the Soviet political elite began to
appear increasingly moribund even as Soviet economic performance deterio-
rated and the international "correlation of forces" seemed to turn against Moscow. By March 1985, when Gorbachev became the new general secretary, the
country was in what Gorbachev characterized as a "pre-crisis situation." Problems were intensifying and the leadership seemed incapable of taking measures
that could overcome those problems, Gorbachev explained, but they were not
yet so acute that society was on the verge of rebellion or that decisive steps by a
more vigorous leadership could not return the country to the proper path. Above
all, there were no signs of imminent antiregime mobilization by the Soviet people generally or by the USSR's non-Russian minorities particularly. This interpretation was generally shared by most outside observers, who assumed that the
USSR's "nationality problem" had been more or less "solved," at least in the
sense that antiunion nationalist mobilization was unlikely.[62]

While it may have been true that, given the repressive apparatus at the dis-
posal of the central authorities, organized opposition to the regime from below
was impossible at the time, it was not true that the USSR's non-Russian minorities were being rapidly or uniformly russified or sovietized, as many nationalists
would later contend. The intensity of national consciousness and durability of
national identities varied significantly, as suggested by a number of behavioral
indicators. Language retention (percentage of passport ethnics who listed their

titular language as their first language) was very high and stable for some national minorities but not others. For Turkmens, for example, it was 98.5 percent in 1989, for Uzbeks 98.3 percent, for Georgians 98.2 percent, and for Chechens 98.1 percent. In other cases it was comparatively low and declining—language retention for Karelians, for example, had declined from 71.3 percent in 1959 to 47.8 percent in 1989. Significant declines were also registered for the Udmurts, Chuvash, Komi, Mordvinians, Koryak, Khanty, Mansi, Chukchi, and Evenk.[63] Intermarriage was relatively common between some nationalities, particularly those that were culturally related (Slavs, Turkic-speaking Muslims), but in other cases it was rare even where there was frequent contact (e.g., between Russians and Central Asians in Central Asia, or between Russians and Georgians in Georgia).[64] Nationalist dissidents were active in some republics and regions (the Baltics, Georgia, and western Ukraine), while in others they were all but absent (the Central Asia republics).[65] Nor can it be assumed that strong national consciousness necessarily equated with strong anti-Soviet sentiments. For example, the Armenians were widely regarded as having a deep and historically rooted national identity, but they were also considered relatively pro-Soviet because of Russia's traditional support for the Christian Armenians during the Ottoman period. In other cases, there was relatively widespread resentment of Soviet power and occupation (e.g., the Baltic peoples, western Ukrainians). And finally, in some cases traditional internationality enmity persisted despite the best efforts of Soviet authorities to promote the "friendship of peoples"—relations between Armenians and Azeris, and between Abkhaz and Georgians, for example, were widely understood as, to use the Soviet euphemism, "complicated."

The character of "nationalist" pressure on central authorities before 1985 varied as well. In some cases there were demands for changes in administrative status (e.g., the demand that Tatarstan or Bashkortostan be made union republics) or administrative affiliation (e.g., the demand that Nagorno-Karabakh be subordinated to Armenia rather than Azerbaijan, or that Abkhazia become an autonomous republic of the RSFSR rather than Georgia). In other instances, Moscow was being pressed to grant union republics or autonomies greater representation in central organs of power (e.g., the appointment of a union republic's first secretary to the Politburo, or greater representation on the Central Committee). Elsewhere there were demands for greater *korenizatsiia* and affirmative action for titulars, as well as pressure to reduce in-migration of non-indigenes (e.g., in the Baltic states and Abkhazia). In still other cases, there were demands that certain territories be returned to their "rightful owners" (e.g., Ingush pressure to have the Prigorodnyi district be made a part of the Checheno-Ingush ASSR), that deported peoples such as the Crimean Tatars, Meskhetian Turks, and Volga Germans be allowed to return to their homelands, and that the autonomous status of regions that had lost administrative recognition under Stalin be restored. Finally, Moscow was under constant pressure from local authorities to provide greater institutional support and resources for the protection of non-Russian languages and cultures, for greater investment in local infrastructure and productive facilities, and for additional subsidies to regional budgets.

There was other evidence that national identities were not abating as well. While a substantial intermingling of peoples and russification had occurred in the interwar period, these trends moderated significantly after 1945.[66] Soviet researchers concluded that "national" prejudices remained significant even in urban areas, which contradicted their expectation that national identities would wither away under socialism in the more "advanced" sectors of society. Likewise migratory patterns suggested that internationality affinities and animosities had yet to give way to the full-blown "friendship of peoples." Most union republic titulars were highly concentrated in their home republics—for example, over 90 percent of Lithuanians (95.3 percent), Latvians (95.1 percent), Georgians (95.1 percent), Estonians (92.9 percent), and Turkmens (93 percent) lived in their home republics, while two-thirds of the least concentrated of the union republic titulars, the Armenians, lived in Armenia. Most out-migration from titular homelands was by Russians, Ukrainians, and Belorussians—by 1989 there were some 25.3 million Russians living outside the RSFSR (17.4 percent of all Russians in the USSR), 6.8 million Ukrainians living outside of the Ukrainian SSR (15.3 percent of all Ukrainians), and 2.1 million Belorussians living outside the Belorussian SSR (21.2 percent). Of these, the majority (56 percent) lived in one of the other Slavic republics. The out-migration of the Turkic-speaking Muslims of Central Asia from their administrative homelands was even lower and was largely limited to republics of similar culture—relatively few would migrate, for example, to Russia or to other republics with traditionally Christian majorities. While the Slavic peoples of the USSR felt comparatively comfortable living in non-Slavic republics, most Muslims were reluctant to live in non-Muslim republics. Similarly, Georgians and the titular peoples of the Baltic republics preferred to live in their "own" republics. Soviet authorities therefore found it difficult to convince many minority peoples to leave their homelands in search of high wage jobs in extraction industries in remote areas, particularly Siberia. Where economic conditions were particularly bad (e.g., the RSFSR's North Caucasus region), many titulars might leave their homelands in search of better jobs, but even then this was often seasonal migration, with many returning regularly to their homes to maintain family ties and friendships.

The political identity of Russians in the late Soviet period presents a special case. As the majority nationality, Russians were less conscious of their ethnicity than minority nationalities (except perhaps Belorussians), just as whites in the United States are less conscious of race than blacks or other racial minorities.[67] Russians were also more likely to think of themselves as Soviet citizens rather than ethnic Russians (again with the possible exception of Belorussians), and they were even less likely to identify politically with the RSFSR.[68] In comparison, non-Russians, and particularly non-Slavs, were more aware of their nationality and tended to view Russians as unfairly privileged—the "first nation" of the USSR, or "elder brother" as Stalin had put it. Nevertheless, the Soviet regime was formally committed to "socialist internationalism," and it had accordingly constructed the Soviet state on an explicitly multinational basis. In order to minimize the danger of "Great Russian chauvinism" and to limit Russian domination of Soviet political life, the RSFSR had been "disadvantaged" relative to the other republics[69]—it did not have its own academy of sciences, Communist Party, Komsomol, interior ministry, or trade union structure, while all-union ministries had jurisdiction over many enterprises in the RSFSR that in other republics were under the control of republic ministries. Russian nationalists could therefore argue with some plausibility that ethnic Russians were being legally discriminated against and that, although the Soviet state was protecting and nurturing minority cultures, it was allowing Russian cultural and traditions to wither away and to degenerate into "sovietism."

While in most cases national identities were relatively well entrenched (even if the substance of those identities was constantly changing), some of the USSR's smaller minorities were being gradually assimilated into locally dominant cultures. Military service made a particularly important contribution to russification, as military authorities were insistent that all recruits be at least minimally competent in Russian, the command language.[70] Moreover, educational opportunities in minority languages gradually diminished, while public administration was increasingly conducted in Russian only.[71] Minority peoples who lived outside their home republics or autonomies were particularly vulnerable to linguistic assimilation, as were those that were dispersed or highly urbanized. In general, the smaller, less concentrated, and more urbanized the nationality, the more prone it was to assimilation. Although in many cases linguistic assimilation and acculturization took the form of russification (e.g., in the case of the RSFSR's Finno-Ugric peoples such as the Karelians, Mordvinians, Chuvash, and Udmurts), in other cases assimilation was to locally dominant, but non-Russian, cultures. For example, many of the small linguistic groups residing on the northern and southern slopes of the Caucasus Mountains were being assimilated by locally dominant Azeris or Georgians, or by larger Dagestani nationalities such as the Avars.

National and political identities in the late Soviet period, like political identities everywhere, were also situational. An ethnic Turkmen visiting relatives in Moscow who was stopped for a traffic infraction by an ethnic Russian militiaman and solicited for a bribe was more likely to be conscious of being Turkmen than a Turkmen collective farmer working alongside other ethnic Turkmens in his home republic. Nor were strong national identities and a Soviet identity necessarily incompatible—it was perfectly possible to have a strong sense of national identity and affiliation with a home republic and also be a Soviet "patriot." An Armenian could be proud of being an Armenian while being at the same time loyal to the Soviet state and proud of its status as an international power. Indeed, Soviet doctrine made a sharp distinction (at least in principle—making the distinction in practice was not always easy) between "nationalism" and "chauvinism" on the one hand, which were regarded as antisocialist, and healthy Soviet "patriotism" and pride in traditional cultures on the other. Consciousness of being either "national" or "Soviet" could also be activated by particular circumstances. A soccer game between a team from Russia and a team from Georgia, for example, would make most Georgians feel very Georgian, but an Olympic basketball game between the Soviet and U.S. national teams would make them feel Soviet.

Differences in economic conditions between regions and national groups were also significant, although the extent to which these inequalities were recognized by the Soviet public or elite was unclear. From its inception, the regime suffered from socioeconomic reductionism in its approach to the nationality question. According to Lenin (and indeed to Marx as well), economic modernization and social mobilization would mean that national identities would be supplanted by class consciousness. Under socialism, the transition to a classless society would mean that class consciousness would disappear as well. The result in the Soviet case would be the emergence of a new nonnational and classless "Soviet people" (*sovetskii narod*). Before this could happen, however, an equalization (*vyravnivanie*) of economic conditions, living standards, and life opportunities between peoples would need to occur, which meant that poorer republics and autonomies would receive disproportionate investments in industries and social infrastructure.

Just as there was little evidence to support the claim that social mobilization and socialism were undermining national identities, there is reason to doubt that significant socioeconomic "equalization" was taking place among union republics, particularly in the final years of the Soviet period, although the evidence in this regard is disputed.[72] Certainly all the republics underwent rapid industrialization, economic growth, and social mobilization after sovietization, but that did not mean that disparities in economic conditions and living standards were necessarily diminishing.[73] In part, persistent disparities between regions and national groups were due to the regime's commitment to rapid industrialization and high growth rates, beginning especially in the 1930s, which required that investment go to areas where it could be employed most productively, and not to the USSR's less-developed regions where labor productivity was low, such as Central Asia. Demographic trends and geographic factors were also important. Whereas the USSR suffered from a general labor shortage, natural resources were most abundant in Siberia, where conditions were harsh and labor particularly scarce. In the Muslim republics of Central Asia and Azerbaijan, on the other hand, the population was growing rapidly but labor productivity was low, job opportunities were comparatively limited, and natural resources relatively scarce. As noted earlier, Central Asians were also very reluctant to migrate to areas where job opportunities were better. As a result, per capita improvements in living standards in Central Asia and other less-developed areas slowed in the late Soviet period.

Nevertheless, central authorities increasingly assumed that industrialization, rapid social mobilization, improved occupational status for minorities, and *korenizatsiia* had brought about an equalization of living conditions between nationalities. As Brezhnev would confidently put it in December 1972, "[T]he problem of the equalization of development of the national republics has been resolved, on the whole." Thus the 1971–1975 Five-Year Plan was the last to identify equalization as a specific goal.[74] Investment decisions made in Moscow accordingly became even less concerned with equalization, and planners began to consider regional development not in terms of the union republics but on the basis of nineteen economic regions that supposedly better reflected economic "rationality."[75] Ten of these regions were located in the RSFSR; three were in Ukraine; Kazakhstan, Belorussia, and Moldavia were treated as distinct economic regions; while the three Baltic republics, the three South Caucasus republics, and the four Central Asian republics (excluding Kazakhstan) were amalgamated into separate planning regions.[76]

With central planners less concerned about interregional equalization, what evidence there is suggests that regional and national inequalities were actually increasing during the Brezhnev period. In general, Tajikistan remained the poorest union republic, followed by the other Central Asian republics and Azerbaijan. Latvia, Estonia, Lithuania, the RSFSR, and Belorussia were the richest. Growth rates per annum between 1961 and 1985 ranged from a low of 4.2 percent in Turkmenistan to a high of 7.8 percent in Armenia. Growth in per capita income in the less-developed Central Asian republics and Azerbaijan averaged 3 percent, compared to 4.4 percent unionwide. Whereas urbanization doubled in Belorussia and Moldavia between 1959 and 1980, it may actually have declined in Turkmenistan and Tajikistan between 1970 and 1985. Per capita consumption was 12 to 28 percent above the all-union average in the Baltic republics, and 40 percent below average in Tajikistan.[77] While all republics were interdependent (although this interdependency was mediated through Moscow), some were more dependent on interrepublic trade than others. In 1988, interrepublic trade as a percentage of GDP ranged from a low of less than 20 percent for the RSFSR to over 75 percent for Turkmenistan.[78] Economic specialization likewise appeared to be increasing over time for all-union republics except Belorussia.[79] Gertrude Schroeder, a leading American specialist on the Soviet economy, summarized the evidence on equalization as follows: "While these regional differentials in living standards are not especially large by international comparison (they are much narrower than in Yugoslavia, for instance), they are substantial nonetheless, and the differences certainly are not being reduced."[80] As we will see, real and (more importantly) perceived inequality among union republics and nationalities would become an important factor in inspiring demands for "economic sovereignty" and eventually "political sovereignty" in the Gorbachev era.

Economic as well as political grievances by titulars in the minority republics were also affected by awareness of conditions in neighboring states. Estonians, Latvians, and Lithuanians, for example, were well aware that living standards in Finland, which had not been substantially different from those of the Baltic republics in the interwar period, were now immeasurably better, and they were accordingly all the more convinced that their republics were being "exploited" in an effort to equalize living conditions in the "backward" republics, notably those in Central Asia.

In general, however, the regime was tolerant of minority cultures, and indeed in many respects it offered them considerable institutional protections and privileges, perestroika-era claims by radical nationalists notwithstanding. The center was intent upon neither rapid cultural sovietization nor russification. And in general it avoided exploiting one national group to the benefit of another. As time passed, the leadership became increasingly willing to acknowledge that national identities were likely to last for a very long time indeed, even under conditions of "mature developed socialism" and an "equality of nations."[81] First Brezhnev, and then Yurii Andropov and Konstantin Chernenko, would frequently cite Lenin in asserting that the national question required tact and sensitivity on the part of central authorities. Andropov in particular held that nationality policy should be based less on dogma and more on the "scientific" study of national identities, and during his brief tenure as Soviet leader ethnographers were encouraged to conduct more objective empirical research on contemporary national identities and to report their findings to the CPSU Central Committee.

Nor can it be assumed that the mobilization of antiunion and separatist sentiments or interethnic conflicts in the Gorbachev period demonstrates conclusively that separatism and interethnic hostilities were widespread or uniform prior to perestroika. In some cases, there is indeed evidence that interethnic enmities and antiregime sentiments predated perestroika, although particular policies and events during perestroika would greatly exacerbate them. In others, however, ethnic conflicts and separatist sentiments resulted from the stresses and strains of perestroika itself, including political struggles over the course of the reform process, deteriorating economic conditions, and mishandling of challenges from antiunion or anti-Communist oppositionists by central authorities. The nationalist mobilization and sovereignty campaigns that began in the Baltic republics would also have a powerful demonstration effect, contributing to the politicization of national identities in places where they previously had been weak or largely apolitical.

While political identities and relations between nationalities in the USSR were thus complex, dynamic, and in many respects opaque, it is certainly the case that the policies of the Soviet state had a powerful impact on the ability of national cultures to reproduce themselves. Those nationalities that lacked administrative recognition (e.g., Germans, Poles, Jews, Finns, Romanians) became more dispersed and urbanized, had correspondingly low, and typically declining, levels of language retention, and were thus particularly vulnerable to assimilation. In other instances, lack of official recognition as a distinct nationality and of institutional protections and preferential treatment meant that certain languages—and the cultures they embodied—were either in decline or, as with the Ubykhs and Shapsugs of Georgia, died out entirely. Placement in the federal ethno-territorial hierarchy likewise had important practical consequences, particularly for titular political and cultural elites whose life opportunities were directly affected by the regime's preferential policies. Federal ranking affected not only the degree of representation in central institutions but the allocation of state funding to the republics for educational opportunities in minority languages, financial support for academies of sciences, indigenous research institutes, books, journals, newspapers, libraries, symphonies, film studios, operas, ballets, and even investment in local infrastructure and the location of new enterprises. At least as important were the symbolic implications. For the officially recognized homeland of a titular people to be designated a mere autonomous *okrug* meant that the titular people had a lower status than those with their own autonomous oblast, autonomous republic, or (best of all) union republic—the implications being that they were somehow less "modern," less distinct, more dispersed, smaller in number, or otherwise more likely to pass into history than more prestigious nationalities with higher ranked homelands. The political and cultural elite of certain nationalities, most notably the Tatars, therefore pressed Moscow repeatedly to raise the status of their national homeland (in the case of the Tatars, from autonomous republic to a union republic).

The formal institutions of Soviet federalism had another practical consequence for local elites—the creation of a vast complex of regional positions and employment opportunities under the control of local Party and government officials. As noted earlier, most important positions in the union republics were on the *nomenklatura* of the republic party apparatus, the sole exception being the RSFSR, which did not have its own Communist Party until late in the Gorbachev period (by which time the *nomenklatura* system had collapsed). Party officials in the union republics appointed members of the republic's legislative and executive organs, and they vetted similar appointments by lower-level Party organs for regional (oblast, krai, autonomous republic, autonomous oblast, autonomous okrug) and local governments (city, raion, urban settlement, village, etc.) within their territory. Key positions in education, culture, health, social welfare, justice, and the local police and militia were likewise on the *nomenklatura* of the relevant Party organizations. Moreover, all the union republics, including the RSFSR, had their own state organs, including their legislative hierarchies (union republic supreme soviets, regional soviets, and city and village soviets) and executive hierarchies (councils of ministers for the union republics, executive committees for regional and local governments). Ministers and the heads of assorted specialized "state committees" of the union republics (heads of administrations or departments at the local level) in turn supervised a considerable assortment of enterprises and organizations located on their territory.[82] Officials in these executive organs were responsible to both the soviet at their equivalent level (which the Soviets referred to as "horizontal" control), as well as to executive organs above them ("vertical" control)—thus the notion of "dual subordination" (*dvoinoe podchinenie*). Equally importantly, executive officials, as well as the managers of the enterprises they supervised, had to comply with, and help "fulfill" (or better "over-fulfill"), plans and directives coming from central planning organs in Moscow, above all Gosplan.

Nevertheless, while all enterprises and organizations throughout the USSR belonged formally to the "all-peoples'" state, the fact that certain enterprises and organizations fell within the jurisdiction of the union republics was understood to mean that in some sense they "belonged" to the individual union republic, not to the Soviet center. This sense of ownership, as well as a widespread perception within some minority communities that the inequalities inherent in the Soviet federal hierarchy were unjust, would prove a powerful stimulus to demands for genuine economic and political "sovereignty" in the Gorbachev era. The elaborate organizational structure of the Soviet system of ethnic federalism would also mean that a highly ramified and entrenched political and economic apparatus existed in each union republic, and to a lesser extent in each autonomous republic, oblast, and krai, prior to perestroika. This apparatus, when controlled by members of the local *nomenklatura* who, for whatever reason, chose to capitalize on the Gorbachev reforms to demand greater autonomy from Moscow or to champion outright separatism, or when it came under the control of antiunion oppositionists who were not members of the traditional *nomenklatura,* would greatly complicate Gorbachev's efforts to preserve the power of the central government and defend the unity of the Soviet state.

It was not only, however, the formal institutions of Soviet federalism and nationality policy that would undermine Gorbachev's efforts to restructure Soviet socialism. Equally important were the normative claims and legitimizing mythologies that the regime had elaborated in defense of Soviet federalism, claims and mythologies that stressed the advantages of "socialist" federalism over mere bourgeois federalism, which ignored the interests of national minorities and failed to respect their right of self-determination. These included the following:

1. The USSR is a voluntary association of equal Soviet socialist republics.
2. The right to the self-determination of nations is entailed in the constitutional right of the union republics to secede.
3. The right of secession means that each union republic is a sovereign state.
4. The union republics voluntarily delegated certain powers to the all-union government by ratifying the 1922 Union Treaty.
5. The USSR's federation structure and nationality policy ensure the de jure equality of all nations of the USSR.

6. The USSR's federation structure and nationality policies provide for the equal opportunity of all nations to flourish culturally (*rastsvet*).
7. Each nation should have its own national intelligentsia, professionals, artists; each should have its cultural institutions and support for traditional practices from the state; and each should have some opportunity to study in its own language. Under these conditions, each nation will contribute equally to the development of the great Soviet multinational state and the further perfection of socialism.
8. Socialism and Soviet federalism have created the basis for an end to interethnic enmity, the genuine "friendship of peoples" (*druzhba narodov*), and a gradual drawing together (*sblizhenie*) of nations.
9. Socialism, modernization, and socioeconomic equalization (*vyranivanie*) are bringing about a gradual withering away (*sliianie*) of distinct national identities, their replacement by a nonnational "Soviet" identity, and the emergence of a new Soviet people (*Sovetskii narod*).

Some of these assertions were unquestionably false—the Soviet Union was not a purely voluntary union of nations; sovereignty and the right of secession were legal fictions; and the powers of the union government had not been delegated from below. But others had a good measure of truth in them, which helped account for the extent to which most Soviet citizens believed them. Soviet nationality policy had indeed contributed to the development of national identities, cultures, and languages; interethnic enmity was moderate for such a diverse society and episodes of interethnic violence extremely rare; there had been substantial improvements in standards of living, health care, education, and job opportunities for all nationalities since 1917, which made the claim to equalization plausible; and most Soviet citizens took considerable pride in their country and its accomplishments. The plausibility of these (and indeed other) legitimizing claims would, as we shall see, have a profound impact on the course of perestroika, above all in the effect it would have in helping account for Gorbachev's highly impractical response to the intensifying "nationality crisis" set in motion by perestroika.

* * * * *

Writing in 1980, the noted American sovietologist Seweryn Bialer presciently argued that, of all the sources of instability in the USSR, the nationality question "is potentially the most devastating for the state in its possible long-range consequences and presents the deepest challenge to the legitimacy of the regime."[83] He went on to suggest, however, that "the nationality problem and the attendant fear of the central elite and most other Great Russians for their power is one of the major brakes on the evolution of the Soviet system away from authoritarianism and on the innovative impulses of the Soviet political leadership."[84] What Bialer did not anticipate was that a reform-minded leader would come to power whose confidence in the basic institutions and legitimizing myths of Soviet socialism—including the legitimizing myths of Soviet federalism—would lead him to underestimate the risk that reform could lead to an explosion of the nationality problem. Ironically, it may have taken a leader like Gorbachev, who assumed that the nationality problem had indeed been solved, to undertake the enormously risky step of fundamentally reforming the Soviet system.

Notes

1. Aryeh L. Unger, Constitutional Development in the USSR: A Guide to the Soviet Constitution (New York: PICA Press, 1981), 26.

2. Unger 1981, 26.

3. Walker Connor, *The National Question in Marxist-Leninist Theory and Strategy* (Princeton, N.J.: Princeton University Press, 1984), 11.

4. Richard Pipes, *The Formation of the Soviet Union: Communism and Nationalism 1917–1923* (Cambridge, Mass.: Harvard University Press, 1954 [1997]), 33.

5. Robert C. Tucker, *Stalin As Revolutionary, 1879–1928* (New York: W. W. Norton, 1973), 150–51.

6. Pipes 1954 (1997), 41.

7. Kaiser 1994, 96.

8. Kaiser 1994, 98.

9. Connor 1984, 36.

10. Quoted in Pipes 1954 (1997), 43.

11. Bruce Franklin, ed., *The Essential Stalin: Major Theoretical Writings, 1905–1952* (Garden City, N.Y.: Doubleday, 1972), 71. To my knowledge, this is the moment when "sovereignty" became a politically important term in Bolshevik political discourse. Why it was used at that particular time, and whether it was meant to connote anything other than the right of secession, is not clear. I can find no use of it by Lenin himself before the October Revolution—notably, it does not appear in *State and Revolution*. I should also note that the term seems to have entered Russian political discourse in general rather late, much later than in Western Europe—it does not, for example, appear in *Tolkovyi slovar' zhivogo velikorusskogo iazyka Vladimira Dalia* (St. Petetsburg: Izd. T-va M.O. Vol'fa, 1882). It is, however, included in the *Entsiklopedicheskii slovar' Brokgauz-Efron,* vol. 31:2 (St. Petersburg, 1901), 892–94, where it is defined as "the supremacy (*verkhoventsvo*) and totality (*sovokupnost'*) of supreme power (*verkhovnykh prav'*) possessed by the state."

12. Quoted in Pipes 1954 (1997), 45.

13. Quoted in Connor 1984, 45.

14. V. I. Lenin, *Selected Works,* vol. 6 (New York: International Publishers, 1943), 399.

15. *Istoriia sovetskoi konstitutsii, 1917–1956 (v dokumentakh)* (Moscow: Gosudarstvennoe izdatel'stvo iuridicheskoi literatury, 1957), 58.

16. Connor 1984, 48.

17. Quoted in Robert Conquest, *The Nation Killers* (London: Macmillan, 1970), 118.

18. Unger 1981, 48.

19. Suny 1993, 85.

20. Quoted in Suny 1993, 88.

21. Unger 1981, 28. The 1918 constitution of the RSFSR did not, however, employ the term "sovereignty." Article 2 asserted that the RSFSR is "established on the basis of a free union of free nations, as a federation of Soviet national republics" (Unger 1981, 25–26).

22. Connor 1984, 46.

23. After occupying much of Belorussia and launching an offensive against Soviet Ukraine in early 1920, Poland under Marshall Pilsudski barely managed to preserve its independence by defeating the advancing Red Army outside of Warsaw in August. The attempt to take Warsaw was made despite the fact that Lenin had earlier identified the Poles and Finns in particular as distinct nations that "could most easily and 'naturally' exercise the rights of separation" from the Tsarist empire, quoted in E. H. Carr, *The Bolshevik Revolution 1917–1923* (New York: W. W. Norton, 1980 [1952]), 292.

24. Ronald Grigor Suny, *The Making of the Georgian Nation*, 2d ed. (Bloomington: Indiana University Press, 1994 [1988]), 201–8.

25. Quoted in Jack F. Matlock, Jr., *Autopsy on an Empire: The American Ambassador's Account of the Collapse of the Soviet Union* (New York: Random House, 1995), 28.

26. Kaiser 1994, 104.

27. The disagreement between Lenin and Stalin over the latter's "autonomization plan" has typically been portrayed by both Western and Soviet historians as reflecting Lenin's interest in accommodating the national minorities and his concerns about "Great Russian chauvinism" on the one hand, and Stalin's desire to subordinate the national minorities to the strong hand of central Party authority on the other hand (see, e.g., Moshe Lewin, *Lenin's Last Struggle* (London: Pluto Press, 1975 [1968]). Terry Martin, however, has argued that Lenin and Stalin were in fact equally concerned about the problem of "Great Russian chauvinism," and that Stalin's objections to Lenin's proposal for a union of equal soviet republics was based on his belief that this would, by giving the Russians there own republic, actually increase the danger of Russian "bourgeois nationalism" and risk transforming the RSFSR from an "all-Russian" (*rossiiskii*) republic into an ethnically Russian (*russkii*) one (Martin 2001, 394–99). Martin also points out that while Lenin's plan was more advantageous to the union republics, Stalin's plan would have been more advantageous to the autonomies, notably Tatarstan and Turkestan (then a part of the RSFSR) (Martin 2001, 396).

28. Initially, the territories of the former Khorezm and Bokhara Emirates in Central Asia, which were also conquered by the Red Army, were not formally incorporated into the USSR and were identified as "peoples' republics" on the grounds that they had yet to rid themselves of feudalism and were thus not ready for socialism.

29. However, only the Georgian, Armenian, and Azerbaijani constitutions identified their titular language as the official state language of their republics. In other cases, both the titular language and Russian were treated as state languages, which typically meant that most public business was conducted in Russian (e.g., the language used at sessions of the republic's Supreme Soviet or Party congresses was Russian). The issue became particularly controversial in 1978 when protests broke out in Georgia against a draft of a new Georgian constitution that would have removed the provision specifying Georgian as the state language. At the urging of Eduard Shevardnadze, then CPSU first secretary in the republic, the attempt to revise the republic's constitution was dropped, Anatoly M. Khazanov, *After the USSR: Ethnicity, Nationalism, and Politics in the Commonwealth of Independent States* (Madison: University of Wisconsin Press, 1995), 15. Similar provi-

sions were dropped that year from the drafts of the new Armenian and Azerbaijani constitutions.

30. Unger 1981, 88. Stalin's 1936 constitution removed this restriction on the legal
powers of the USSR legislature, but a 1957 constitutional amendment restored it. Moreover, the all-union legislature never actually adopted a unionwide legal code between
1936 and 1957.

31. There were also over 5,000 "nationality" village soviets and raions (districts),
including distinct "aboriginal" (*tuzemnye*) soviets, "tribal" (*rodovye*) soviets, and "nomadic" (*kochevye*) soviets, but these were abolished under the Stalin constitution of 1936
(Kaiser 1994, 109–10).

32. The exceptions were Dagestan, Gorno-Badashkhan, Nagorno-Karabakh, and
Nakhichevan. In Dagestan, an ASSR within the RSFSR, the 1989 census listed thirty-
four nationalities, the largest of which, the Avars, made up only 28 percent of the population. As a result, none of Dagestan's nationalities was eponymous ("Dagestan" has Turk-
ish roots meaning "mountainous land"). Gorno-Badashkhan, in Tajikistan, was populated
by highlander peoples known colloquially as Pamiris, most of whom spoke a distinct
language (the principal dialect of which was known as Shughni), and who were also
distinguished from other Tajiks by the fact that they were traditionally Ismaili Muslims
while the Tajiks, like the great bulk of Muslim peoples of the USSR, were traditionally
Sunni. Nevertheless, the Pamiris were required to classify themselves as Tajiks after 1937
on their internal passports and census forms. Nagorno-Karabakh and Nakhichevan, both
formally part of Azerbaijan, were "shared" by Armenians and Azeris, neither of which
was "titular." Other anomalies in the Soviet system of ethnic federalism and nationality
classification also warrant mention. Jews were classified as a nationality despite the fact
that their traditional distinctiveness as a "people" was primarily religious/cultural, not
linguistic. They were also "awarded" their own homeland (the Jewish AO, now Biro-
bidzhan) in the remote Far East, despite the fact that there was no Jewish claim to the
territory as a traditional homeland and very few Jews lived in the area. Adzhars, traditionally Muslim Georgians who live along Georgia's border with Turkey, were initially
treated as a separate nationality from Georgians, again the argument being that in this
case "religion-as-culture outweighed language and became a crucial ethnic marker in its
own right" (Slezkine 1994, 429). However, the Abkhaz later lost their designation as a
nationality, despite the fact that the Adzhar ASSR retained its status as an autonomous
republic within Georgia. Apparently it had been decided that their traditional religious
beliefs were insufficient to justify treating them as having a distinct culture from other
Georgians, at which point Adzhars had no choice but to list themselves as "Georgians"
on their internal passports. Examples of nationalities sharing the same administrative
homeland included the Karbardins and Balkars in Kabardino-Balkaria, the Chechens and
Ingush in Checheno-Ingushetia, and the Karachai and Cherkess in Karachai-Cherkessia.

33. Philip G. Roeder, "Soviet Federalism and Ethnic Mobilization," *World Politics*
23, no. 2 (1992): 196–233, reprinted in Rachel Denber, ed., *The Soviet Nationality
Reader: The Disintegration in Context* (Boulder, Colo.: Westview Press, 1992), 147–78.

34. Slezkine 1994.

35. For example, the Tatars and Bashkirs, like the Chechens and Ingush, spoke languages and shared histories that were close enough that they might well have been identified as a single nationality by Soviet ethnographers. Had they done so, the smaller groups
(in these cases, the Baskhirs and the Ingush) would have been partially or entirely assimilated culturally and linguistically into the larger groups, which would in turn have meant
very limited or no national consciousness by the end of the Soviet era.

36. In designating the nomadic Kazakhs, Kyrgyz, and Turkmen as distinct nationalities, the regime's ethnographers were influenced by the strength of their traditional clan identities and beliefs in common descent from a single founding ancestor of their respective clans (Slezkine 1994, 429).

37. Audrey L. Altstadt, *The Azerbaijani Turks: Power and Identity under Russian Rule* (Stanford, Calif.: Hoover Institution Press, Stanford University Press), 1992.

38. The passports were first introduced in December 1932. Initially, however, they were available to urban residents only, which meant that collective farmers were denied the opportunity to leave their collective farms, Mikhail Heller and Aleksandr M. Nekrich, *Utopia in Power: The History of the Soviet Union from 1917 to the Present* (New York: Summit Books, 1986), 260.

39. Victor Zaslavsky, *The Neo-Stalinist State: Class, Ethnicity, and Consensus in Soviet Society* (Armonk, N.Y.: M. E. Sharpe, 1982), 92–93.

40. Peter A. Blitstein, "Stalin's Nations: Soviet Nationality Policy between Planning and Primordialism, 1963–1953" (Ph.D. dissertation, UC Berkeley, 1999).

41. Blitstein 1999, 9.

42. Slezkine 1994, 442.

43. Joseph Stalin, *Leninism* (London: G. Allen & Unwin, 1942), 399–400.

44. Unger 1981, 89 and 160.

45. John N. Hazard, "Managing Nationalism: State, Law, and the National Question in the USSR," in *The Post-Soviet Nations: Perspectives on the Demise of the USSR,* ed. Alexander J. Motyl (New York: Columbia University Press, 1992), 114.

46. Quoted in Unger 1981, 87, citing Michael Browne, ed., *Ferment in the Ukraine: Documents by V. Chornovil [and Others]* (London: Macmillan, 1971), 51.

47. Adam Ulam, *Expansion and Coexistence: Soviet Foreign Policy, 1917–1973,* 2d ed. (New York: Praeger, 1974), 372–74.

48. In contrast, the U.S. government accepted the legality of Moldavia's incorporation into the USSR despite the fact that it, too, had been seized by Soviet troops after it had been placed in Moscow's sphere of influence by the Molotov-Ribbentrop Pact in 1939. Washington did so on the grounds that the United States had been a party to the treaty in which Romania, which was under Moscow's hegemony at the time, had ceded the region to the USSR after World War II.

49. While the Crimean Tatar, Volga German, and Meskhetian Turks were absolved of the charge of collaborating with the Germans, they were not allowed to return to their former lands, and neither was the Crimean or the Volga German ASSR reestablished. Moreover, several territorial adjustments made in the Khrushchev era—most notably, the transfer of Crimea from the RSFSR to Ukraine in 1954, the decision to allow North Ossetia to keep the traditionally Ingush area of Prigorodnyi raion, and the decision to allow Dagestan to keep traditionally Chechen regions in what is now western Dagestan in exchange for two traditionally Cossack regions of Stavropol Krai north of the river Terek that were made a part of the reconstituted Chechen-Ingush ASSR—would provoke bitter territorial disputes in the late Soviet and post-Soviet eras.

50. On "crypto-politics" in the USSR, see T. H. Rigby, "Crypto-Politics," *Survey* 50, no.1 (January 1964): 183–94.

51. *Izvestiia,* 1 January 1988, *CDSP,* vol. 40, no. 1, 4.

52. Roeder 1992, 152.

53. Gertrude Schroeder, "The Soviet Economy on a Treadmill of 'Reforms,'" in *The Soviet Economy in a Time of Change,* ed. The Joint Economic Committee, U.S. Congress (Washington, D.C.: US GPO, 1979), 312–40.

54. Seweryn Bialer, *Stalin's Successors: Leadership, Stability, and Change in the Soviet Union* (Cambridge: Cambridge University Press, 1980), 214–15.

55. Michael Voslensky, *Nomenklatura: The Soviet Ruling Class* (Garden City, N.Y.: Doubleday, 1984), 287.

56. On the other hand, as Michael Voslensky explained in describing the relationship between Party organs in the union republics and central Party officials in the Central Committee Secretariat in Moscow, "But Moscow is far away, and to the average citizen of a federated [i.e., union] republic, power means the local *nomenklatura*" (Voslensky 1984, 284).

57. Vakhii Akaev, "Informatsiia o natsional'nom voprose v rasstanovke kadrov v Checheno-Ingushetii (1934–1991 g.)," (unpublished manuscript, 1992). Until historians have access to the relevant archives, it is impossible in most cases to know why Moscow treated certain nationalities and certain republics differently. Chechen nationalists are convinced that in their case, Moscow believed that the highlander Chechens and Ingush harbored anti-Soviet sentiments and feared that these sentiments would flourish under a titular Party boss. It is possible, however, that Moscow treated Checheno-Ingushetia differently because it feared that strong kinship and communal ties among Chechens and Ingush would increase tendencies toward *mestnichestvo*. Yet another possibility is that because Checheno-Ingushetia was one of the USSR's dual titular autonomies, central authorities feared that appointing a Chechen as first secretary would have offended the Ingush, while appointing an Ingush would have offended the Chechens.

58. Bialer 1980, 214.

59. Quoted in Grey Hodnett, "The Debate over Soviet Federalism," *Soviet Studies* 28, no. 4 (April 1967): 458–81, reprinted in Denber 1992, 124.

60. "State sovereignty," the 1976 edition of the Great Soviet Encyclopedia explained, was "the supremacy (*verkhovenstvo*) and independence (*nezavisimost'*) of state power, which manifests itself in corresponding forms of the internal and external activity of the state," *Bol'shaia Sovetskaia Entsiklopediia*, vol. 25, 3d ed. (Moscow: Sovestskaia Entsiklopediia, 1976), 26.

61. The original draft did not describe the republics as sovereign, reflecting a general desire to strengthen the powers of the all-union government at the expense of the republics now that the "all-people's state" and "developed socialism" had been established (Unger 1981, 201–4). The term was restored only after the draft was presented for "mass discussion" before ratification.

62. Alexander J. Motyl, "The Sobering of Gorbachev: Nationality, Restructuring, and the West," in *Politics, Society, and Nationality inside Gorbachev's Russia*, ed. Seweryn Bialer (Boulder, Colo.: Westview Press, 1989), 149–73. Moreover, most Western scholars who felt that the Soviet Union was vulnerable to centrifugal pressure argued that the principal threat to regime stability came from the USSR's Muslim peoples, who were said to be culturally the most distant from the Slavic majority, were generally disadvantaged economically, and represented a steadily growing share of the Soviet population as a result of higher fertility rates, Helene Carrere D'Encausse, *Decline of an Empire: The Soviet Socialist Republics in Revolt*, trans. Martin Sokolinsky and Henry A. LaFarge (New York: Newsweek Books, 1979); Aleksandr Bennigsen and Marie Broxup, *The Islamic Threat to the Soviet State* (London: Croom Helm, 1983). As it turned out, the USSR's Muslim peoples proved the firmest supporters of the Union in the Gorbachev era.

63. Kaiser 1994, 253–95.

64. Kaiser 1994, 295–317.

65. Ludmilla Alexeyeva, *Soviet Dissent: Contemporary Movements for National, Religious, and Human Rights*, trans. Carol Pearce and John Glad (Middletown, Conn.: Wesleyan University Press, 1987 [1985]).

66. Kaiser 1994.

67. Rogers Brubaker, *Nationalism Reframed: Nationhood and the National Question in the New Europe* (New York: Cambridge University Press, 1996), 49.

68. Kaiser 1994, 371.

69. Martin 1991, 401.

70. Ellen Jones, *Red Army and Society* (Boston: Allen & Unwin, 1985), 190–92.

71. Khazanov 1995, 13.

72. Donna Bahry and Carol Nechemias, "Half Full or Half Empty? The Debate over Soviet Regional Equality," *Slavic Review* 40, no. 3 (Fall 1981): 366–83, reprinted in Denber 1992, 287–304.

73. Comparing life opportunities and living standards between nationalities rather than between union republics was made more difficult by the way Soviet economic statistics were gathered and reported. In practice, differences between nationalities were almost certainly considerably greater than between union republics, in part because titulars lived disproportionately in rural areas in union republics other than Armenia and the RSFSR, which meant they tended to have lower than average levels of education and poorer paying jobs, Gertrude E. Schroeder, "Nationalities and the Soviet Economy," in *The Nationalities Factor in Soviet Politics and Society,* ed. Lubomyr Hajda and Mark Beissinger (Boulder, Colo.: Westview Press, 1990), reprinted in Denber 1992, 263 and 268. Focusing on differences between union republics also ignored the often substantial differences between nationalities within the union republics, where in many cases, such as the RSFSR's North Caucasus region, living standards for national minorities were well below average.

74. Schroeder 1992, 262.

75. Richard Ericson, "Soviet Economic Structure and the National Question," in *The Post-Soviet Nations: Perspectives on the Demise of the USSR,* ed. Alexander J. Motyl (New York: Columbia University Press, 1992), 248.

76. Schroeder 1992, 275.

77. Schroeder 1992, 264.

78. *The Economist,* 14 September 1991, 77.

79. Schroeder 1992, 265.

80. Schroeder 1992, 268.

81. Gail W. Lapidus, "Ethnonationalism and Political Stability: The Russian Case," *World Politics* (July 1984): 562.

82. Donna Bahry, "The Union Republics and Contradictions in Gorbachev's Economic Reforms," *Soviet Economy* 7, no. 3 (1991): 215–55. It is important to note, however, that all-union ministries and state committees oversaw enterprises that were responsible for the great majority of Soviet economic production. There was also, as Bahry noted, a strong "sectoral bias" in the federal division of labor, with heavy industry being primarily the responsibility of central authorities, and light industry, food processing, and agriculture and infrastructure more within the jurisdiction of the union republics (Bahry 1991, 218). Moscow also had the last word on governmental budgets at all levels and controlled foreign trade and the distribution of foreign currency earnings.

83. Bialer 1980, 207.

84. Bialer 1980, 212.

Chapter 3

Perestroika and the Parade of Sovereignties

> The sovereignty of the Estonian Republic means that, through its supreme bodies of power and administration and judicial bodies, it wields supreme power in its territory. The sovereignty of the Estonian Republic is one and indivisible. . . . [The Estonia Supreme Soviet] declares the priority of its laws over Estonian SSR territory. (Declaration of the Estonian Supreme Soviet on the Sovereignty of the Estonian SSR, 16 November 1988)

Shortly after his selection as Soviet leader in March 1985, Mikhail Gorbachev announced that the renewal of Soviet socialism could be achieved only through a frank and open assessment of the accumulating problems of the "era of stagnation." To this end, he made what would prove a fateful decision to allow a gradual expansion of the boundaries of permissible public discussion about the realities of Soviet life, a policy that became known as glasnost (loosely translated as "openness"). The initial result was a series of sensational articles in the Soviet press about societal malaise and alienation, pervasive alcoholism, drug addiction, crime, economic waste and the misallocation of resources, and official privileges, corruption, and patronage networks—all "bourgeois" ills that Soviet propagandists long claimed had disappeared from Soviet life.

While the focus of the early glasnost campaign was on the manifestations of what Gorbachev would later call the "pre-crisis situation in society," this was followed after the watershed Central Committee plenum of January 1987 by an increasingly frank analysis of the causes of the USSR's accumulating problems. Soviet analysts began to emphasize that among the many failings of "mature, developed socialism" were manifestations not only of *mestnichestvo* but *vozhdizm* ("leaderism"), or the bullying of subordinates by state and Party officials, including regional Party officials. These problems had become so acute, the argument went, that a virtual "feudalization" of the Party-state had led to its segmentation along horizontal (local-regional) lines.[1] Party officials at all levels of the federal hierarchy, including union republic and regional first secretaries, were accused of having engaged in widespread corruption and to have relied on patron-client networks to increase their own power and privileges at the expense of society as a whole. Indeed, the Soviet media began to portray many Brezhnev-era first secretaries as virtual tyrants with their own Stalin-like personality cults.

This critique of what became known as the "command-administrative system" was accompanied by a relaunching of an anticorruption drive that had begun under Gorbachev's erstwhile patron, Yurii Andropov, during his brief tenure as Soviet leader in 1982–1984. The campaign was directed above all at ending the bribery, embezzlement, fraud, nepotism, cronyism, and report padding that were said to have been pandemic in the Brezhnev era, but the particular target of the anticorruption drive was the political elite of the Central Asian republics. As Gorbachev explained in his keynote speech to the January 1987 Central Committee plenum, Uzbekistan, Kazakhstan, and Turkmenistan had become areas where "negative processes that related to a degeneration of cadres and breaches of socialist legality manifested themselves in extremely ugly forms."[2] Several months later, the so-called "Cotton Affair" scandalized the Soviet public with revelations about massive overreporting of cotton production in Uzbekistan, embezzlement of state funds, and bribery during Brezhnev's tenure.

While the anticorruption campaign was taken by many as an indication that Gorbachev was committed to a decisive break with Brezhnevism, it had the added effect of unsettling elites in the union republics and regions and discrediting them in the eyes of their constituents. In some cases, particularly in Central Asia, traditional elites concluded that the campaign was directed at the implicit contract between central and regional authorities whereby political quiescence was exchanged for local autonomy and preferential treatment for titular peoples. Thus the first serious incident of "ethnic violence" under Gorbachev came in response to a Politburo decision to replace an ethnic Kazakh, Dinmukhamed Kunaev, with an ethnic Russian, Gennadii Kolbin, as first secretary in Kazakhstan in December 1986. This violation of the unwritten norms of cadres policy led to protest demonstrations in Alma Ata (Almaty), the Kazakh capital. After riot police were brought in to suppress the demonstrations, violence broke out that lasted for several days and led to at least two deaths and some 200 injuries, and drew front page coverage in newspapers around the world.[3]

Signs of internationality tensions and antiunion sentiments increased in early 1987, particularly in the Baltic republics. Violent clashes between Latvians and Russians were reported in Riga, the capital of Latvia, in January and again in March. That same month, the Lithuanian Party first secretary informed a meeting of the republic's Central Committee that additional measures were needed to counter growing manifestations of nationalism and religious practices in the republic. In June, a group of Crimean Tatars demonstrated in Moscow demanding that the Crimean Tatars be allowed to return to the Crimea from their places of internal exile in Central Asia and Siberia.

It was not until early 1988, however, that the first sustained interethnic violence of the perestroika era broke out, as ethnic Armenians and Azeris clashed over the status of the Nagorno-Karabakh Autonomous Oblast (Karabakh). Signs that Karabakh could cause a serious political rift between Azerbaijan and Armenia had surfaced in late 1986 when a letter was sent to Gorbachev reiterating the long-standing Armenian demand that the autonomous oblast, where the population was then roughly three-quarters Armenian, be transferred from the jurisdiction of the Azerbaijani SSR to the Armenian SSR. The letter was essentially ignored, but some 75,000 Karabakh Armenians signed a petition in support of the letter during 1987. The petition was rejected by the Politburo in February 1988, which prompted unsanctioned mass demonstrations by Armenians first in Stepanakert, Karabakh's capital, and then in Yerevan. The size and duration of these demonstrations induced Moscow to dispatch Soviet troops to the Armenian capital to "restore order," at which point protest leaders agreed to a one-month moratorium to avoid bloodshed. Two days later, anti-Armenian riots erupted in the Azerbaijani town of Sumgait that led to over thirty deaths. Soviet troops were brought in to quell the rioting, but the result was months of intensifying violence and eventually full-scale war.

The Armenian-Azeri conflict was essentially intercommunal—neither party was primarily interested in wresting greater autonomy from Moscow or asserting its "sovereignty" at the expense of the central government. Indeed, both Azerbaijan and Armenia initially tried to win Moscow's support in pressing their claims. In the Baltic republics, in contrast, the nationalist movements that began to mobilize in late 1987 were motivated primarily by demands for genuine autonomy and a devolution of authority from Moscow. In June 1987, a small demonstration was held in Riga to mark the anniversary of the deportation of thousands of Latvians to labor camps after the republic's initial occupation by Soviet troops in 1940. Two months later, protest demonstrations were attended by several thousand participants, still a very unusual phenomenon in the USSR, in all three Baltic capitals on the anniversary of the August 1939 signing of the Molotov-Ribbentrop Pact and the secret protocol that gave Stalin a green light from Hitler to annex Estonia, Latvia, and Lithuania. In the fall, an Estonian economist publicly proposed that the republic become self-sufficient in budgetary terms, neither transferring taxes to, nor receiving budgetary transfers from, the federal government. In early February 1988, a nationalist demonstration in Estonia was broken up by Soviet militiamen carrying shields and truncheons and equipped with gas masks, the first such show of force in the region in the perestroika era. Later that same month, some 4,000 people demonstrated in Tallinn on the anniversary of the independence of the interwar Estonian Republic, despite being photographed by plainclothed agents and surrounded by police. In August, peaceful mass demonstrations took place in all three republics on the anniversary of the Molotov-Ribbentrop Pact, with between 100,000–200,000 participating in Vilnius alone.

The Soviet leadership was clearly taken by surprise by both the violence over Karabakh and the nationalist mobilization in the Baltic republics in 1987–1988. As he would later admit, Gorbachev had genuinely believed that the nationality problem had been more or less solved by the time he took office, as he suggested in a speech shortly after becoming general secretary: "Into the consciousness and heart of every [Soviet citizen] there has deeply entered the feeling of belonging to a single family—the Soviet people, a new and historically unprecedented social and international community."[4] In his five-and-a-half-hour speech at the 27th Party Congress in February 1986 (the speech would take up over 100 pages in the third volume of his collected speeches and articles), he spent but a few short minutes on the nationality question, reminding his audience that "healthy interest in all that is valuable in each national culture should not degenerate into attempts to remain isolated from the objective process of mutual cooperation and the drawing together (*sblizheniia*) of national cultures."[5] Even in his 1987 book, *Perestroika,* which was published after the Alma Ata riots in December 1986, he would confidently assert that, despite some "negative phenomena" in nationality relations, the USSR was reaping the "fruits of the nationality policy launched by Lenin," as a result of which the nationality question had been "solved in principle." As for "negative phenomena," the Party was required, as Lenin had prescribed, "to combat any manifestations of nationalist narrow-mindedness and chauvinism, parochialism, Zionism, and anti-Semitism, in whatever forms they may be expressed."[6] What "nationalist narrow-mindedness" there was, he believed, was concentrated within the intelligentsia, from where it spread to the masses as a result of deliberate manipulation by extremist intellectuals. As he would put it to the Politburo in March 1988: "The virus of enmity is cultivated not by the masses but by intellectuals. They are the bearers of nationalism."[7]

Nevertheless, by late 1987 it was becoming increasingly clear that the nationality problem had not been solved even "in principle." This was particularly true in the Baltic republics, where nationalists, emboldened by glasnost, continued to organize. Initially, they directed their efforts against environmental degradation from Soviet industrialization and the dangers of the Soviet nuclear power plants in the region, particularly the Ignalina plant in Lithuania, the dangers of which had been dramatically demonstrated by the Chernobyl disaster the previous year.[8] They also took advantage of the modest economic reforms adopted by Moscow in mid-1987, the principal themes of which were "self-financing" (*samofinansirovanie*), "self-management" (*samoupravlenie*), and "self-accounting" (*khozraschet*), as well as the legalization of limited forms of private and semiprivate economic activity (individual labor activity and cooperatives) and an "experiment" in economic decentralization (once again) in several regions, including the Baltics, to press for greater control over republic budgets, productive activity, and interrepublic trade.[9] Finally, they appealed to the principle of glasnost in demanding that the authorities face up to the "historical truth" of the forceful annexation of the Baltic republics in 1940 and the illegitimacy of the Molotov-Ribbentrop Pact.[10]

As 1988 progressed, "popular front" movements formed in all three Baltic republics, and by the fall each had convened a founding congress. Initially, the popular fronts presented themselves as committed supporters of perestroika— the Estonian popular front, for example, called itself the "Popular Front for Perestroika." Their programs demanded greater autonomy for regional governments over cultural affairs (including language and education policy), the accurate representation of national history, the preservation of traditional monuments and culturally significant buildings, and environmental protection measures. Soon, however, they began to demand the restoration of "Leninist norms of federalism" and respect for the constitutionally recognized status of the union republics as "sovereign states" as the central themes of their campaigns, themes that were potentially far more radical in their challenge to the authority of the center. As a statement adopted at a key meeting of cultural figures in Latvia on 1–2 June 1988 put it:

> The Latvian SSR's participation in the USSR's economic and social development is not taking place on the basis of the equitable principle of a sovereign state within an alliance of free states. . . . We must eliminate the situation whereby rights stipulated by the constitution cannot be enjoyed because there is no relevant law defining the method of implementing these rights [i.e., the right of secession].[11]

The document went on to call for the establishment of "political and diplomatic relationships such that its status as a republic will allow Latvia to be internationally recognized as a sovereign and nationally constituted nation within the Soviet federation." It also demanded UN representation; membership in UNESCO; separate representation at the Olympic Games; the right to participate in international political, cultural, scientific, and sports forums "under the colors and symbols of our sovereign national state"; greater control over the activities of the Soviet military and the KGB within the republic's territory; the right to limit the inflow of Russians; recognition of Latvian as the republic's sole state language; greater freedom for Latvians to travel abroad; and the right of Latvians to maintain contact with their ethnic kin abroad.[12]

To Western ears, these demands sounded curious—sovereignty before the international community and UN representation but at the same time membership in the USSR and limited internal "sovereignty," including the implicit right of the USSR to station troops on Latvian soil. Indeed, the assumption of many Westerners was that the Latvian nationalists and their counterparts in Estonia and Lithuania were in fact pressing for full independence. However, while the program was certainly radical in its implications, it consisted for the most part of demands to respect rights that the union republics supposedly already possessed or that other republics had already acquired. Like Ukraine and Belarus, Latvia would send its own delegation to the United Nations. Like Georgia, the language of its titular people would be recognized as the sole state language of the republic, and government business would be conducted in Latvian. International recognition of the republic's "sovereignty" and its status as a nationally constituted state "within the Soviet federation" was simply a request that the international community endorse the "Leninist" principles that Soviet federalism was supposedly based upon. Finally, most of the individual rights demanded in the document, such as the right of Latvian citizens to travel freely abroad, were already de jure guaranteed by the Soviet constitution.

While most of the demands of Baltic nationalists were consistent with the central themes and slogans of Gorbachev's reform program, "sovereignty" was not. It was therefore a slogan that Gorbachev preferred to ignore, particularly because it could be interpreted to mean anything from regional *khozraschet* to the right to determine unilaterally the extent of authority devolved from the center. But most alarmingly, it could be interpreted to mean respect for the right of secession, something that was still well beyond the limits of permissible political discourse. Gorbachev could not, however, simply reject the claim that the republics were truly "sovereign" because of the term's entrenchment in the Soviet constitution and its centrality to the normative mythology of Soviet federalism.

While preexisting constitutional provisions and traditional legitimation helped tie Gorbachev's hands, these same factors as well as the deep ambiguity of the term helped make "sovereignty" an extremely effective mobilizational slogan for the nationalist movements in the Baltic republics. "Sovereignty" could be embraced by radical nationalists, including those few who felt that full independence was possible in the foreseeable future, as well as by moderates who hoped that Moscow would afford their republic greater autonomy over language, education, and cultural policies. The slogan was even reasonably reassuring to ethnic Russians and other nontitulars, who by mid-1988 were increasingly alarmed by the nationalist mobilization under way in the Baltics. After all, what was being demanded was that the founding principles of Soviet federalism, principles that had been "distorted" by the excesses of Stalinism, be respected and that the USSR be allowed to return to the true "Leninist" path, a claim that Russians could interpret as entailing not only regional autonomy but respect for the principles of socialist internationalism and the rights of nontitular minorities.

Most importantly, support for "sovereignty" did not necessarily mean support for independence, as made clear by the following statement by Algirdas Brazauskas, the Lithuanian Communist Party first secretary who proved a supporter of Lithuania's sovereignty drive and whom the conservative Yegor Ligachev would refer to as "the classic Liquidator":[13]

> First of all this word and concept, and therefore, the understanding of the concept "independence" or "sovereignty"—and I treat them as absolute synonyms—is of great importance to us today . . . independence and sovereignty are possible when nations join the union of their own free will. . . . Therefore, a state which is within the union can also be a sovereign and free state.[14]

The notion that "sovereignty" was perfectly compatible with the preservation of the union, and indeed with the preservation of the "leading role" of the Communist Party (albeit possibly a decentralized or federalized Party) as well, helps account for the extent of the support the Baltic nationalist movements would receive from regional Party officials like Brazauskas. Titulars in the republics' Party apparatuses who sympathized with the nationalists or who wanted to see the devolution of state authority from Moscow would begin to carve out a measure of independence from the CPSU's central organs by appealing to the principles of "Leninist federalism":

> The Central Committee of the Communist Party of Lithuania proposes that the Leninist interpretation of a Soviet federation should, first of all, be rekindled. It is necessary to specify . . . the concept of the USSR itself, including its component and functional principles—including the separate status of the union republics as sovereign socialist states—and to define a union republic as a sovereign state . . . without ambiguity.[15]

This support from local Party officials greatly facilitated the mobilizational efforts of the popular fronts. For example, the Estonian popular front's first congress, which was attended by some 3,000 delegates, was officially sanctioned and convened in the Lenin Palace of Culture in Tallinn, which would have been impossible without support from the local Party. Indeed, an estimated quarter of the delegates were Party members, and the front received assurances during the session of access to the media.[16] In other instances, local Party officials would give the nationalists access to both Party and state newspapers and state-owned publishing houses, afford them extensive radio and television coverage, and give them permits to hold increasingly large demonstrations.[17] In Ukraine, in contrast, nationalist mobilization would be effectively repressed by the republic's conservative first secretary, Vladimir Shcherbitsky, until his removal from office in September 1989, despite evidence of strong nationalist sentiments in western Ukraine.

Thus, the ambiguity of the notion of "sovereignty" contributed to its political potency by allowing it to function as a unifying slogan for a broad coalition of political forces with disparate political agendas. As the central government weakened in the face of the deepening political struggle in Moscow between Gorbachev and his conservative and radical opponents, and as economic conditions began to deteriorate in 1989 and especially 1990, the "sovereignty" coalitions in the republics would strengthen and their demands would radicalize as fence-sitters concluded that the risks of supporting the antiunion opposition were diminishing while the odds of realizing genuine autonomy and even full independence were growing. At the same time, antiunionists would continue to employ the term, with its traditional legitimation, as a cover that masked the reality of their increasingly radical demands. And finally, supporters of perestroika could embrace it as an overarching slogan that seemed consistent with the core themes of perestroika, particularly the stress on self-reliance implicit in the slogans *samofinansirovanie, samoupravlenie,* and *khozraschet.*

In the summer of 1988, nationalist mobilization in the union republics was given a powerful stimulus by the convening of a special CPSU conference in Moscow. At Gorbachev's insistence, delegates to the Nineteenth Party Conference made two critical decisions. First, they announced that perestroika required a renewed emphasis on respect for the law and legal norms by both society and officialdom, a theme that in 1989 would develop into a campaign to transform the USSR into a "law-governed state" (*pravovoe gosudarstvo*). Second, they endorsed Gorbachev's plans for a far-reaching reform of the Soviet political system. The reforms provided for the establishment of a Congress of Peoples' Deputies (CPD) as the USSR's supreme legislative body; limited competition in elections for the new legislature (no political parties would be able to sponsor candidates other than the CPSU, and Article 6 of the constitution remained in force, thereby effectively banning the formation of alternative parties), which would eventually be held in March 1989; the establishment of a new standing legislature, the Supreme Soviet, to be elected by delegates to the Congress; and the creation of a powerful new post of chairman of the presidium of the Supreme Soviet as the USSR's chief executive and head of state (colloquially referred to as "president"), who would be elected indirectly by the delegates to the CPD. These delegates would number 2,250: 750 were to be selected by the Party from various "all-union social organizations"; 750 would be elected by the USSR's nonethnic oblasts and krais; and 750 would be elected by the USSR's "national territories." Representation from the latter was divided as follows: thirty-two deputies would be elected in each union republic, eleven in each autonomous republic, five in each autonomous oblast, and one in each autonomous okrug. The new Supreme Soviet would in turn be bicameral, with one house being a "Council of Nationalities" elected from the CPD deputies from the national territories, as follows: eleven from each union republic, four from each autonomous republic, two from each autonomous oblast, and one from each autonomous okrug.

As intended, Gorbachev's commitment to *demokratizatsiia* (democratization) contributed to a further reduction in popular fears of engaging in public debate and unsanctioned political activity. By early 1989, the Soviet public had enthusiastically taken up Gorbachev's challenge to become directly engaged in the reform process, particularly as the only partially competitive but nevertheless dramatic elections to the new CPD approached in March 1989. At the same time, however, *demokratizatsiia* had the unintended effect of making nationalist mobilization in the union republics more meaningful. The election of delegates to the new legislature in predetermined numbers based on federal status, and direct representation in the upper house of the new standing legislature for the USSR's ethno-federal units, reinforced the tendency for political mobilization to take place on the basis of regional rather than all-union identities. Moreover, nationalists in the union republics were alarmed to learn that an initial draft of the constitutional amendments affecting the political reforms approved in the

June Party conference included a provision giving the new Supreme Soviet the right to approve or disapprove a petition of secession from a union republic.

While the nationalist mobilization in the Baltics attracted some media attention in the West that summer and early fall, the "shot heard round the world" that alerted the international media and foreign governments to the seriousness of the mounting challenge to Moscow from the Baltic republics came on 16 November 1988. With little advance notice, the Estonian Supreme Soviet issued its now-famous "Declaration of the Estonian Supreme Soviet Regarding the Sovereignty of the Estonian SSR," which asserted the republic's "sovereignty" and the primacy of Estonian laws over those promulgated by the all-union government in Moscow: "The sovereignty of the Estonian Republic means that, through its supreme bodies of power and administration and judicial bodies, it wields supreme power on its territory. The sovereignty of the Estonian republic is one and indivisible."[18] Estonian laws would henceforth have primacy over those of the center on Estonian territory: "[T]he top organ of the Estonian SSR people's power—the Estonian SSR Supreme Soviet—declares the priority of its laws over Estonian SSR territory before USSR laws, until the Union contract is concluded." Amendments to the Soviet constitution would come into effect only after being approved by the Estonian parliament.[19]

In a separate law passed that same day, Estonia's parliament laid claim to the republic's land, mineral deposits, inland waters, forests, and other natural resources located within its borders, as well as to "the basic means of production in industry, construction, and agriculture, means of transportation and construction, state banks, the property of state-organized trade, municipal services and their enterprises and the basic urban housing stock, as well as other property necessary for fulfilling the tasks of the Estonian Republic."[20] And it reiterated that the Estonian Supreme Soviet "has the right to suspend or establish limits to the application of a USSR legislative act if this act violates the sovereignty of the Estonian Republic or regulates questions that, according to the Estonian Constitution, fall within the jurisdiction of the Estonian Republic, or if it does not take the republic's specific features into account."[21] Nevertheless, the declaration made clear that it was not intended as an assertion of full independence for the republic. Rather, Estonia's relationship with the USSR, if any, would have to be negotiated: "The future status of the republic within the Soviet Union *could* be determined by a union treaty" (emphasis added). Thus only if a negotiated settlement were reached would the republic consider signing a treaty of union with the federal center.

Over the next two years, first the more assertive union republics (Latvia, Lithuania, Azerbaijan, and Georgia), then the RSFSR, Moldavia, Ukraine, and finally all other republics except Armenia[22] would issue their own sovereignty declarations (see table 3.1). The "parade of sovereignties," as Soviet writers would come to call it, even spread to union republics with conservative leaderships and little nationalist mobilization. Failing to declare sovereignty, leaders in those republics realized, would undermine their leverage in bargaining over the

Table 3.1. Union Republic Sovereignty Declarations

Estonian SSR	16 November 1988
Lithuanian SSR	18 May 1989
Latvian SSR	28 July 1989
Azerbaijan SSR	23 September 1989
Georgian SSR	18 November 1989[23]
Russian SFSR	12 June 1990
Uzbek SSR	20 June 1990
Moldavian SSR	23 June 1990
Ukrainian SSR	16 July 1990
Belorussian SSR	27 July 1990
Turkmen SSR	22 August 1990
Tajik SSR	24 August 1990
Kirghiz SSR	24 October 1990
Kazakh SSR	25 October 1990
Armenia	none (see footnote 22)

federal budget, over the pace and costs of economic reform, and (later) over the terms of the new union treaty. It would also risk a loss of popular support for regional leaders who allowed Moscow or other republics to dominate the political agenda.

In most respects, the sovereignty declarations of the union republics differed little in substance.[24] They demanded greater autonomy, the right of the republics to define their relationship with the federal center, and ownership of local assets. Most importantly, they asserted the priority of republic laws over those of the center. Republic legislatures were soon passing laws that clearly violated the Soviet constitution and federal legislation, including laws banning military service outside the borders of the republic, laws denying nontitular peoples the right to communicate with officials in Russian or to be educated in their own languages, and laws that implied that Soviet citizens who were legal residents in the republics were not necessarily citizens of that republic. The republics also began to assert their "economic sovereignty" by seizing control of local enterprises, attempting to set prices for goods and services on their territories, and claiming authority to limit exports both abroad and to other Soviet republics regardless of the interests of the union as a whole.[25]

Gorbachev and his allies responded by arguing that the sovereignty campaigns of the union republics were making a centrally directed reform program impossible and the country ungovernable, and this in turn risked provoking a conservative backlash against Gorbachev's reforms. They pointed out that the USSR constitution empowered the federal government to promulgate laws on matters within its jurisdiction (which included almost everything of significance); that federal laws were supreme throughout the territory of the USSR; and that these laws went into effect immediately (i.e., they did not require approval by the republics' legislatures). Nevertheless, the republics continued to pass laws and adopt policies that directly contradicted those of the center. This in turn induced federal bodies to respond with countering laws, resolutions, or decrees intended to nullify those of the republics. A "war of laws," as Soviet journalists called it, was accompanying the "parade of sovereignties."

Despite Gorbachev's obvious distaste for nationalist politics and violations of "socialist legality" by the union republics, the Soviet leader was extremely reluctant to use force to impose central writ. In part, this was for normative reasons—as he reportedly put it to the Politburo in May 1989: "Use of force is out of the question. It's been ruled out in foreign policy, and definitely should be in domestic policy."[26] There were, however, many practical considerations as well. A crackdown would have provided political ammunition to conservative opponents of his reforms, opponents who already were openly warning that perestroika threatened to destroy the Party and break up the country. Redressing the grievances of particular minorities or accommodating the sovereignty demands of the Baltic republics could also lead to an escalation of group grievances throughout the country. And finally, he had been stressing since his arrival in power that a benign international environment was needed if perestroika were to succeed, and he was accordingly worried that a crackdown would lead to a rapid deterioration in relations with the West.

In fact, although the Western public generally sympathized with the Baltic nationalist movements, Western governments were extremely cautious about taking any steps that might be construed as deliberate efforts to encourage separatism or the breakup of the USSR.[27] Fearful that the dissolution of the USSR would be accompanied by violence and disorder, they worried about possible threats to the command and control of the Soviet Union's nuclear arsenal from a fragmented military. Internal chaos might also place nuclear weapons in the hands of local warlords or terrorists, or encourage the sale of nuclear weapons technology, or indeed the weapons themselves, to rogue states. There might even be war between nuclear-armed successor states, which could lead to the first use of nuclear weapons since World War II. At the least, the dissolution of the USSR would confront the international community with four new states with strategic nuclear weapons on their territory—Russia, Ukraine, Belorussia, and Kazakhstan.

There were other concerns as well. Encouraging secession or dissolution might provoke conservatives in Moscow to oust Gorbachev, thereby putting an end to the "new thinking" in Soviet foreign policy, rekindling the Cold War, and jeopardizing cooperation with the USSR on a whole host of issues, from arms control, an end to the war in Afghanistan, and liberalization in Eastern Europe. Conflict and disorder in the Soviet Union could cause a massive humanitarian disaster that would drive a huge wave of refugees into Western Europe, while the breakup of the country could affect the ability or willingness of any successor states to service the USSR's external debt. There was also a personal dimension—Western leaders, including not only U.S. presidents Reagan and Bush, but also German chancellor Helmut Kohl, French president François Mitterrand, and

British prime ministers Margaret Thatcher and John Major, developed close personal ties with the Soviet president and came to feel that they had a personal and political stake in the success of perestroika. And finally, most states are generally loath to legitimize secession, not only because it is impossible to agree on criteria for determining which groups qualify as "nations" and accordingly have a right to exercise "self-determination," but also because most governments fear encouraging separatists within their own borders or separatist violence elsewhere in the world.

Thus, despite the nominal commitment to the "self-determination of peoples" in the UN charter, the General Assembly's 1960 "Declaration on Colonial Countries," and other international treaties and conventions,[28] Western governments made clear that they supported liberalization and democratization in the Soviet Union but wished to see the union preserved. To this end, they indicated that they would respect the principles of the 1975 Helsinki Accords regarding the inviolability of Europe's international borders. This was true even for the Baltic republics, despite the policy of nonrecognition of their original incorporation. Thus, when in June 1989 the U.S. ambassador to Moscow, Jack Matlock, agreed to meet with representatives of the Lithuanian popular front (a break with the traditional U.S. policy of refusing to meet officially with Baltic representatives because doing so, it was felt, could be interpreted as recognition of their annexation), he informed them, as he recalls in his memoirs, that

> the United States government and virtually all Americans would sympathize with Lithuania if it declared independence. Nevertheless, immediate recognition would be unlikely since recognition involves a judgment that a government actually controls the territory it claims. If Lithuania remained under effective Soviet control, the American government could probably not recognize its government as independent, no matter how much it might sympathize.

As for economic aid, he notified them that "it would be impossible for outsiders, be they Americans, Germans, Swedes, or anyone else, to supply economic aid in the event of a Soviet blockade." Mindful of the guilt that many Western governments had felt after their failure to help the Hungarians after encouraging them to rise up against the Soviets in 1956, Matlock also warned them "under no circumstances" should they assume that "the United States or any other foreign country would be able to help them directly if their actions brought on military or economic sanctions from Moscow."[29]

Despite the lack of support from foreign governments, nationalist mobilization in the Baltics proceeded apace over the course of 1989, particularly in the wake of the strong performance of oppositionists in the March 1989 CPD elections. Meanwhile, a devastating earthquake had struck Armenia in late 1988, causing some 25,000 deaths and prompting a visit to the republic by Gorbachev. The Soviet leader was shocked by the hostile reception he received in the republic, as local Armenians repeatedly asked him not about disaster relief but about Moscow's failure to support Armenia in its struggle with Azerbaijan over Karabakh. In an interview on Soviet television Gorbachev indicated that he had nothing but contempt for those who refused to put aside ethnic differences in the face of tragedy, adding apocalyptically, "This is the edge of the abyss. One more step and it's the abyss."[30] He also made clear his conviction that nationalist passions, interethnic enmity, and violence were being deliberately provoked by intellectuals and self-interested politicians, telling a journalist in an interview in Yerevan:

> Yes, the Karabakh problem is real. But you know, the Karabakh issue is played up by dishonest people, by political demagogues, adventurists, moreover, by corrupted people. They see *perestroika* is going on, it is coming to Armenia and Azerbaijan, there are new leaders, and the new leaders are taking up positions of *perestroika*. That means this kind of folks [*sic*] will be hit. The parasitic folks, who are holding the people in their hand by intimidation, they are going to be hit. . . .
>
> They are playing on the Karabakh issue. . . . They have long not needed Karabakh and it has never worried them. They are fighting for power, they want to preserve power in their hands. This applies to all illegal operators, all profiteers sponging on the working class, collective farmers, and the professions. This is the crux of the matter.[31]

This tendency to assume that nationalism and ethnic violence were products of elite manipulation rather than manifestations of genuine popular grievances or fears would remain an important part of Gorbachev's understanding of the "nationality crisis" throughout his remaining years in power.

Gorbachev's warnings that the Soviet Union was "on the edge of an abyss" of rising nationalism and ethnic conflict were borne out in the following months. In January 1989, Karabakh was placed under direct administrative control from Moscow, but incidents of violence between Armenians and Azeris continued. The first large-scale nationalist demonstrations took place in Moldavia in late 1988. In Ukraine, increasingly open calls for Shcherbitsky's resignation were accompanied by signs of mounting nationalist unrest and antiunion sentiments, especially in the west. In April 1989, participants in a gathering of Georgian nationalists in Tbilisi who were demonstrating against greater autonomy for Abkhazia were set upon by Soviet troops, leading to an estimated twenty deaths. In June 1989, approximately 100 people were killed in Uzbekistan's Ferghana Valley in eight days of rioting pitting ethnic Uzbeks against Meskhetian Turks (a Turkic-speaking, traditionally Muslim minority who had been deported from Georgia by Stalin in 1944). Similar clashes were reported a week later between ethnic Kazakhs and non-Kazakhs, particularly Chechens, in the Kazakh town of Novy Uzhen. In July, clashes between Abkhaz and Georgians in the Abkhaz capital, Sukhumi, led to a reported fourteen deaths and the hospitalization of over 100.

Signs of a mounting challenge to Communist power appeared from nationalists in Eastern Europe as well. In Poland, a deteriorating economy led to a new round of labor unrest in April 1988 and again in August. By the end of the year,

Wojciech Jaruzelski's Communist government was openly discussing the possibility of legalizing Solidarity, the opposition labor movement. "Roundtable Talks" between the government and Solidarity began in February 1989, which led to a historic agreement in early March that provided for a power-sharing arrangement and free elections in June to the existing legislature, the Sejm, and to a newly reinstated upper house. The elections, which took place on 4 June 1989 (that same day, the Chinese Communist Party was violently suppressing the Chinese democracy movement in Tiananmen Square), resulted in an overwhelming defeat for the Polish Communist Party. By the end of the summer, a Solidarity candidate had become Poland's prime minister, effectively ending forty-five years of Communist rule, and a new government was planning a rapid transition to a market economy. On 1 January 1990, the Polish experiment in economic "shock therapy" was launched with full-price liberalization.

By then, even more dramatic events had taken place elsewhere in Eastern Europe. Encouraged by the Roundtable Talks in Poland, the Hungarian Communist Party, long the most liberal of the ruling Communist parties in Eastern Europe, had opened negotiations in June 1989 with opposition groups on the possibility of organizing contested elections in the spring. The talks continued intermittently in the following months, until in early September the Hungarian government unexpectedly announced that it would open up its border with Austria, in effect tearing a hole in the "Iron Curtain" that had divided Europe since the end of World War II. Immediately, tens of thousands of East Germans hoping to escape the highly repressive policies of the German Democratic Republic (GDR) and to resettle in Western Germany began crossing the border into Austria, which prompted the East German government to announce that henceforth its citizens would have to obtain exit visas to travel to Hungary.

By the time Gorbachev arrived in Berlin in early October to celebrate the fortieth anniversary of the founding of the East German state, the extent of the regime's domestic unpopularity and the precariousness of its hold on power was obvious. The visit by the still-popular father of perestroika prompted even larger antigovernment demonstrations. East Germany's hard-line leader, Erik Honecker, responded by ordering the police to use force if necessary to disperse the demonstrations, but the halfhearted attempt at a "Chinese solution" to the crisis only enraged the population further. On 17 October, the German Politburo, over Honecker's objections, ordered the police not to use force, which prompted Honecker to resign the following day. Mass demonstrations continued regardless, with some 300,000 participating in a pro-democracy march in Leipzig on 23 October, which prompted Gorbachev, then in Finland, to announce that Soviet troops would not be used to save the East German regime from its own people. Finally, the Communist government in Berlin resigned in early November, East German border guards allowed a flood of East Germans to cross directly into West Germany, and the Berlin Wall was torn down by a jubilant East German public.

The collapse of communism in East Germany, which would be followed by full German unification a year later, sparked a series of equally dramatic regime collapses elsewhere in Eastern Europe. Under pressure from Moscow to introduce perestroika-type reforms lest it suffer the same fate as its East German counterpart, the Bulgarian Communist Party ousted its conservative and corrupt leader, Todor Zhivkov, in mid-November. His replacement called for a dialogue with opposition forces, the convening of a constitutional commission, and an end to the Party's monopoly of power, but popular protests forced the regime to agree in December to talks with the opposition on multiparty elections and marketization. In Czechoslovakia, the Communist Party was likewise forced to cede power to the opposition, led by Vaclav Havel, after weeks of massive street protests beginning in mid-November in what would become known as the "Velvet Revolution." In Romania, the fall of communism was accompanied by widespread violence, which culminated in the execution of the Communist dictator, Nicolae Ceauşescu, and his wife on Christmas day 1989. By the end of the year, Communist power in Eastern Europe was all but dead.

The astonishing dramas that unfolded in Eastern Europe in the final months of 1989 complicated an already extraordinarily difficult political situation for Gorbachev. As early as the summer of 1989, some four years after his arrival in power and two-and-half years after the launching of perestroika at the January 1987 Central Committee plenum, it was already clear that Gorbachev's reform program was in trouble. His efforts to revitalize the tottering Soviet economy were proving at best inadequate and at worst counterproductive. In April 1989, the U.S. Central Intelligence Agency (CIA) and Defense Intelligence Agency (DIA) in their joint annual report to Congress on the Soviet economy estimated that GNP growth in 1988 had been only 1.5 percent, which was not enough to maintain living standards. Agricultural production had declined by approximately 2 percent, while the budget deficit had increased under Gorbachev from 3 percent in 1985 to 9 percent in 1988. Poor economic performance, the report concluded, had led the government to postpone needed price reform and to increase consumer goods production at the expense of investment in machinery and the technology needed to sustain, let alone improve, growth rates.[32] The likelihood that growth rates would turn around quickly became even more remote after a mass strike broke out among coal miners in the Kuznets Basin in Siberia and the Donets Basin in Ukraine in July, the first of what would prove to be many such strikes in the final years of the Gorbachev era.

The sense of crisis that these proliferating economic and political problems were giving rise to among the leadership is conveyed starkly by an entry at the time in Chernyaev's diary:

Journal. May 1989.

All around Gorbachev has unleashed irreversible processes of "disintegration". . . .

Socialism in Eastern Europe is disappearing. Communist parties are collapsing in Western Europe and everywhere else they were they couldn't "latch on" to the national idea. . . . Everywhere things are turning out different from what had been imagined and proposed.

But most important is the disintegration of myths and the other unnatural forms of our society—the planned economy is living its last days and the "image" of socialism is fading. Ideology doesn't exist anymore. The empire-federation is falling apart. The Party is in disarray, having lost its place as a ruling, dominating, and repressive force. Governmental authority has been shaken to the breaking point. And nothing has yet been created to take its place. Chaos is breaking out . . . and no one has the power to enforce the strict laws designed to preserve discipline."[33]

* * * * *

By the summer of 1989, then, even before the regime collapses in East/Central Europe at the end of the year, Gorbachev was facing a host of extraordinary challenges in domestic politics, foreign policy, and economy, challenges that threatened to overload the regime's decision-making circuits. It was the deepening "nationalities crisis," however, that presented the most serious political challenge to regime stability. At the beginning of 1988, after the bloody events in Sumgait and Karabakh, Gorbachev had argued during a Politburo meeting that the nationalities problem was "one of the most complex problems in the entire life of the country."[34] That problem had only grown worse in the period since. Clearly, the leadership needed some kind of strategy for addressing those problems. Several years earlier, after the December 1986 disturbances in Alma Ata, Gorbachev had suggested to his colleagues on the Politburo that a special plenum on "internationality relations" might be needed, but the idea was initially ignored.[35] Gorbachev returned to it after the Nineteenth Party Conference in the summer of 1988, and this time the Politburo agreed.[36] However, the plenum itself was repeatedly postponed, suggesting both the complexity of the problem as well as the fact that the Party leadership was finding it difficult to reach a consensus over how to respond. Finally, a date was set for 19–20 September 1989.

A month before the plenum, Soviet newspapers published a draft of the Party's "nationalities platform," which was to serve as a basis for discussion at the plenum.[37] Entitled "The Party's Nationalities Policy in Today's Conditions," the platform, like all policy platforms submitted to the Central Committee, had been carefully drafted and redrafted by the professional staff of the Central Committee Secretariat under the guidance of the general secretary and responsible members of the Secretariat, with contributions from government experts and outside scholars. It represented the clearest expression of the Party leadership's strategy for dealing with the nationality question at that time. And after its approval by the plenum, it was intended to serve as the Party's blueprint for overcoming the crisis. As it turned out, it would prescribe a course of action that would prove fatal to the union.

In its opening lines, the platform recognized the seriousness of the challenge the Party was confronting: "The nationalities question in the Soviet Union has become exceptionally acute recently. The Party recognizes that a solution to the problems that have arisen in this connection is of enormous importance for the fate of restructuring and the future of our country." A brief review of the history of Soviet federalism and nationality policy followed. Predictably, current problems were blamed on "deformations" in nationality policy that had begun after Lenin's death. It also offered a typical Soviet bromide that would be repeated endlessly by both defenders and opponents of the union in the remaining years of the USSR's existence: "The main idea on which the Soviet federation is based is expressed in the universally recognized formula: Without a strong union there can be no strong republics." This, it asserted, required that the separate jurisdictions of the union and the republics be defined more clearly, and it went on to list in general terms a reasonable set of powers (e.g., foreign policy, defense policy, "general tasks" in economic policy, etc.) that would be reserved for the federal government in a renewed Leninist federation.

The document made no mention of a right of secession—Gorbachev and the Party leadership were firmly committed to defending the territorial integrity of the USSR in its entirety. However, the document included three other provisions that would have an enormous impact on relations between the center and the union republics in the final two years of the USSR's existence. First, it repeated the traditional canard that "the pledge of the durability of our federation is the completely voluntary nature of the unification of the Soviet republics into a single federal state, in which each republic retains its independence and has the right to participate in the adoption of general decisions." Second, it asserted, again in line with traditional Soviet claims about socialist federalism, that the union republics were "empowered to resolve all questions of state and public life, with the exception of those that they voluntarily transfer to Union jurisdiction." Third, it asserted that "the question is being raised of drafting and signing a new federal treaty to replace the 1922 Treaty on the Formation of the USSR, as well as preparing a new Declaration on the USSR," and it then appeared to endorse the proposal by suggesting that a new foundational document "could be regarded as an organic part of the USSR Constitution."[38] These themes—that the secession of any of the union republics was politically unacceptable; that the union was a purely voluntary association; that the republics retained all powers other than those they delegated to the union; and that the union needed to be renewed on the basis of a new foundational document—would serve as the cornerstones of Gorbachev's strategy for solving the USSR's intensifying "nationalities problem." That strategy would prove disastrous, above all because convincing the leaders of all fifteen union republics to sign a revised treaty, and the legislatures of those same republics to ratify it, would turn out to be impossible.

The immediate effect of the nationalities plenum, coupled with the unfolding drama of the anti-Communist revolutions in Eastern Europe, was a deepening of antiunion sentiments in the republics. The well-publicized plenum offered representatives of both the union republics and the autonomies an opportunity to articulate grievances and to reassert their claims against the center in a public forum specifically devoted to their problems. Gorbachev, for the first time in the perestroika era, had staked out a decidedly conservative position—he was no longer pushing simply for a radicalization of the reform process but was now at least as concerned with preventing the reform process from spinning out of control.[39] He therefore chose not to use the plenum as a forum for co-opting even part of the program of the antiunion opposition. Instead, he defended the CPSU's traditional nationalities policy and bluntly argued that "attempts to distort and belittle the genuine achievements in relations between nationalities are a desecration of the memory of several generations of Soviet people, and they do not stand up to criticism when compared to the facts of our lives." He also insisted, the historical record notwithstanding, that there was "no reason to call into question the decision that was made concerning the entry of the Baltic republics into the USSR, or the choice that was made by their peoples." As for the sovereign status of the union republics:

> First of all, it should be stressed that the Party will work consistently to implement the Leninist nationalities policy, including the basic principle of the right of nations to self-determination. Allegations that the self-determination of peoples of the USSR has not occurred, and attempts to interpret it merely as secession, thus weakening this universal principle for resolving the nationalities question, are fruitless and should be condemned. All our experience, and not just our experience, indicates that self-determination should not be viewed simply as a one-time act involving the exercise of one's right of secession. It is a complicated, multifaceted process involving affirmation of national dignity, development of language and culture, strengthening of political independence, and economic and social progress.[40]

This characterization of the meaning of "self-determination," and its implications for the union republics' "sovereignty," would doubtless have been endorsed by most Western governments. Gorbachev's problem was that it was Lenin himself who had held that sovereignty and the right of secession were the institutional embodiments of the principle of self-determination. Arguing that the Party would continue to "implement the Leninist nationalities policy" but refusing to recognize the right of the union republics to secede was thus a non sequitur, as the antiunion opposition in the republics was happy to point out.

Despite the hard-line tone of Gorbachev's speech, Moscow made some significant concessions in the wake of the plenum. On 27 November 1989, the USSR Supreme Soviet adopted a law that afforded the Baltic republics significant economic autonomy. Union republic governments were given control of the land and natural resources on their territory and the right to raise their own taxes, to adopt their own budgets, to regulate all economic activity, and to control investment on their territory, including investment by the all-union government.[41] The USSR was to retain the right to levy its own taxes, to control the ruble (which was to be the currency for all interrepublic trade), and to issue binding state orders (*goszakazy*) on state enterprises. These same rights were afforded the other republics, as well as the autonomies, in a Supreme Soviet law of 10 April 1990.[42] Adopting these laws and implementing them, however, were rather different matters—in particular, it was difficult to see how the union republics could levy and collect their own taxes when the federal center controlled the tax inspectorate and claimed ownership of the bulk of the enterprises on republic territory. Moreover, the right of central planners to continue to issue state orders meant that in effect enterprises were still subject to federal jurisdiction.

That April a number of additional federal laws were passed that reflected the Party's strategy for addressing the nationalities problem as laid out in its August 1989 program. A law prohibiting discrimination against individuals based on nationality, religion, or language and banning any activity directed at "stirring up enmity and discord between nationalities" was signed by Gorbachev on 2 April 1990.[43] A second law, entitled "On the Languages of the Peoples of the USSR" and adopted by the Supreme Soviet on 24 April 1990, established Russian as the official language of the USSR and as the language of international communication. However, the law granted the union republics the right to choose their own state languages.[44]

A more important law was passed on 3 April 1990. Entitled "Law on the Procedure for Resolving Questions Connected with a Union Republic's Secession from the USSR," it was the first piece of legislation in Soviet history that made it possible, at least legally, for the union republics to exercise their constitutional right of secession. The procedures established by the law for effecting secession, however, were so onerous that they made that right meaningless. To secede, a union republic would have to hold a referendum in which all Soviet citizens legally resident in the republic (e.g., ethnic Russians in Latvia) could participate. Two-thirds of all eligible voters, not just those who turned out for the vote (Article 6), would have to vote for secession. Campaigning during the "referendum period" was not allowed, which would have made it very difficult to attain the extremely high turnout required for approval by two-thirds of voters. The results of the referendum would have to be reviewed by the USSR Supreme Soviet and Congress of Peoples' Deputies to determine whether the referendum had been carried out in accordance with the law, which would have given both bodies the opportunity to rule that the strictures against campaigning had been violated. At that point, a five-year transition period would begin during which a host of technical economic and political problems would have to be worked out through a complicated process specified by the law. If the initial referendum failed to garner at least two-thirds support, another referendum on secession could not be held for another ten years (Article 9). Finally, in the last year of the transition period, another referendum would have to be carried out if one-tenth of the residents of the republic demanded it. If the second referendum failed to receive two-thirds majority support from eligible voters, "the decision of the union republic to withdraw from the USSR shall be considered rejected and the process provided for by the law ended" (Article 19).[45]

Complicating the law further were provisions specifying that in those union republics with autonomous republics, autonomous oblasts, or okrugs (i.e., the RSFSR, Armenia, Azerbaijan, Georgia, Uzbekistan, and Tajikistan), referendums would be "held separately," and the electorates of the autonomies would retain the right "to decide independently the question of remaining in the USSR or within the seceding union republic, and also to raise the question of their own state-legal status" (Article 3). In areas within the seceding republic "that are densely populated by ethnic groups constituting a majority of the population in question" (e.g., Crimean Tatars or Russians in Ukraine, Russians in northern Kazakhstan or the Baltic republics, Abkhazians or even Mingrelians, depending on what was meant by an "ethnic group," in Georgia, as well as the many minority peoples without a homeland in the RSFSR), a separate tally of the results of the referendum on secession would have to be gathered and agreement would have to be reached between the USSR and republic government on how to deal with those compactly settled territories (Article 3 and Article 14.8). A similar procedure was specified for areas not belonging to the republic at the time of its entry into the USSR (e.g., Crimea, which had been part of the RSFSR until 1954) (Article 14.7). For obvious reasons, the law was widely referred to as the "law on nonsecession" by the antiunion opposition and was viewed as an insulting violation of the sovereignty of the union republics.

A fifth law adopted in April would prove equally important in the coming months. Entitled "On the Delineation of Powers between the USSR and the Subjects of the Federation" and adopted on 26 April 1990, the law was expected to become part of the USSR constitution by amendment. Its opening article affirmed that the USSR is "a sovereign socialist federated state" that "possesses powers (*obladaet polnomochiiami*) that the subjects of the federation jointly place within the competence of the USSR." As in the 1977 constitution, the union republics were described as "sovereign soviet socialist states," but it now made explicit the traditional myth that the constituent units of the union "voluntarily, on the basis of the free self-determination of peoples and equal rights, unite in the Union of Soviet Socialist Republics." The union republics were again granted a right of secession, but the law now made clear that the right could only be exercised in accordance with federal law. The union republics, as well as all the other autonomies, could enter into economic agreements with each other but only on condition that those agreements did not contradict the interests of the USSR or of other republics or the autonomies. The union republics (but not the autonomies) would be allowed to enter into direct relations with foreign governments and sign treaties (*dogovory*) and exchange diplomatic representatives, but again only to the extent that doing so did not violate federal laws or treaties signed by the USSR.

Article 6 of the law enumerated a long list of matters that fell within the jurisdiction of the federal government, including a common foreign policy, a uniform monetary system, defense, state banks, federal taxation, and so on, as well as a very broad provision for "working out the prospects for the social-economic development of the country, and the drawing up and implementation of an all-union program" (Article 6.7). Article 8 then enumerated a series of policy arenas that fell within the joint competence of the USSR and the union republics.[46]

On the face of it, the 26 April 1990 law went a considerable distance toward accommodating the demands of the union republics. Unlike the drafts of a new union treaty that would be published in the coming months (see below), the law provided for a reasonable degree of authority for the central government that was similar to the powers afforded federal governments elsewhere in the world. And like most federal constitutions, it provided a broad framework for intergovernmental relations without trying to specify too much.

Unfortunately for Gorbachev, however, the package of laws adopted in April 1990 failed to ameliorate the centrifugal pressures on the USSR, for two reasons. First, they appeared to be directed above all at sowing dissension between the union republics and the autonomies (see below). And second, they confirmed that the center was intent on preventing secession at almost any cost. Had a reasonable law on secession been adopted, and had Moscow refrained from its shortsighted effort to mobilize the autonomies against the union republics, the law on the delineation of powers might have served, as Gorbachev hoped, as the basis for a renewed union. Instead, Gorbachev's allies would spend the next twenty months trying to negotiate a new union treaty from a position of increasing weakness. He and his aides would help draft a series of proposed treaties, each of which would provide for an ever weaker federal center, indeed to the point where it was unclear whether what was being provided for was a "renewed" union or no union at all.

Indeed, rather than placating the antiunion opposition in the union republics or providing local authorities with a legal basis for cracking down on individuals who were contributing to internationality violence in the Caucasus and Central Asia, the April laws had the opposite effect. Most dramatically, their impending passage, as well as Gorbachev's proposal to create a powerful new position of Soviet president, helped prompt the Lithuanian parliament to take the dramatic step of declaring full independence on 11 March 1990. Lithuania's parliamentarians, who had been elected in February in a vote that resulted in a resounding victory for the Lithuanian popular front (Sajudis) and its allies, wanted to make clear that the laws were inapplicable to their republic before they were passed in Moscow, and they feared that Gorbachev, who was certain to assume the new position of Soviet president (as indeed he did on 15 March), would use his new powers to order a crackdown.

Lithuania's independence declaration was approved by a unanimous vote (there were six abstentions). It asserted that "the execution of the sovereign power of the Lithuanian state, heretofore constrained by alien forces in 1940, is restored, and henceforth Lithuania is once again an independent state. . . . The Supreme Council of the Republic of Lithuania, expressing sovereign power, by this act begins to achieve the state's full sovereignty."[47] Additional resolutions were passed that same day that invalidated the USSR law on military conscription in the republic, established a border guard and border controls, changed the name of the republic from the Lithuanian Soviet Socialist Republic to the

Lithuanian Republic, and replaced the Communist hammer and sickle with Lithuania's traditional coat of arms. A new non-Communist government was then formed to negotiate the terms of Lithuania's independence with Moscow.

Four days later, the USSR Congress of Peoples' Deputies responded with a resolution nullifying the declaration on the grounds that the USSR had yet to adopt a law on secession (it would not be adopted until several weeks later) and directing Gorbachev to take steps to protect Soviet citizens and property in the republic. Earlier in the month, Lithuanian officials had reported that Gorbachev had raised questions about the republic's borders and suggested that Lithuania would have to surrender Klaipeda and other territory if it pressed for independence. He also reportedly demanded $33 billion as a "divorce settlement," including $17 billion in compensation for previous capital investments, $4 billion for undelivered production, and compensation for the costs of relocating ethnic Russians and Poles who would want to leave the republic.[48] Gorbachev, who presided during that same session over the abolition of Article 6 of the Soviet constitution that institutionalized the CPSU's monopoly of power, ruled out direct talks with the Lithuanians. "There can be no question of talks," he asserted. "We hold talks only with foreign states."[49] Instead, he ordered authorities in Vilnius to retract their declaration within three days. Soviet planes began dropping leaflets on Vilnius that urged residents to attend anti-independence rallies; telephone links to the West were cut off; and Lithuanian radio and television broadcasts were interrupted. The Lithuanians nevertheless held firm and refused to rescind the declaration. Gorbachev responded by issuing a decree on 21 March 1990 that instructed the KGB to take "necessary measures to enhance the security of those USSR borders which lie along the territory of Lithuania" and ordering all Lithuanian residents to turn in their firearms within a week. The decree also banned travel to the republic by foreigners.[50] Two days later, all foreign diplomats were ordered to leave the republic. As Soviet troops carried out threatening movements inside the republic, the Soviet prime minister, Nikolai Ryzhkov, ordered an embargo on oil and gas supplies to the republic on 17 April 1990.

With the conflict between Moscow and Vilnius intensifying, Gorbachev found himself under growing pressure from conservatives to declare presidential rule and use force to dissolve the Lithuanian parliament, replace the government, and seize key media and other assets in the republic. These pressures intensified after the Estonian parliament adopted a declaration on 30 March 1990 that asserted that "the state power of the USSR in Estonia has been illegal from the moment of its imposition and proclaims the restoration of the Republic of Estonia (*restitutio in integrum*)." It also proclaimed "a period of transition lasting until the formation of the constitutional organs of state power of the Republic of Estonia."[51] On 4 May 1990, the Latvian parliament followed suit, declaring the "*de facto* restoration of a free, democratic, and independent Republic of Latvia," characterizing the incorporation of the republic into the USSR as illegal, and restoring the validity of Latvia's 1922 constitution.[52]

Despite the growing pressure on Gorbachev from conservatives to take forceful action, and despite the West's reluctance to encourage secessionist aspirations in the union republics, Washington and its allies made it clear that a crackdown in the Baltics would have serious international repercussions.[53] In part, Western interest in a peaceful resolution of the standoff in the Baltics was tied to the nonrecognition policy of the Western governments. But there were other considerations as well: the proximity of Estonia, Latvia, and Lithuania to frontline NATO countries, particularly Germany; a belief (party mythological) in the close historical and cultural ties of the Baltic states to the Nordic countries, and to lesser extents to Poland and Germany; the sympathy that Western publics felt for such numerically small and evidently "European" peoples; the relatively large and vocal Baltic diasporas in the West; and the negative reaction of Westerners to the bullying tactics of "less European" Russians (the distinction between Russians and Soviets, or between the Russian and Soviet governments, did not enter public consciousness). Moreover, in contrast to the crackdown in Baku in January 1990, where widespread rioting and anti-Armenian pogroms preceded the introduction of Soviet troops, the Baltic peoples were using peaceful means to pursue their political ends. Finally, whereas in the April 1988 crackdown in Tbilisi it had been unclear whether Gorbachev or other members of the central leadership had endorsed the decision to use force, it was clear that the mounting pressure on the Baltic governments, including the threatening maneuvers by Soviet military units, was being directed from Moscow.

Nevertheless, Western governments continued to be extremely cautious about encouraging separatism in the union republics. In part, this was because they wished to avoid undermining Gorbachev politically at home. Neither did they wish to provoke separatist wars in the Soviet Union. The rapidly changing political situation in Eastern Europe led Western governments to fear that conservatives would oust Gorbachev and halt Soviet troop withdrawals or even use the USSR's still considerable military presence in the region to preserve Communist power by force. It was also becoming increasingly clear that a breakup of the Yugoslav federation might spark war in the Balkans, and supporting separatists in the Baltic republics might well encourage separatists in Slovenia or Croatia to take up arms.[54] Finally, after Iraq invaded Kuwait on 1 August 1990 and Washington began to build the military coalition that would eventually drive Iraqi forces out of Kuwait, the United States and its coalition allies found themselves in even greater need of Gorbachev's cooperation on the international front.[55]

* * * * *

While the deepening conflict between the Soviet central government and Baltic states was the subject of enormous international attention in the first six months of 1990, the period also witnessed the beginning of another process that received far less attention but ultimately proved fateful to the Soviet Union—the mobilization of Russian democratic forces in opposition to the Soviet center under the leadership of Boris Yeltsin. Yeltsin had been removed as a candidate (nonvoting) member of the Politburo and as the Party first secretary of Moscow in November 1987 for having openly attacked Politburo conservatives at a Central Committee plenum. Publicly humiliated and deeply resentful of his treatment by Gorbachev in particular, Yeltsin had been demoted to Deputy Minister of Construction. His political resurrection began in early 1989 when he ran successfully for a seat as a delegate to the USSR Congress of Peoples' Deputies. A year later, with support from radical reformers in the recently formed political movement, Demokraticheskaia Rossiia (Democratic Russia), Yeltsin ran for a seat in the new RSFSR Congress of Peoples' Deputies, which he hoped would allow him to establish an independent political base from which to challenge Gorbachev and conservatives in the Kremlin.

Despite the earlier success of the Baltic popular fronts in using "sovereignty" to mobilize the antiunion opposition in their republics, Yeltsin was rather slow to embrace the term as a theme in his political campaign. His platform of 5 February 1990 called for the elimination of the Communist Party's constitutionally entrenched monopoly of power; the formation of an independent "Russian" Communist Party; the adoption of a new, essentially liberal, constitution for Russia; the establishment of a Russian presidency and presidential elections through a "direct, universal, equal, and secret vote"; the marketization of the Russian economy; and pluralism in forms of ownership (i.e., the legalization of private property in the means of production).[56] Other than a brief reference to the need to restore Russia's "economic sovereignty," the platform did not mention "sovereignty" or stress the importance of devolving power to the union republics. It reflected Yeltsin's principal concern at the time—the need to accelerate political and economic reforms for the union as a whole and the exploitation of the RSFSR elections to pressure Gorbachev to adopt a more radical course.[57]

Within a matter of weeks, however, the character of his platform began to change. By the time the RSFSR's Congress of Peoples' Deputies convened for the first time in mid-May 1991, "sovereignty" for Russia had become the centerpiece of Yeltsin's political strategy. Running from his hometown of Sverdlovsk, Yeltsin won a seat in the Congress with 84 percent of the vote on 4 March 1990. The elections were considerably more "free and fair" than the elections to the USSR Congress the previous year, and democrats did well, winning control of the Moscow and Leningrad city soviets. Approximately 25–33 percent of the delegates to the RSFSR Congress were aligned with DemRossiia, approximately the same percentage were considered pro-Communist conservatives, while the remainder were middle-of-the-road swing voters, including a number of illiberal and anti-Yeltsin Russian nationalists. Immediately after the returns were reported, Yeltsin had his close advisor, Mikhail Bocharov, form a DemRossiia parliamentary umbrella organization, which convened in late March and nominated Yeltsin as its candidate for chairman of the RSFSR Supreme Soviet. Bocharov went on to convene a number of working groups from the group's supporters, one of which was given responsibility for drafting a sovereignty declaration. The draft was approved at a DemRossiia meeting on 14 April.[58]

Thus when the first RSFSR Congress of Peoples' Deputies session opened in mid-May, Yeltsin was in a position to present the draft sovereignty declaration to the assembled delegates. In his speech submitting the draft for consideration, Yeltsin argued that genuine sovereignty was just as necessary for Russia as it was for the other republics: "The center is for Russia today the cruel exploiter, the miserly benefactor, and the favorite who does not think about the future. We must put an end to the injustice of these relations. Today it is not the center but Russia that must think about which functions to transfer to the center, and which to keep for itself."

"The problems of Russia," he went on, "cannot be solved without full-blooded political sovereignty." He argued that laws adopted by the USSR should not violate either the new constitution that Russia should adopt or the proposed USSR-RSFSR treaty; that there should be a single republic-wide Russian citizenship; and that Russia's "economic sovereignty" should be realized through Russian ownership of "land, the soil beneath and the air above, forests, water and other natural resources, enterprises, all produced output and its scientific-technical and intellectual potential." He then articulated a radical understanding of "sovereignty" that went well beyond sovereignty for the RSFSR government alone:

> The most important, primary sovereignty in Russia is the person and his rights; further on, the enterprise, the collective and state farm, and other organizations—that is where the primary and strongest sovereignty must be, as well as, of course, the sovereignty of the *raion* [local districts] Soviet or any other primary Soviet.[59]

Just what Yeltsin meant by "sovereignty" generally, let alone "sovereignty" for individual citizens and enterprises, was far from obvious (presumably something close to "liberty" or "freedom"). He did assert, however, that a declaration of sovereignty did not mean that "we are talking about some kind of confrontation with the center. The main thrust is in just one direction—the strengthening of the Union."[60] At no point did he indicate that he wanted full-blown independence or the dismantling of the Soviet state, as he made clear in another address to the RSFSR Congress several days later: "I have never advocated Russia's secession. I am in favor of the Union's sovereignty, equal rights of all republics, the autonomy of the republics, so that the republics are strong and so that, with this strength, they reinforce our strong Union."[61]

Given an opportunity to address the assembly the day after Yeltsin's address, Gorbachev agreed that the sovereignty of the RSFSR should be "strengthened." For him, however, this meant "providing full power to the Soviets at all levels and creating in Russia an integral system of bodies of state power." It also meant establishing a Russian Communist Party on a par with those of the other republics. He then went on to criticize Yeltsin explicitly: Yeltsin "wants, with one stroke of the pen, as it were, to invite us to bid farewell to the socialist choice of 1917. . . . For us citizens of the Russian republic, as for all the peoples of our country, the socialist choice and power of the Soviets are not empty phrases. They are our fundamental values, or reference points." He made it clear that he believed that Yeltsin was seeking, "under the banner of restoring Russian sovereignty, to break up the Union,"[62] a claim that he would reiterate frequently and include in his 1996 memoirs.

In fact, there is no evidence that Yeltsin was hoping to bring about the dissolution of the Soviet Union at the time. While Yeltsin was perfectly clear that he hoped that the RSFSR would adopt a more radical reform program if the center would not, he also repeatedly asserted that he wanted a strong and sovereign union along with strong and sovereign republics. And while his argument that the "sovereignty" of the federal government and the "sovereignty" of the union republics were compatible may seem contradictory, this was a position that was shared not only by Gorbachev but by the great majority of Soviet analysts at the time.[63]

Neither did Yeltsin appear the slightest bit interested in a precise legal definition of the meaning of sovereignty—far more important was its political effect in putting Gorbachev and the central leadership on the defensive. As an instinctive politician who, unlike Gorbachev, showed little interest in doctrinal issues or programmatic statements, he probably gave little thought to the term's meaning, although he apparently felt that "sovereignty," however defined, was something that Russia and the other republics deserved if for no other reason than it had been long denied them.

There is also no evidence that Yeltsin was opposed in principle to the adoption of a new union treaty. Like most of his colleagues, he believed that some kind of treaty could and should be negotiated to provide for a "renewed union," and that this new union would consist at least of Russia, Ukraine, Belorussia, and Kazakhstan. What *was* critically important to him, however, were the terms of the treaty and the extent to which the RSFSR government would control the reform process in the RSFSR. As time passed, his views about the optimal delineation of power between the central government and the republics would become more radical. But while his belief in the viability of a very weak confederal union may have been highly impractical, so too were those of most Soviet politicians and scholars at the time, including Gorbachev's.

Despite Gorbachev's campaign to oppose him, Yeltsin was elected Chairman of the Presidium of the RSFSR Supreme Soviet on the third ballot in an extremely close vote on 29 May 1990 (he received 535 votes to 467 for his primary opponent and 11 for a third candidate). His victory came despite the fact that the "democratic" bloc of delegates represented a minority in the new Congress. That his championing of Russian "sovereignty" played an important, perhaps decisive, role in his election victory was suggested by the fact that the Congress would approve a declaration of state sovereignty on 12 June 1990 by a comfortable margin of more than two to one. "Sovereignty" for Russia, with all its ambiguity, was clearly more popular than Yeltsin or his liberal-democratic program.

The substance of the RSFSR's sovereignty declaration was similar in most respects to those of the Baltic republics. Its first two articles stated that the RSFSR was "a sovereign state" and that the "sovereignty of the RSFSR constitutes the natural and necessary condition for the existence of the statehood of Russia with its centuries-old history, culture, and traditions." Article 5 asserted "complete authority for the RSFSR in resolving all questions relating to state and public life with the exception of those which it voluntarily hands over to USSR jurisdiction" and the "primacy of the RSFSR Constitution and RSFSR laws throughout the territory of the RSFSR." It continued: "[O]n its territory, the republic suspends the operation of USSR acts that contravene RSFSR sovereign rights. Differences between the republic and the Union are resolved according to the procedure established by the Union Treaty." Article 7 asserted that the RSFSR "reserves the right to leave the USSR freely according to the procedure established by and for [*sic*] the legislation established by the Union Treaty," while its final provision called for a new RSFSR constitution, the conclusion of a new union treaty, and corresponding legislation.[64]

The Russian legislature, under Yeltsin's leadership, thus proclaimed the primacy of its constitution and laws over those of the USSR and demanded that a new union treaty be negotiated by the members of a newly constituted union. Unlike Serbia under Milosevic, Russia under Yeltsin would not fight to preserve the "federation" of which it was the principal part. On the other hand, Yeltsin and the overwhelming majority of the deputies to the RSFSR Congress were in favor of a reconstituted union, unlike many of the proponents of sovereignty in the Baltic republics. While most Russian democrats were willing to accept that the Baltic republics, or conceivably Moldavia or one or more of the South Caucasus republics, might well opt out of a new union, most assumed that a central state would survive as a legally recognized entity with a seat in the UN General Assembly and membership in the UN Security Council. Whether the new union would be a "federation" or "confederation," or indeed what was meant by those terms, and how much "sovereignty" would be afforded the center and the union republics, would have to be worked out in the negotiations over the new union treaty.

Before turning to the drama of Gorbachev's efforts to ratify a new union treaty for a reformed USSR, however, we will first take a short detour and consider another unfolding drama—the struggle of the autonomies to follow the lead of the union republics and demand greater authority and genuine autonomy. This time, however, the proposed devolution of power was to come at the expense not only of the all-union center but of the union republics as well.

Notes

1. An additional traditional evil—*vedomstvo* (departmentalism), or the placement of the interests of particular departments above those of society as whole and the consequent feudalization of the party-state hierarchy along vertical (branch ministry, state committee) lines was also the subject of much criticism in the early glasnost era. The campaign against *vedomstvo*, however, had less direct relevance to antiunion mobilization than the campaigns against *mestnichestvo* and *vozhdizm*.

2. Mikhail S. Gorbachev, *Izbranniye rechi i stat'i,* vol. 3 (Moscow: Izdatel'stvo politicheskoi literatury, 1987), 307.

3. Gorbachev would concede in his memoirs that the decision to replace Kunaev with Kolbin had been a mistake and that the leadership's response to the Alma Ata riots had been misguided, failures that he explained as follows: "In reacting to these events, we were ruled by obsolete stereotypes—that everything must take place in unity and friendship, and that the only danger lay in spontaneous outbreaks of nationalism," Mikhail Gorbachev, *Memoirs,* trans. Wolf Jobst Siedler and Tatjana Varsavsky (New York: Doubleday, 1995), 331.

4. Quoted in Motyl 1989, 156–57.

5. Gorbachev 1987, vol. 3, 234.

6. Mikhail Gorbachev, *Perestroika: New Thinking for Our Country and the World* (New York: Harper & Row, 1987 [b]), 118–22.

7. Anatoly S. Chernyaev, *My Six Years with Gorbachev,* trans. and ed. Robert English and Elizabeth Tucker (University Park: Pennsylvania State University Press, 2000), 183. Chernyaev was Gorbachev's closest foreign policy advisor throughout the perestroika years. According to Chernyaev, the statement is lifted directly from his diary, where he transcribed notes taken during many of Gorbachev's key meetings, including verbatim statements from Politburo sessions as well as meetings with foreign leaders. In a preface to the book, the U.S. ambassador to Moscow for most of the Gorbachev era, Jack Matlock, writes, "As one who was present at many of the events and encounters Chernyaev describes, I can testify to the accuracy of his descriptions, at least of those matters that I, too, observed" (Chernyaev 2000, foreword, x). In general, Chernyaev's memoirs are frank and often self-critical, and they strike me as credible. I therefore place this passage as well as additional diary entries below in quotes, albeit with the caveat that there is no way to confirm that the diary entries are entirely accurate.

8. Dawson 1996.

9. Anders Aslund, *Gorbachev's Struggle for Economic Reform* (Ithaca, N.Y.: Cornell University Press, 1989).

10. See, for example, Charles F. Furtado, Jr., and Andrea Chandler, *Perestroika in the Soviet Republics: Documents on the National Question* (Boulder, Colo.: Westview Press, 1992), 65–66.

11. Furtado and Chandler 1992, 111.

12. Furtado and Chandler 1992, 111–14.

13. E. K. Ligachev, *Inside Gorbachev's Kremlin: the Memoirs of Yegor Ligachev,* trans. Catherine A. Fitzpatrick, Michele A. Berdy, and Dobrochna Dyrcz-Freeman (New York: Pantheon Books, 1998), 174. The reference is to Lenin's epithet for those Mensheviks who, during the Stolypin reform era when the Tsarist regime was becoming more tolerant of political opposition, argued that the Russian socialist parties should adopt nonviolent methods for promoting change. Lenin accused them of advocating a premature "liquidation" of the RSDLP. Ligachev's use of the term therefore implied that Brazauskas was an anti-Leninist and an enemy of the Party.

14. FBIS-SOV-89-170, 59.

15. Furtado and Chandler 1992, 154.

16. *New York Times,* 2 October 1988.

17. Roeder 1992, 155–56.

18. Furtado and Chandler 1992, 70.

19. Furtado and Chandler 1992, 71–72.

20. Furtado and Chandler 1992, 69.

21. Furtado and Chandler 1992, 70.

22. In early December 1989, the Armenian Supreme Soviet and the Armenian-dominated National Council of Nagorno-Karabakh issued a joint declaration on the "re-unification" of Karabakh and Armenia. The declaration has sometimes been treated as the equivalent of a sovereignty declaration, particularly in view of the fact that, although the USSR Supreme Soviet ruled the following month that the declaration violated the Soviet constitution, Armenia initially refused to rescind it.

23. Georgia adopted an additional set of laws reaffirming and expanding the republic's "sovereignty" on 14 November 1990.

24. As I will discuss in some detail in chapter 4, an important exception was the RSFSR's sovereignty declaration, which was explicit in adopting a nonethnic understanding of Russian statehood and citizenship.

25. As a 1 July 1989 Latvian draft law bluntly explained, "[T]he main meaning of the republic's incipient economic sovereignty is that all local economic possibilities are to be utilized to satisfy the vital needs of the population [of Latvia]."

26. Chernyaev 2000, 227.

27. Western parliaments and NGOs, on the other hand, were less circumspect. For example, during the 23 August 1988 demonstrations in Vilnius on the anniversary of the Molotov-Ribbentrop Pact, the crowd was read a letter from the U.S. Senate condemning the 1940 invasion as an "illegal occupation." It is also true that Baltic diaspora organizations were active in supporting the popular fronts, and they may well have contributed to a false impression among nationalist activists about the extent of the support they would receive from Western governments.

28. Under the UN Charter, "the self-determination of peoples" was mentioned in Articles 1(2) and 55, but it was treated initially as a "principle" rather than a "right." It was referred to as a "right" for the first time in the 1960 Declaration on the Granting of Independence to Colonial Territories and Countries, as follows: "All peoples have the right to self-determination; by virtue of that right they freely determine their political status and freely pursue their economic, social, and cultural development" (UN General Assembly Resolution 1514 [XV], 14 December 1960, 89:0:9). At the same time, both documents referred to the principle of the preservation of the territorial integrity of existing states. On the ambiguity of the concept under international law, see Mortin H. Halperin, David J. Scheffer, and Patricia L. Small, *Self-Determination in the New World Order* (Washington, D.C.: Carnegie Endowment for International Peace, 1992), 45–69; and Hannum 1990, 27–49.

29. Matlock 1995, 230–31.

30. *New York Times,* 12 December 1988.

31. Supplement to *Moscow News,* no. 51 (3351), 1988, 5.

32. *New York Times,* 23 April 1989.

33. Chernyaev 2000, 226.

34. Chernyaev 2000, 182.

35. Chernyaev 2000, 93.

36. Chernyaev 2000, 181.

37. *Pravda* and *Izvestiia,* 17 August 1989, *CDSP,* vol. 41, no. 33, 1–8.

38. In endorsing the need for a new "declaration," the Party was attempting to stake out an intermediate position between those who argued that a new union treaty had to be negotiated between the federal government and the union republics, either jointly or individually, and then ratified by their respective parliaments, and those who were advocating that greater autonomy for the union republics should be accomplished by amending the USSR constitution, which would have required only a two-thirds vote by the Congress of Peoples' Deputies. As we will see, the leadership in fact gave up on the need for a "decla-

ration" and instead initially adopted a federal law on the delineation of powers within the federation on 26 April 1990. Less than two months later, however, Gorbachev would come out publicly for a new union treaty that would need to be ratified by all the union republics as the panacea for the USSR's federation crisis.

39. Several weeks after the plenum, Gorbachev would further alienate liberal reformers by sharply criticizing the media in general for, as he put it, "an orgy of irresponsibility and incitement" (Chernyaev 2000, 242). He attacked the editor of the proreform weekly, *Argumenty i fakty,* Vladislav Starkov, in particular, as well as the proreform historian, Yuri Afanasyev. Accounts of the two-hour meeting were leaked to the Western press, which gave Gorbachev's apparent retreat on glasnost considerable coverage (see, for example, *New York Times,* 23 October 1989). The speculation was that *Argumenty i fakty* had published polling data that suggested Gorbachev was losing popular support.

40. *Pravda,* 20 September 1989, *CDSP,* vol. 41, no. 38, 7.

41. Hazard 1992, 120–21.

42. Hazard 1992, 121.

43. *Izvestiia,* 5 April 1990, *CDSP,* vol. 42, no. 16, 15.

44. *Vedomosti,* 1990, no. 19, 421–28.

45. *Izvestiia,* 6 April 1990.

46. *Vedomosti,* 1990, no. 19, 429–34.

47. Furtado and Chandler 1992, 182.

48. *New York Times,* 8 March 1990.

49. *New York Times,* 14 March 1990.

50. Furtado and Chandler 1992, 187.

51. Furtado and Chandler 1992, 102–103.

52. Furtado and Chandler 1992, 139–40.

53. Matlock, for example, repeatedly informed Soviet officials that a crackdown would inevitably undermine U.S.-Soviet relations. He also recalls an interesting exchange with Yevgenii Primakov, then chairman of one of the two houses of the USSR Supreme Soviet and later Russia's foreign minister. Primakov responded to a warning by U.S. Ambassador Matlock not to use force in the Baltics by asking whether the U.S. president would negotiate with the governor of a state that had declared independence. Matlock responded, "Maybe not, but our Constitution does not give states the right to secede" (Matlock 1995, 342).

54. The Western response to the Yugoslav crisis during this period is worth noting. Washington pressed its West European allies to take the lead in preventing a war in the Balkans. Initially, the European Community (later the European Union) enthusiastically took up the challenge. It insisted that the unity of Yugoslavia be preserved, and argued that this could best be accomplished through successful democratic and economic reform. This position became untenable, however, after Slovenia and Croatia declared independence in June 1991 and war broke out. As it became clear that keeping the country together was no longer possible, the EC changed its position, arguing only that any changes in international borders could not be brought about by force. The implication, then, was that a general settlement on Yugoslavia's dissolution would have to be negotiated by all parties before diplomatic recognition was afforded any new state or states. As fighting in Croatia spread, the Western public, and most Western governments, became increasingly convinced that Serbia was the main aggressor in the war. Germany in particular began to agitate for recognition of Slovenia and Croatia. West Germany, it is worth noting, treated citizenship largely as a matter of ethnicity—ethnic Germans who had lived in Russia for centuries, for example, were automatically afforded German citizenship if they applied for it, while ethnic Turks who lived in Germany for decades or had been born there had

great difficulty acquiring citizenship. The West German government was also committed to unification with the former GDR, and it had no ethnic minorities on its territory that might press for secession. Accordingly, it has traditionally been considerably more sympathetic to the principle of national self-determination than other Western states. Under German pressure, the EC recognized the independence of Slovenia and Croatia in mid-January 1991. A special Arbitration Commission of the Hague Conference, which had been established at the EC's initiative, provided legal justification for the move (after the fact, of course) by arguing that the Yugoslav Federation was "in a process" of dissolution at the time Slovenia and Croatia were recognized. This same position was then adopted by the United States after it began advocating the "preemptive recognition" of Bosnia in 1992 in the hopes of deterring Serbia from sending troops into the republic, Woodward 1995, and Mihailo Crnobrnja, *The Yugoslav Drama* (Montreal: McGill-Queen's University Press, 1994).

55. In his memoirs, written jointly with Brent Scowcroft, National Security Advisor during the Bush presidency, President Bush described his reaction to the escalating confrontation between the Baltic republics and Moscow in March 1990 as follows: "I was concerned, very concerned. We could not be in a position of opposing an independent Lithuania. On the other hand, if we pledged support, the minute it declared independence, that might cause Gorbachev to fall, or the Soviet military to act on its own. If there was violence, realistically there was not a thing the United States could do about it, and we would have blood on our hands for encouraging the Lithuanians to bite off more than they could chew. It was a worrisome picture," George W. Bush and Brent Scowcroft, *A World Transformed* (New York: Alfred A. Knopf, 1998), 214. Scowcroft would add, "The reality was that the only way the Baltic States [*sic*] could achieve lasting independence was with the acquiescence of the Kremlin. Our task was to bring Moscow to that point. The very worst way to do that was to confront the Soviets (Bush and Scowcroft 1998, 216).

56. Furtado and Chandler 1992, 317–19.

57. For an analysis of the relationship between Gorbachev and Yeltsin, their contrasting political styles, and Yeltsin's success in politically "outbidding" Gorbachev, see George W. Breslauer, *Gorbachev and Yeltsin as Leaders* (New York: Cambridge University Press, 2002). As Breslauer notes, "Yeltsin played a polarizing role during these two to three years of Gorbachev's leadership. No matter what Gorbachev proposed in domestic policy, Yeltsin criticized the Party leader for conservatism and half-measures. . . . When Gorbachev accommodated radicalizing forces, Yeltsin typically upped the ante by endorsing a still more radical option" (Breslauer 2002, 124–25).

58. Jerry F. Hough, *Democratization and Revolution in the USSR, 1985–1991* (Washington, D.C.: Brookings, 1997), 300.

59. Furtado and Chandler 1992, 322–24.

60. Furtado and Chandler 1992, 324.

61. Quoted in John Morrison, *Boris Yeltsin: From Bolshevik to Democrat* (New York: Dutton, 1991), 147.

62. *Pravda,* 25 May 1990, *CDSP,* vol. 42, no. 21, 4.

63. That sovereignty can be shared is a widely held view in the West (consider, for example, the notion of "pooled sovereignty" in the European Union). It is also the view of many American constitutional scholars, and indeed the U.S. Supreme Court, which has repeatedly taken the position that U.S. states share sovereignty under the constitution with the federal government.

64. Furtado and Chandler 1992, 325–26.

Chapter 4

Sovereignty for the Autonomies

Take all the sovereignty you can swallow. (Boris Yeltsin, to Russia's autonomous regions, August 1990)

In two important respects, Russia's sovereignty campaign was different from those of the Baltic republics. First, it relied less on the legitimizing rhetoric of anticolonialism and national liberation and more on the rhetoric of anticommunism and the need to remove the *nomenklatura* from power. It was thus a classic political struggle between Gorbachev and the all-union government on the one hand, and Yeltsin and the newly empowered RSFSR government on the other, with both parties appealing to the same constituency for support. Its driving force, up until the final days of the USSR, was the destruction of the ancien régime, not secession or the dissolution of the union. Second, and relatedly, the legitimating rhetoric of the RSFSR sovereignty campaign was less "ethnic" in character. Yeltsin and his allies were careful to adhere to the traditional Soviet doctrine of multinationalism (*mnogonatsional'nost'*)—the Russian state, they insisted, would be the sovereign representative not of ethnic Russians but of all the "peoples" (*narody*) resident on the RSFSR's territory. Accordingly, its sovereignty declaration would refer not to ethnic Russians (*russkie*) but to the "multinational people of the Russian Federation" (*mnogonatsional'nyi narod Rossiiskoi federatsii*).

In part, these differences resulted from the ambiguous status of Russians in the USSR described earlier. Not only were ethnic Russians more likely to see

87

themselves as citizens of the multinational Soviet state than were other nationalities, they were considerably less likely to identify the RSFSR rather than the USSR as their homeland. As Yeltsin himself confessed in a revealing interview in late 1990:

> I recognized myself to be a citizen of the country [i.e., the USSR] and not of Russia. Well, I also considered myself to be a patriot of Sverdlovsk, in as much as I had worked there. But the concept of "Russia" was so relative to me that, while serving as first secretary of the Sverdlovsk party obkom, I had not turned to the Russian [*rossiiskie*] departments on most questions. I would first turn to the Central Committee of the CPSU, and then to the union government.[1]

The weakness of affective ties to the RSFSR as a political entity (as opposed to respect for traditional Russian culture, the "Russian soul," or simply the land—*zemlia*) made it difficult for partisans of Russian sovereignty to employ the rhetoric of national self-determination and national liberation in challenging the center. While Russians may have been as much the victims of Soviet exploitation as other peoples of the Soviet Union, this victimization hardly resulted from political exploitation by non-Russians, despite the efforts of some extreme Russian nationalists to claim that most Bolsheviks were Jews. Rather than liberation from foreign oppression, it was liberation from an oppressive and hidebound center under the control of Communist ideologues and opportunists that served as the principal motivating force behind the RSFSR's sovereignty drive.

There was another, equally important, constraint on Russian ethnic nationalism. According to the Soviet 1989 census, the RSFSR had a population of 147.4 million, 81.5 percent of which was ethnic Russian. The rest were non-Russian minorities, many of whom lived more or less compactly on land that they considered traditionally theirs, a belief that was in many cases entrenched by administrative recognition. Moreover, the RSFSR was the only union republic that had formally been constituted as a federation, and by the time the Gorbachev era began, thirty-one of its eighty-eight constituent units were ethnically defined autonomies—sixteen autonomous republics, five autonomous oblasts, and ten okrugs.[2] While they tended to be lightly populated, the autonomies nevertheless included some 15 percent of the RSFSR's total population and covered approximately 50 percent of its territory. Advocates of Russian sovereignty were therefore constrained to adopt an inclusive understanding of Russian citizenship lest they provoke the autonomies to attempt to secede from the RSFSR, thereby undermining the very sovereignty they were promoting.

That the autonomies could create serious political problems for the union republics had first been demonstrated outside the borders of the RSFSR. As noted earlier, the first sustained political violence of the Gorbachev era broke out between Armenians and Azeris in February 1988 over the administrative subordination of the Nagorno-Karabakh Autonomous Oblast to Azerbaijan. Tensions would also surface that same year over the status of Abkhazia and South Ossetia, where local governments began pressing to "secede" from Georgia and join the RSFSR. They would eventually demand full independence, prompting two additional secessionist wars in the South Caucasus (see chapter 7).

Despite its heterogeneous population and numerous autonomies, Russia would manage to avoid significant violence between central authorities and minority governments during the Gorbachev era. Nevertheless, by late 1987—that is, at approximately the same time that antiunion mobilization was getting under way in some of the union republics—the RSFSR found itself facing escalating demands from some of its autonomies for a devolution of authority. The most serious initial challenge came from the Tatar ASSR, where Tatar intellectuals began articulating many of the same grievances being expressed in the Baltic republics. Initial complaints were directed at the treatment of Tatar draftees in the Soviet military, Moscow's decision to construct a nuclear power plant in the republic, the lack of opportunity for Tatar children to be educated in their native language, and the underrepresentation of the autonomies in the USSR Council of Nationalities and other central institutions. In February 1988, a new nationalist organization, the Tatar Public Center (*Tatarskii obshchestvennyi tsentr,* or TOTs) held a founding congress in Kazan. A Tatar deputy to the USSR Congress of Peoples' Deputies expressed some of the grievances of the republic in June 1989 as follows:

> Why . . . do union republics get to elect 32 Deputies from national-territorial districts, while autonomous republics elect only 11? What, in essence, distinguishes union republics from autonomous republics? Even at our Congress the union republics are being put into a special class, while we are relegated to the role of listeners. . . .
>
> Why, for example, is the Tatar nation of 7 million people deprived of its own film art? . . . Why, for example, do Tatar or Bashkir, Chuvash, Mari and other autonomous peoples' radio and television stations have far less time for their broadcasts than those in the union republics? . . .
>
> I think it is necessary to equalize the status of all the national republics, without dividing them into union and autonomous republics.[3]

By the summer of 1989, the status and powers of the autonomies had become important subjects of public discussion and were on the agenda of the Central Committee's September nationalities plenum. Already, there were suspicions that the Party leadership and other defenders of the union were going to use the autonomies as a point of leverage against the union republics. Thus the CPSU's draft nationalities platform of 17 August called for the expansion of the rights of the autonomous republics "in all fields of state, economic and cultural construction," and the elevation of the legal status and powers of the autonomous oblasts and okrugs. In his report to the plenum that September, Gorbachev referred to these provisions in the Party Platform, but he made clear that he was against redrawing the USSR's internal borders or otherwise changing its federation structure: "Embarking now on a path aimed at redrawing the administrative and territorial map of the country would only complicate an already difficult situation."[4]

Despite its suggestion that the Party would consider expanding the rights of the autonomies, representatives of the autonomies criticized the draft platform as inadequate at the November plenum. As the Party first secretary of Yakutia put it, the platform "does not go deep enough in disclosing the present-day problems of federalism and national autonomous units, it does not contain scientifically substantiated criteria for defining Union and autonomous republics." The rights of the autonomous republics should be broadened "so that they would have a real right to run things within their territories—in other words, the rights of the autonomous republics must be brought as close as possible to those of the union republics."[5] Likewise, the first secretary of Tatarstan argued that the Tatar ASSR should be afforded greater economic autonomy, including the right to choose its own "model of economic accountability" and budgetary independence, and he complained the republic had retained almost none of the estimated $250 billion of earnings from petroleum produced in Tatarstan since oil was discovered shortly after the end of World War II.[6] Particularly revealing was the address of the Party first secretary of the Bashkir SSR. The draft platform, he complained, "maintains inviolate the hierarchical structure of the national-state system." "In Estonia," he continued, "with a population only 40 percent that of Bashkiria, 105 magazines and other periodicals are published. We publish only 10 periodicals, and in the publication of books per capita our Estonian comrades publish 28 times what we do." He also pointed out that Bashkiria, with its population of almost four million, had far fewer representatives in the national parliament than union republics with substantially smaller populations. He then reminded his colleagues that the people and leadership of the republic had repeatedly demanded that the status of the ASSR be raised to that of a union republic:

> During the discussion of the draft USSR Constitution of 1936, proposals were made concerning the possibility of transforming the Bashkir and Tatar Autonomous Republics into union republics. But at that time, the only formal obstacle was their lack of external borders. Life has proven the far-fetched nature of that condition. Bashkiria's working people have never intended to go anywhere.[7]

In the wake of the plenum, central authorities took a number of steps in response to these complaints. As noted earlier, the USSR Supreme Soviet approved a law on 10 April 1990 that provided the autonomies with the same degree of economic autonomy that had been afforded the Baltic republics in the law of 27 November 1987, including ownership of land and natural resources on their territory, the right to raise taxes, control their own budgets, and regulate most economic activity, including investment by the all-union government.[8] The law on secession passed that same month gave the autonomies the right to remain within the USSR in the event that a union republic met the onerous requirements for seceding established by the law. Finally, the 26 April 1990 law on the delineation of powers defined their status in Article 1 as follows:

> [T]he autonomous republics are soviet socialist states (*gosudarstva*) and subjects of the federation of the USSR. Autonomous republics and autonomous formations [i.e., the autonomous oblasts and autonomous okrugs] are a part (*vkhodiat v sostav*) of union republics on the basis of the free self-determination of peoples, and they possess the entirety (*vsei polnotoi*) of state power on their territory, except for the powers that they transfer to the jurisdiction of the USSR and union republics.
>
> Relations between the autonomous republics and autonomous formations and the union republics in which they are located are defined by treaties (*dogovory*) and agreements (*soglasheniia*) that are concluded within the framework of the USSR constitution, the constitutions of the union republics and autonomous republics, and this law.[9]

The law went on to equalize the powers of the union republics and autonomous republics in certain areas: "[I]n the field of economic, social, and cultural construction on its territory, an autonomous republic has the same rights as a union republic, with the exception of those that, by mutual agreement, are assigned to the union republic's jurisdiction."

The law thus had the effect of putting the relationship between the autonomies and their host union republics on the same footing as the relationship between the USSR and the union republics—that is, the autonomies would supposedly retain all powers other than those they voluntarily delegated to the union republics and the USSR on the basis of negotiated treaties. The autonomous republics would also argue that their identification as "subjects of the federation" meant that they had a right to participate individually in the effort to draft and to ratify the new union treaty that Gorbachev hoped would solve the USSR's federation crisis (see below). The opening paragraph of the law, they noted, provided that the USSR government "possesses the powers that the subjects of the federation jointly assign to the jurisdiction of the USSR"—that is, *all* the subjects of the federation, not just the union republics.

While the 26 April 1990 law clearly strengthened the hand of the autonomies, it did not equalize their status or powers with that of the union republics, as some representatives of the autonomies and Western scholars would later claim.[10] Article 5, for example, provided that *only* the union republics had a right to enter into "relations with foreign states, to conclude treaties with them, to exchange diplomatic and consular missions, to conduct foreign-economic relations, and to participate in the activity of international organizations." Likewise Article 8, which identified the many areas subject to the joint jurisdiction of the USSR and the union republics, made no mention of the autonomies. Finally, the autonomies, unlike the union republics, were not identified as "sovereign," and they were not afforded a right of secession from either the USSR or from the union republics of which they were a part.

Nationalists in the union republics were nevertheless convinced that the law was designed to intimidate the union republics by promoting a rift between them and the autonomies. These suspicions were reinforced by the fact that pro-center hard-liners were encouraging the minority populations in the Baltic republics, most of whom were ethnic Russians, to mobilize in opposition to titular nationalism through the formation of "internationalist" organizations called "interfronts" (they were in fact made up mostly of Russians) that opposed the "parochial" nationalism of the popular fronts. Moreover, Gorbachev was warning ominously that the Russian Federation, like the USSR, was a multinational state that was vulnerable to the same centrifugal pressures as the Soviet Union, and many interpreted these warnings as implicit threats.

How extensive and concerted the effort was to mobilize the autonomies in opposition to their host union republics is unclear. The law on the delineation of powers had been in preparation for some time, and its provisions for increasing the rights of the autonomies had been anticipated in the 1989 nationalities platform, well before the RSFSR (the republic that, along with Georgia and Moldavia [Moldova], was the most vulnerable to pressure from the autonomies) declared sovereignty or elected Yeltsin as chairman of its new parliament. The provisions in the law giving the autonomies a right to remain within the union should a union republic secede therefore appeared to have been directed primarily at making secession more difficult, not at encouraging the autonomies to secede from the union republics. Had Gorbachev really wanted to stir the pot with the autonomies, he could have taken the position that internal border changes and changes in status were open for discussion. The effort to appease the autonomies apparently began, then, as a response to their demands for greater autonomy, but once it became clear that they could be used politically against the union republics, particularly Russia, Gorbachev took advantage of the opportunity they presented him.

Representatives of the union republics have argued that conservative forces in Moscow, particularly the KGB and its allies in the hard-line "Soiuz" faction in the USSR legislature, provoked conflict between the union republics and the autonomies in the hopes of undermining Gorbachev and his reform program. Both Armenians and Azeris, for example, have asserted that the February 1988 anti-Armenian pogrom in Sumgait and the January 1990 anti-Armenian pogrom in Baku were deliberately instigated by conservatives who spread false rumors and committed other "provocations," and that Azerbaijani authorities allowed the pogroms to continue for several days before calling in troops. Similarly, Georgians argue that Moscow conservatives encouraged the Party first secretary in Abkhazia to support the demands of Abkhaz nationalists in an effort to pressure Georgia (see chapter 7), and that without this encouragement differences between Abkhaz and Georgians might not have turned violent. It is impossible to verify these claims, and at best their truth will not be known until historians have access to the relevant archives.

Regardless, by the time Yeltsin began his campaign for a seat in the RSFSR Congress of Peoples' Deputies in early 1990, Russia's autonomies were posing a serious challenge to the RSFSR government. Initially, Yeltsin appeared rather insensitive to their concerns. In his February 1990 election platform, he went so far as to propose a scheme that was anathema to representatives of the RSFSR's national minorities—the creation of "self-governing socioeconomic territories and regions" in the central, northern, and southern regions of European Russia and the Urals, Siberia, and the Far East to replace the existing units of the Russian Federation.[11] This plan, which was supported at the time by many liberal democrats who believed that politics and ethnicity should be separated and viewed the U.S. system of nonethnic federalism as a model, would have meant a return to the Tsarist system of large, nonethnic *gubernii*.[12] It would have required the dissolution, or at least the subordination, of the governments of the existing autonomies to these new territorial governments, and it thus presented a profound threat to the political elites in the autonomies. Yeltsin appears to have become aware of the extreme reaction such a plan would have provoked from the autonomies, and accordingly he began to modify his position shortly after the platform was published. In an interview published on 24 January 1990, he said the preservation of "autonomous formations is essential."[13] In another interview three weeks later, he went even further: "I believe that we must give independence [*samostoiatel'nost'*] to all the autonomies within the borders of the Russian Federation. And then create, for example, six independent Russian territories where the majority of the population is Russian."[14]

Like Lenin before him, then, Yeltsin understood rather quickly that he would need political support from the autonomies, and he quickly modified his position. As he continued to press forward with his radical program of sovereignty for the RSFSR (see chapter 5), it was critical that the autonomies not become "land mines" (as Soviet analysts described them) that would blow up in Russia's face. Yeltsin desperately needed the support of Moscow's liberal intelligentsia, which had long been suspicious of Yeltsin's brand of populism, if he was to mount a successful challenge to Gorbachev. By early 1990, the intelligentsia was already souring on Gorbachev, and it was coming around to the view that Yeltsin was the principal champion of democratic reform. Opposing the autonomies, which after all were only asking for what Russia and the other union republics were demanding, would have appeared hypocritical and "antidemocratic" according to the views of the time, thereby undermining Yeltsin's support from the intelligentsia. It also would have meant that Yeltsin, who was desperate to differentiate himself from the Soviet president, was taking the same approach toward Russia's autonomies that Gorbachev was taking toward the union republics. And it would have come shortly after the death of Andrei Sakharov, the hero of the liberal intelligentsia (he died on 15 December 1989), who in the last month of his life had drawn up a draft constitution for a new "Union of Sovereign States" that would have equalized the status of all autonomies and union republics and afforded each a right of secession.[15]

As a result, Yeltsin began to insist that Russia's relations with the autonomies be "renegotiated." By the time he and his supporters in DemRossiia began working on the draft of the RSFSR's sovereignty declaration late that spring, he had committed himself to a program of increased rights for the autonomies. As he put it in an interview on the eve of the first session of the RSFSR CPD, "I think the chief requirement today is to grant independence to all nationalities. . . . As early as the first congress of Russia we must declare the economic independence and sovereignty of each autonomous republic. . . . The autonomous republics should be granted the right to leave the federation."[16] While the RSFSR's Sovereignty Declaration did not go that far, it nevertheless reflected Yeltsin's views about the need "to broaden substantially the rights of autonomous republics, autonomous oblasts, autonomous okrugs, along with RSFSR krais and oblasts."[17] At the same time, Yeltsin began to articulate a radical doctrine of "sovereignty from the ground up" in which "the lowest government unit closest to the people in villages or towns, delegates power to the next highest level, then to the republic parliament, then to the national parliament."[18] He would describe this arrangement a month later as "a kind of inverted pyramid."[19] The fact that only the union republics were described as "sovereign" in the USSR constitution did not seem to matter.

It was at this point that Yeltsin began to articulate a decidedly civic and liberal understanding of Russian statehood rather than an ethnic one.[20] The RSFSR's sovereignty declaration would not claim that ethnic "Russians" (*russkie*) were "indigenous" to Russia.[21] Rather, it was the "multinational people" (*mnogonatsional'nyi narod*) of the Russian federation who were the "repository of sovereignty and are the sources of state power in the RSFSR" (Article 3).[22] The declaration's preamble stated that the Congress of Peoples' Deputies was "attesting to its respect for the sovereign rights of *all peoples* that make up the USSR" and that it was "expressing the will of the *peoples* [i.e., not *people* in the singular] of the RSFSR." Similarly, Article 1 reaffirmed that the RSFSR is "a sovereign state created by the *peoples* historically united within it." Article 4 went on to aver that sovereignty was being proclaimed "for the most lofty purposes—of guaranteeing the inalienable right of every person to a worthy life, free development, and use of his native language and of every people (*kazhdomu narodu*) to self-determination in their chosen national-state and national-cultural forms" (emphasis added in each case). It was not, in other words, being asserted on the basis of self-determination for ethnic Russians (*russkikh*).

In August 1990, several weeks after his election as chairman of Russia's new legislature, Yeltsin took a three-week trip around the RSFSR in which he made his support for the autonomies even clearer. Addressing an audience in Tatarstan, he informed them:

> I will repeat once again what I said at the Congress of Peoples' Deputies: the formation of each portion of state power must take place from the bottom up— from city to republic, whatever autonomy (*samostoiatel'nost'*) Tataria chooses for itself, we will welcome it. . . . I say the following: if you want to govern yourselves completely, go ahead. And it seems to me that the Russian parliament will vigorously defend those powers that Tatarstan delegates to Russia.[23]

In Yeltsin's opinion, the autonomies would be better off sticking with the RSFSR government in opposition to Gorbachev and the center. But he also suggested that the RSFSR leadership should not "repeat the mistakes" made by Gorbachev in dealing with the union republics: "The republics should have been given independence three years ago, before the centrifugal processes gained force. When national feelings are suppressed, they gain momentum and take on an abnormal character."[24] Continuing on to Ufa, the capital of Bashkiria, he made a statement that would soon become famous: "We are saying to the Bashkir people, the peoples of Bashkir [*sic*], we are saying to the Supreme Soviet and the government of Bashkir [*sic*]: You take the share of power which you yourselves can swallow."[25]

Taken literally, Yeltsin's support of "sovereignty from the bottom up" was a prescription for anarchy—if each individual or collectivity in a political community has unlimited sovereignty, there can be no authoritative state power. However, a measure of anarchy was doubtless welcomed by Yeltsin, who by then was engaged in his dramatic struggle over Russian sovereignty with the central Soviet government. And again, it was not clear what he actually meant by "sovereignty"—most notably, he never explicitly stated that the autonomies should have a right of secession and full independence under international law (*nezavisimost'*). Regardless, it was enough that he was able to score political points with elites and electorates in the autonomies as well as with the Moscow intelligentsia by his seemingly unequivocal support for "democracy" and "sovereignty" for the autonomies.

On 10 August 1990, several days after Yeltsin's visit to Tatarstan, the autonomous republic of Karelia issued a sovereignty declaration.[26] In the following months, virtually every other autonomous republic within the RSFSR would follow suit (see table 4.1).[27] The substance of these sovereignty declarations were for the most part similar and differed little from those of the union republics.

The "parade of sovereignties" in the autonomies prompted a number of RSFSR officials to express their reservations about Yeltsin's notion of "sovereignty from the ground up." Russia was indeed vulnerable to centrifugal pressures, they suggested, and might well suffer the same fate as the Soviet Union should the latter dissolve. Ruslan Khasbulatov, then the first deputy chairman of the RSFSR Supreme Soviet, and Ramazan Abdulatipov, chairman of one of the two houses of the RSFSR Supreme Soviet, made clear that the RSFSR's legislature would refuse to allow the autonomies to change their status unilaterally.[28] Andranik Migranian, a well-known (and controversial) political analyst in Moscow (and a russified Armenian), expressed these mounting doubts about "sovereignty from the bottom up" as follows:

> The idea that everything should be restructured from the bottom up has led to a situation in which the republics are issuing a challenge to the Union, the cities and provinces are challenging the republics, and the boroughs are challenging

Table 4.1. Sovereignty Declarations by Autonomous Republics, Autonomous Oblasts, Transdniestra, Crimea, and Gagauzia

Nagorno-Karabakh	2 December 1989
North Ossetia	20 July 1990
Karelia	10 August 1990
Khakassia	15 August 1990
Gagauzia	19 August 1990
Abkhazia	25 August 1990
Tatarstan	30 August 1990
Komi	30 August 1990
Transdniestra	2 September 1990
Udmurtia	19 September 1990
South Ossetia	20 September 1990
Yakutia/Sakha	27 September 1990
Chukotka	29 September 1990
Koryakia	9 October 1990
Buriatia	11 October 1990
Bashkiria	11 October 1990
Kalmykia	18 October 1990
Mari-el	21 October 1990
Gorno-Altai	24 October 1990
Chuvashia	27 October 1990
Karachaevo-Cherkessia	17 November 1990
Checheno-Ingushetia	26 November 1990
Mordvinia	8 December 1990
Tuva	12 December 1990
Karakalpakstan	19 December 1990
Kabardino-Balkaria	31 January 1991
Dagestan	13 May 1991
Adygeia	2 July 1991
Crimea	5 September 1991

the cities. Under these conditions, how can fulfillment of the higher-level Soviets' decisions by the lower level Soviets be secured? . . .

Our attempts to create all state institutions from scratch on a contractual basis are attempts to put into effect yet another grandiose utopia, something that will lead to a situation in which society finds itself without an organizing core. . . .

The bomb planted under the USSR by the declaration of Russian sovereignty is, it seems to me, facilitating not only the destruction of the USSR but also—to an even greater extent—the destruction of Russia itself. . . . Where are the geographical boundaries of the republic that is supposed to represent ethnic Russians?[29]

Despite these concerns, Yeltsin continued to express his sympathy for the autonomies and to solicit their support. On a trip to Yakutia in December, he asserted that the autonomous republic should "decide the fate of its natural resources [i.e., of the diamond mines in its territory]."[30] Nevertheless, with opposition from RSFSR officials mounting to their sovereignty campaign, leaders of the autonomies began to conclude that the principal barrier to their demands for greater autonomy came from Yeltsin and his democratic allies in Moscow, not from Gorbachev and the dying Soviet center. The conflict between the autonomies and the RSFSR government would therefore intensify in the coming months, particularly after Gorbachev, Yeltsin, and the leaders of the other union republics became engaged during late 1990-early 1991 in a deepening conflict over Gorbachev's proposal to negotiate a new union treaty for the USSR.

Notes

1. Quoted in Dunlop 1993, 55.
2. Shortly after the Soviet collapse, the Russian parliament recognized the bifurcation of what had been the Chechen-Ingush ASSR into separate Chechen and Ingush Republics and amended the Russian constitution accordingly.
3. *Izvestiia,* 8 June 1989, *CDSP,* vol. 41, no. 29, 20.
4. *Pravda,* 20 September 1989, *CDSP,* vol. 41, no. 38, 8.
5. *Pravda,* 21 September 1989, *CDSP,* vol. 41, no. 39, 7.
6. *Pravda,* 22 September 1989, *CDSP,* vol. 41, no. 40, 14.
7. *Pravda,* 21 September 1989, *CDSP,* vol. 41, no. 39, 5.
8. Hazard 1992, 120–21.
9. *Vedomosti,* 1990, 430–34.
10. Hough describes the law as follows: "The terms *union republic* and *autonomous republic* disappeared, and *subjects of the federation,* which was said to encompass both kinds of republics, was inserted. Both former types of republics were subordinated directly to the USSR government" (Hough 1997, 381). This is simply incorrect—the terms "union republics," "autonomous republics," and "autonomous formations" in fact appear throughout the law, and, as the above quotation indicated, the autonomies were expected to define their relationship with both union republics and the USSR through treaties and agreements. He also ascribes the law to the "fears of radical and liberal reformers" who were "very suspicious of democratically elected oblast governments" and did not want to see regional governments in the RSFSR acquire more power because the "outlying areas in Russia were less supportive of radical reform than the largest cities" (Hough 1997, 382). This seems very implausible—"radical reformers" were at the time focused on the struggle with Gorbachev and the federal center, and Yeltsin was already attempting to woo the autonomies by supporting their demands for a devolution of power. Nor were the leaders of the autonomies as of yet "democratically elected."
11. Furtado and Chandler 1992, 318.

12. Calls for the amalgamation of Russia's federal units would continue into the post-Soviet period. Taking such a step, however, would have encountered enormous resistance from regional elites and required a politically fraught constitutional overhaul. Instead, soon after his election as Russia's president in May 2000, Vladimir Putin established seven federal districts, each of which was overseen by a presidential envoy whose mandate was to coordinate federal activities in their district and ensure that regional and republic governments comply with the federal constitution and federal laws.

13. *Literaturnaia gazeta,* no. 4, 24 January 1990, FBIS-SOV-90-201, 69.

14. *Sovetskaia Estoniia,* 20 February 1990, FBIS-SOV-90-050, 77. "*Samostoiatel'nost,*" which could be translated as "self-sufficiency" (or "autonomy, although there is a Russian cognate for autonomy, *avtonomiia*) has a decidedly different meaning from "*nezavisimost',*" which is the term used to refer to full political independence in the legal sense. It is doubtful, however, that Yeltsin was particularly sensitive to these differences in meaning or their implications at the time.

15. An English-language version of the "Sakharov" draft constitution can be found in *New Times,* 1989, no. 52, 26–28. It is available in Russian from the Sakharov Foundation. Another key figure in the democratic reform, Galina Starovoitova, was equally committed to the principle of "national self-determination" in general and to the equalization of the status of the ethnic units in the Soviet federal hierarchy in particular. She advocated equal representation of "all peoples, irrespective of their number and form of their present ethnic statehood," in representation in the USSR's Soviet of Nationalities (see her interview, along with the Western political scientist and nationalities specialist, Gail W. Lapidus, in *Moscow News,* no. 24, 1990). These views on the "national question" were not shared by many other supporters of democratization and liberalization, however, including the well-known head of the Institute of Ethnography and Anthropology, Valerii Tishkov (see Tishkov 1997, especially 55, where he criticizes the "political naiveté" of the Sakharov constitution).

16. Interview on Bulgarian radio, DUMA, 17 May 1990, in FBIS-SOV-90-101, 39.

17. Furtado and Chandler 1992, 325–26.

18. *New York Times,* 31 May 1990. See also *Izvestiia,* 12 June 1990, translated in *CDSP,* vol. 42, no. 23, 14.

19. Morrison 1992, 162.

20. Later, Ukraine under the leadership of Leonid Kravchuk would also adopt a generally civic understanding of statehood, which accounts in part for the extent of the support for Ukraine's sovereignty campaign from ethnic Russians in the SSR, most notably in the referendum on Ukrainian independence in December 1991 (see chapter 6). The Ukrainian sovereignty declaration did, however, state that sovereignty of the republic was being affirmed "on the basis of the exercise of the Ukrainian nation of its inalienable right to self-determination" (Furtado and Chandler 1992, 237). There was no such reference to the "Russian nation" or a right of self-determination in the Russian case. Moldova, too, was a partial exception—its sovereignty declaration also did not refer to the Moldovan nation. At least in part, however, this was because it was rather difficult to argue that there was such a "nation," at least if understood in ethnic terms, because the "Moldovans" of the late 1980s had been "Romanians" living in Bessarabia and surrounding regions when the territory was annexed by the USSR during World War II. The Moldovan declaration thus did not claim that the republic's sovereignty was being asserted in the name of the self-determination of the Moldovan people. Instead, it merely stated that the "people" were the "bearers and source of sovereignty." The Moldovan nationalist movement in 1988 and 1989 did, however, reject the argument of the then Party first secretary, Semeon Grossu, that Romanian should not become the state lan-

guage because Moldova was a "multinational" republic, Jonathan Eyal and Graham Smith, "Moldova and the Moldovans," in *The Nationalities Question in the Post-Soviet States,* ed. Graham Smith (London: Longman, 1996), 232. And unlike the RSFSR, Moldova did not use the terms "multinational people" (*mnogonatsional'nyi narod*) or "peoples" (*narody*) in the plural in its sovereignty declaration. Its independence declaration of 1991 would assert that independence was being established "in awareness of the one thousand year existence of our people and its uninterrupted statehood within the historical and ethnic boundaries of its national formation" (Eyal and Smith 1996, 239).

21. By way of contrast, the Estonian sovereignty declaration made clear that its drafters were making a distinction between ethnic Estonians and other residents of the republic: "The Estonian People have tilled the land here, on the shores of the Baltic Sea, and developed their culture for over 5,000 years. In 1940, the relatively homogenous people—approximately 94 percent Estonian within today's boundaries, with cultural autonomy for many minority nations—and the sovereign Estonian state were incorporated into the Soviet Union. . . . [I]n Estonia, an unfavorable situation has developed demographically for Estonians, who are the indigenous population on Estonian land" (Furtado and Chandler 1992, 70).

22. *Zakony i postanovleniia Rossiiskoi Federatsii, 1991.* Similar language was introduced into the RSFSR constitution by amendment and would later be included in the constitution of the Russian Federation adopted in December 1993, Edward W. Walker, "Designing Center-Periphery Relations in the New Russia," *East European Constitutional Review* 4, no. 1 (1995): 54–60. Interestingly, the 1978 RSFSR constitution did not employ the term "multinational people" although its preamble asserted that Soviet power had "guaranteed to all the peoples of Russia equality and free self-determination." Likewise it affirmed that the establishment of the RSFSR guaranteed to "the Russian people (*russkomu narodu*) and all the nations (*natsiiam*) and peoples (*narodam*) of the Russian Federation propitious conditions for all-around economic, social, and cultural development," *Konstitutsiia (osnovnoi zakon) Rossiiskoi Sovetskoi Federativnoi Sotsialisticheskoi Respubliki* (Moscow: Izdatel'stvo Sovetskaia Rossiia, 1979). Again, it was clear that the "people" of the RSFSR included not just Russians. It may well be, then, that the RSFSR federal character made it easier for Russian politicians to define Russian statehood in civic rather than ethnic terms in 1990–1991.

23. *Pravda,* 9 August 1990, 2.

24. *New York Times,* 3 September 1990.

25. Moscow Television Service in Russian, 12 August 1990, FBIS-SOV-90-156, 83. The Russian word used by Yeltsin was "*proglatyvat.*"

26. *New York Times,* 13 August 1990.

27. The Transdniestr and Gagauz republics, both located within the Moldavian SSR (Moldova after 5 June 1990), were not autonomous formations under the 1977 Soviet constitution but declared themselves autonomous and established local governments in the perestroika era. The declaration establishing the Transdniestr Soviet Socialist Republic of 2 September 1990 proclaimed the new entity to be a full union republic (hence endowed with "sovereignty") and a constituent unit of the USSR that was no longer a part of Moldova. Crimea was also not an autonomy under the 1977 Soviet constitution, but it held a referendum on its status in January 1991, after which the Ukrainian government designated the region an autonomous republic in February. Also unique was the Karabakh "sovereignty" declaration, which came in a joint statement by the Armenian-dominated National Council in Karabakh and the Armenian Supreme Soviet on 2 December 1989 and that provided for unification of the autonomous oblast with Armenia. The "sovereignty" claim was thus implicit in that it asserted a right to determine Kara-

bakh's fate irrespective of either Soviet or Azerbaijani law. The sovereignty declarations of Chukotka and Koryakia took the form of declarations of changes in status from autonomous okrug to an autonomous republic. The Adzhar, Gorno-Badashkhan, and Nakhichevan cases were also somewhat different. Soviet nationality policy did not recognize separate Adzhar, Gorno-Badashkhan, or Nakhichevan nationalities—the traditionally Muslim and Georgian-speaking Adzhars were classified as "Georgians," the Pamiri people of Gorno-Badashkhan as "Tajiks" (as noted earlier), and the traditional residents of Nakhichevan as either Azeris or Armenians. Notably, none of the three declared sovereignty.

28. This despite the fact that Khasbulatov was an ethnic Chechen and Abdulatipov was an Avar from Dagestan.

29. *Izvestiia,* 20 September 1990, *CDSP,* vol. 42, no. 39, 2.

30. Quoted in Dunlop 1993, 62.

Chapter 5

Multiple Sovereignty and the New Union Treaty

[T]he sovereignty of the republics is a historically irreversible step in the development of our multinational state. But, while getting away from excessive centralization and a unitary approach, we must not allow the Union to turn into an amorphous formation, let alone to disintegrate. (Mikhail Gorbachev, December 1990)

The USSR's crisis of territorial integrity had taken a dramatic turn with Lithuania's independence declaration of 11 March 1990, the Estonian declaration of a transition to independence of 30 March 1990, and the Latvian declaration of a "free, democratic, and independent Republic of Latvia" of 4 May 1990. Rather than giving in to pressure from conservatives to declare presidential rule, Gorbachev decided to concentrate political, economic, and psychological pressure on Lithuania, which had been the first to declare independence and had made clear that independence was effective immediately. This pressure met with some initial success. On 23 June 1990, the Lithuanian parliament approved a 100-day "moratorium" on its independence declaration, with the proviso that the moratorium was to take effect only with the start of negotiations with Moscow. Vilnius was not, however, rescinding its independence in full. Moreover, by the time the moratorium was announced, Gorbachev was already confronting the profound challenge of the RSFSR's sovereignty declaration.

On 11 June 1990, the day before sovereignty for Russia was proclaimed, Gorbachev made a fateful decision. Abandoning his effort to solve the "federation crisis" through federal laws and constitutional amendments, he announced to the Federation Council that he had been persuaded that a new "union treaty" could serve as the basis for a renewed federation of sovereign states.[1] His plan was to have a group of experts prepare a draft treaty that would be signed by the Soviet president and leaders of the union republics (and possibly the leaders of autonomies as well) and then ratified by the legislatures of the signatory parties. The result, he hoped, would be the establishment of a truly voluntary union in which the sovereign status of the union republics would be accommodated by their participation in the drafting process and final ratification. In the meantime, however, Gorbachev would not allow any of the republics to secede except under the burdensome terms of the April 1990 law on secession.

Gorbachev's strategy for saving the union would prove catastrophic. It meant that he would have to convince the leaders of the union republics, including those that were fully intent on secession, those that wanted a weak confederation, and those that favored a stronger central government, to endorse a comprehensive legal document that would somehow accommodate their very different concerns. Moreover, he hoped that this could be accomplished by having "experts" in Moscow draft a text, albeit with input from the republics, that the republics would then accept. As the republics quickly made clear, however, they would not approve a draft prepared by the center but would insist instead on being directly involved in the drafting process. Eventually, Gorbachev would be compelled to negotiate a draft text directly with the leaders of the republics, with each participant in the process in a position to veto each provision. Complicating the political challenge further was the fact that the negotiators were themselves not free agents—each would have to consider whether local legislatures would approve the final text. While this probably would not have been a problem for some union republic leaders, for others, including Yeltsin, parliamentary approval was far from guaranteed.

Negotiating a "voluntary union" with sixteen different parties would have been an enormous political challenge under the best of circumstances. It had been made more daunting by the attempt of central authorities to use the autonomies and national minorities as leverage against the union republics, not only because it made the union republics in which they were located even more suspicious of the central authorities, but because it raised the prospect that the autonomous republics would be included among the already numerous parties to the negotiating process. Moreover, the proposed treaty would have to be drafted and ratified at a time when the Soviet economy was beginning a wrenchingly painful downward spiral, and it required the consent of union republics that were extraordinarily diverse in culture and economic structure—indeed far more so than the original thirteen states in the United States or even the members of today's European Union.

Gorbachev would have been far better advised to take a different approach. Rather than committing to a negotiated union, he could have provided the union republics with an exit option through the promulgation of a reasonable law on secession. For example, the law might have required approval of independence by a super-majority—say, two-thirds or 60 percent of those voting, with a minimum turnout threshold of 50 percent—in a clearly worded referendum in which all legal residents would be allowed to participate. To be sure, this would have been vigorously resisted by Party conservatives, but there is no reason to believe that Gorbachev would have been less able to push through such a law than he was able to push through the equally fundamental question of the elimination of Article 6 from the Soviet constitution. Indeed, he was being urged to give the Baltic republics an opportunity to leave by some of his key advisors, including Anatoly Chernyaev, who recalls telling the Soviet leader in mid-summer 1989, after the massive demonstration of support for independence in the Baltic republics on 23 August 1989 (the fiftieth anniversary of the signing of the Molotov-Ribbentrop Pact): "The process [of independence] is irreversible. We will have to let the Baltic countries go, otherwise an abscess will develop that will bring incalculable harm to all our new national-international policies throughout the country."[2] Some seven months later, shortly after Lithuania's independence declaration and a few weeks before the adoption of the law on secession, Chernyaev recalls telling Gorbachev, "Letting Lithuania go, we don't incur any economic loses, it has no other place to turn . . . while Georgia is considered our internal affair, Lithuania's case is recognized by the United States, by Western Europe, by the international community. Where's our common sense, our grasp of political priorities?"[3]

Indeed, a law that made secession practicable for Lithuania could have been coupled with a federal law that, like the 26 April 1990 law on the delineation of powers, provided for a workable division of powers between the federal government and the republics. Such a law could have been incorporated into the Soviet constitution by means of amendment, which would have required approval by two-thirds of the delegates to the USSR Congress of Peoples' Deputies. Additional amendments might then have defined the status and powers of the autonomies, which could have been provided with considerable autonomy over education, cultural affairs, environmental protection, independent powers of taxation, and independent legislatures, executives, and judiciaries. There would have been no need, given the legacy of Soviet constitutional law, to give the autonomies a new right to secession from either their host union republic or the USSR, a move that would have been interpreted, with good reason, by nationalists in the union republics as a deliberate "provocation" by Moscow directed at deterring them from attempting to secede by legal means.

While these measures might not have satisfied more radical nationalists, the political energy of the nationalist movements would then have been channeled into effecting secession where secession was politically feasible. The Baltic states, and possibly Georgia, Moldavia, and Armenia, might have taken advantage of the opportunity to secede (although both Moldova and Georgia might have been deterred by separatist movements within their own borders, while Armenia, given its difficult geostrategic position bordering on Azerbaijan and Turkey, might well have preferred to remain within the union). Regardless, the population of these six republics totaled only 7.3 percent of the USSR's population, and their secession would not have been a mortal blow to the union. Above all, allowing the secession of the Baltic republics, and perhaps a few of the others, would have provided the union with a critical safety valve, venting the steam of the most antiunion nationalist sentiments. Gorbachev would then have been in a position to concentrate his energies on overcoming the country's mounting economic crisis, a development that would have made his effort to save the union considerably easier.

The Soviet leader believed, however, that even in the Baltic republics a majority of the population wanted to remain part of the "friendship of peoples." All that was needed, as he had told the Politburo back on 13 October 1988, was to find "honest, well-respected people, genuinely concerned with the people's interest," with whom it would be possible "to find a common language."[4] Ever the rationalist, Gorbachev was convinced that only extremists could fail to appreciate the enormous costs of secession. Ultimately, reason would triumph over irrational nationalist passions being whipped up by irresponsible "adventurists." He also apparently believed that ethnic Russians would be deeply opposed to the secession of any of the minority republics, telling Chernyaev on several occasions that Russians would never forgive him for "the collapse of the empire."[5] That many Russians would prove ambivalent about the benefits of "empire" and come to resent what they viewed as the economic subsidization of minority republics by the RSFSR came as a considerable surprise to him.

The extent to which Gorbachev consistently misread both the popular mood in the Baltics as well as the political dynamics of nationalist mobilization generally is suggested by a statement he had made to the Politburo in mid-May 1989: "If we hold a referendum, not one of the three [Baltic] republics will 'walk out.' What we need to do is bring the Popular Front leaders into government, give them positions in the administration. . . . In general, we should trust the people's common sense more. . . . And in general, we must keep thinking how to transform our federation or else everything will really fall apart."[6] Again in early 1990, when he visited Lithuania for the first time since becoming general secretary (he had visited Latvia and Estonia in February 1987), he found himself heckled by Lithuanian nationalists during a talk at a factory. He would tell a second audience of factory workers, "Lying in front of me are letters and notes citing instances of statements such as the following: You've occupied us for 70 years, and now we'll teach you a good lesson, etc. I pay no attention to this, it's plain old nationalism. But if it enters into arguments for the adoption of decisions, then, comrades, worse times are in store for us. . . . Let's try and listen to each other. Let's reason together."[7]

As it turned out, Gorbachev would find himself engaged in a long and ultimately futile effort to convince the leaders of the union republics to endorse what would prove to be highly impractical institutional arrangements in a series of draft treaties, each of which would provide fewer powers for the central government. In fact, the immediate effect of Gorbachev's announcement that he intended to push for a new union treaty was to increase incentives for other republics to declare sovereignty. As Ambassador Matlock pointed out, the RSFSR's sovereignty declaration and Gorbachev's support for a new union treaty "*required* the remaining republics to declare their own sovereignty if they were to be in a position to negotiate a new treaty of union as an equal."[8] In the following months, those union republics that had yet to declare sovereignty did so, the only exception being Armenia, which on 23 August 1990 declared "the start of the process of the establishment of independent statehood."[9]

Work on the text of the treaty began over the summer. On 24 November 1990, Soviet newspapers published what would prove the first of five published draft treaties.[10] The first "basic principle" of the treaty for a "Union of Sovereign Socialist Republics" (the term "Soviet" would thus be omitted but the acronym "USSR" would be preserved) asserted that the USSR "is a sovereign federal state formed as a result of the voluntary association of republics and exercises state power within the limits of the powers (*polnomochii*) it is endowed with by the parties to the Treaty." Because acceding to the union was "voluntary," the constituent units of the proposed union were not listed. The 1922 Union Treaty would become "null and void" only for the signatories to the new treaty (Article 22), which meant those union republics that refused to sign would continue to be subject to laws adopted under the terms of the original treaty.

In a particularly confusing formulation, the draft implied that at least some of the autonomies would be signatories to the treaty and that their status with the union republics would be equalized—"Member-republics," Article 1 read, "that are parties to the treaty enter the Union directly or as part of other republics." Moreover, the draft was accompanied by a statement that the Soviet president was presenting the draft to the Supreme Soviets not only of the union republics but also the autonomous republics, the autonomous oblasts, and even the okrugs. In a statement to the USSR legislature, Gorbachev later confirmed that the treaty was open to signing by the autonomies.[11]

Other provisions specified that the federal government would have its own constitution and would be responsible for "protecting the sovereignty and territorial integrity of the Union," organizing the defense of the Union, declaring war and peace (Article 5.2), and determining the union's foreign policy (Article 5.3). Areas of joint jurisdiction in which policy would be determined by the federal government "in conjunction with the republics" were extensive. They included developing a common economic program, a uniform financial, credit, and monetary policy; preparing the federal budget; managing unified fuel, power, and railroad, air, maritime, and trunk pipeline systems, defense enterprises and energy reserves, and working out a common social policy, including programs on job safety, social security and insurance, and public health (Articles 5.4–5.6). The federal government would also "coordinate inter-republic cooperation" in, inter alia, culture and education (Article 7) and establish "principles of legislation in conjunction with the republics" while "coordinating activity to safeguard public order and combat crime" (Article 5.8). How this would be effected in practice was specified by Article 9: "USSR laws in areas within joint jurisdiction of the Union and the republics take effect if the republic whose interests are affected by the given laws does not object." Thus the republics would have had a right to veto all-union legislation on their territory on the numerous issues of joint jurisdiction.

Notably, the draft did not provide for a right of secession, in contrast to the four subsequent draft treaties that would be published in the following months. Other provisions nevertheless suggested that the republics would have attributes and obligations normally associated with independent states. The first basic principle asserted that "each member-republic of the Union is a sovereign state that possesses the entirety of state power (*vsei polnotoi gosudarstvennoi vlasti*) on its territory." Article 4 provided that the republics would "construct their relations within the Union on the basis of equality, respect for sovereignty, territorial integrity, noninterference in internal affairs, the resolution of all disputes through peaceful means, cooperation, mutual assistance, and the conscientious implementation of commitments under the Union Treaty and inter-republic agreements." Neither the USSR's constitution nor the constitutions of the republics could contradict the terms of the treaty, while only those federal laws that were "adopted in areas within the Union's jurisdiction have supremacy and are binding on the territory of all republics" (Article 9). For all areas not within the jurisdiction of the union or identified as subject to joint jurisdiction, republic legislation would have "supremacy on all questions." The republics would be the owners of the land, mineral wealth, and other natural resources on their territory, as well as all state property other than that "necessary for the exercise of the USSR's powers" (Article 7). They would be free to decide on the structure of their own governments (Basic Principle No. 5). A constitutional court would have the authority to settle jurisdictional and other disputes between the center and the republics (Article 16).

As the sovereignty campaigns in the union republics radicalized over the course of 1990, the Soviet Union's economic difficulties continued to worsen—indeed, the "nationality crisis" and the economic crisis were mutually reinforcing. Nationalists in the union republics could argue with increasing credibility that the republics would be better off economically by ridding themselves of the apparently counterproductive economic policies coming out of Moscow. To address the deteriorating national economy, Gorbachev and Yeltsin agreed over the summer to cooperate on the drawing up of an economic reform plan. A commission was formed under the directorship of a well-known reform economist, Stanislav Shatalin, and a reform program was quickly prepared that provided for rapid price liberalization and privatization in a mere 500 days (the "Shatalin Plan" or "500-day Program," as it was alternately referred to in the Soviet press, was based on an earlier plan—the "400-day Plan"—that had been prepared for the RSFSR government). While the 500-day plan was unrealistic in the extreme (in every case, the transition to a market economy would take far longer than 500 days), it at least held out the possibility that the half measures of the Soviet government adopted to date, measures that had resulted in an unworkable hybrid economy in which limited market mechanisms coexisted with centrally determined prices and state ownership of the bulk of the means of production, would be abandoned and some of the prerequisites for a functioning market economy would be put in place. In a surprise move in view of his earlier support, Gorbachev rejected the 500-day plan late that summer. He instead instructed the Soviet prime minister, Nikolai Ryzhkov, to work out a compromise program that would combine the 500-day plan with a more conservative proposal drafted by the Soviet government. The government made public its compromise plan in mid-October. To no one's surprise, it failed to provide for price liberalization, privatization, or significant decentralization of economic decision making in favor of the union republics. By then, however, the RSFSR legislature had voted to approve the 500-day plan and instructed the Russian government to draw up plans for implementing it.

Thus the temporary cease-fire in the "war of laws" came to an end, and indeed a new front opened up as the RSFSR and other union republics began to insist on a "single channel tax system" that would allow them to collect all taxes on their territory, a fixed percentage of which they would turn over to the federal government. When the union government rejected their demands, some of the republics, again including Russia, began to reduce their contribution to the federal treasury unilaterally. Efforts were made to reach a compromise, but on 27 December 1990 the Soviet finance minister announced that negotiations between the USSR and the RSFSR over the budget had broken down and that Russia was deeply in arrears to the federal treasury.

Gorbachev's rejection of the 500-day plan was part of a decided "tilt to the right" by the Soviet president in late 1990-early 1991. With goods disappearing from store shelves amidst predictions of hunger and heating shortages that winter, as well as mounting antiunion mobilization in the republics, conservative criticism of the Soviet president was becoming increasingly public and vitriolic. Gorbachev's approval rating was falling rapidly, dropping from 52 percent who "wholly approved" of his performance and another 32 percent who partly approved of it in December 1989, to 17 percent who wholly approved of it and 39 percent who partly approved in December 1990.[12] Fearful that the country was on the verge of civil war, Gorbachev began to take steps to "restore order." He presented a plan to the Supreme Soviet in mid-November that strengthened the powers of the president; established a position of vice-president; replaced the existing Council of Ministers with a smaller "Cabinet" (which required a government shuffle and the replacement or reappointment of all ministers, including the prime minister); replaced the relatively weak Presidential Council (which had been in existence for less than a year) with a smaller Security Council with representation from all the "power ministries"; and transformed the Federation Council (which had been established earlier to give the leaders of the union republics a forum for communicating directly with the Soviet president) into a consultative body with primary responsibility for relations between the federal government and the members of the federation.

Gorbachev also made a series of personnel decisions that suggested a preference for a firmer hand in dealing with the opposition. The reform-minded interior minister, Vadim Bakatin, was replaced by Boris Pugo, a Latvian with a reputation as a hard-liner. (There was speculation at the time that Gorbachev felt that Pugo's Latvian ethnicity would reduce the popular backlash if Interior Ministry troops were ordered to impose presidential rule in the Baltics.) General Boris Gromov, who had commanded the Soviet forces in Afghanistan, became first deputy interior minister. Ryzhkov was replaced by the former finance minister, Valentin Pavlov, who was widely viewed as an economic conservative. Gorbachev nominated a little-known Party apparatchik, Gennadii Yanaev, to be his vice-president. Finally, the Soviet president appointed another conservative, Leonid Kravchenko, as chairman of Gosteleradio, the USSR State Committee for Television and Radio. Kravchenko promptly made clear that glasnost had its limits by announcing that "state television does not have the right to engage in criticism of the leadership of the country," and he removed a highly popular program, *Vzgliad,* from the airwaves.[13]

Gorbachev also began to step up efforts to intimidate the Baltic republics, apparently in the belief, once again, that the Baltic peoples were souring on nationalism and separatism and thus were ready to reject the "maximalist" policies of Landsbergis and his ilk. As he told Helmut Kohl in a meeting on 9 November:

> The nationalists sense that their time is passing. Lithuanians have already realized that the policies of Landsbergis are leading to a dead end. . . . It's good to go to rallies of course, but you also have to live somehow! They saw what nationalism did in Moldova, Azerbaijan, Armenia, Central Asia. People there are getting more sober by the day, realizing more and more that nationalism and separatism will bring no good, that their venomous shoots have to be destroyed.[14]

Ten days later, he told Bush in Paris:

> [T]he people want more drastic, even tough measures, without waiting for the Union Treaty and other decisions. . . . Landsbergis is being severely censured. . . . Peasants, workers, and leading members of the intelligentsia now express extreme displeasure with him. . . . At the same time, there are people peering out from behind the government's back who are even worse extremists—those who collaborated with Nazis in their time, or the children of these people. In short, we have lots of information that the situation there is explosive.[15]

As Chernyaev commented in his memoirs, Gorbachev was drawing "the conclusions that he found most 'comforting' . . . he was 'driving' reality into the mold necessary for his policies."[16]

Another sign that Gorbachev had decided to take new "tough measures" in the Baltic republics came that same month when the head of the USSR's elite paratrooper forces was made a deputy minister of defense, which meant that he now reported directly to the hard-line defense minister, Dmitrii Yazov, instead of the head of the Soviet air force, Yevgenii Shaposhnikov, who was considered more pro-reform. Additional troops were ordered into the Baltics in late November, and Yazov announced that his troops would use force if necessary to protect military installations, monuments, and themselves against nationalist threats in the Baltics. On 1 December, the day that Pugo replaced Bakatin as interior minister, Gorbachev signed a decree that banned the union republics from forming their own militias. Pugo warned that Gorbachev had ordered him to see to it that the USSR constitution was being observed throughout the country. Finally, the head of the KGB, Vladimir Kryuchkov, informed the Congress of Peoples' Deputies that the time had come to take "defensive measures" against ethnic violence, which he claimed was being incited by "destructive forces" from abroad.

Gorbachev was simultaneously distancing himself from some of his long-time reform allies. Aleksandr Yakovlev, who had been a member of Gorbachev's team even before he came to power in March 1985 and was one of the intellectual architects of perestroika, was left without a formal position after the Presidential Council was dissolved. Yakovlev would later report that his relations with Gorbachev were never the same again. Chernyaev later recalled, "In those dramatic days, [Gorbachev] didn't want to talk to any of 'us' [his more reform-minded aides]. . . . He'd apparently 'limited' himself to Lukyanov and Kryuchkov [conservatives who would later participate in the failed August 1991 coup].[17] The most visible evidence that Gorbachev was alienating the more reform-minded members of his political team came on 20 December 1990 when Eduard Shevardnadze, who was closely associated in the public mind with the perestroika-era "new thinking" in Soviet foreign policy, abruptly resigned as Soviet foreign minister after warning ominously that "a dictatorship is coming."[18]

Despite these efforts to demonstrate a "firm hand" at the center, Gorbachev continued to press for the adoption of a new union treaty. In mid-December, he presented the draft published on 24 November to a session of the USSR Congress of Peoples' Deputies for approval. Consistent with his long-held belief that elites in the union republics were more antiunion than the electorate, he proposed that a referendum be held asking the Soviet people whether they supported the preservation of a renewed Union. While the results of the referendum would not be legally binding, Gorbachev felt that popular endorsement of the union would make it far more difficult for leaders in the union republics to reject the treaty.

The Congress approved the draft and Gorbachev's proposed referendum, although it refused to accept the proposed change in the name of the country, voting instead to retain the terms "soviet" as well as "socialist." Predictably, the draft was flatly rejected by the Baltic republics, while Moldovan, Georgian, and Armenian officials made clear that they did not expect their republics to become members of the new union. The Baltic republics and Georgia also rejected the authority of the newly empowered Federation Council on their territories, and Estonia and Lithuania refused to send representatives to the Council's meeting in late December. Azerbaijan, Ukraine, and Russia were more circumspect.

While they continued to insist that they did not wish to see the USSR dissolve, they indicated that they opposed the current draft because it provided for an excessively strong federal government. Ukrainian officials also stated that Kiev would put off consideration of the treaty until after a referendum on sovereignty had been held and a new Ukrainian constitution adopted for the republic, which was not expected to take place for some months. As for Russia, while Yeltsin himself was equivocal, his allies in DemRossiia rejected it outright as an infringement of Russia's sovereignty. Gorbachev would later write that DemRossiia had by then launched an all-out "propaganda war" against him, "blazing away in an organized political frontal assault to weaken and eventually destroy the Union, the center, and the President."[19] Only the five Central Asian republics and Belorussia seemed likely to sign the treaty without revision.

In late 1990, yet another threat to the authority of the center emerged. Earlier that summer, Yeltsin had indicated on Latvian television that the RSFSR would be willing to sign bilateral treaties with the Baltic republics that would provide for the recognition of their mutual sovereignty. While the Baltic states did not immediately take him up on his offer, the RSFSR and Ukraine signed a formal treaty on 19 November that recognized the two parties' borders and established formal interstate relations. A similar treaty was signed between the RSFSR and Kazakhstan two days later, while a trade agreement was signed between Russia and Ukraine that provided for economic exchanges that ran counter to the state orders being issued by Gosplan. Gorbachev responded by signing a decree nullifying all trade agreements that violated the directives of the USSR's central planners. The RSFSR and Belorussia promptly ignored the decree and signed a bilateral trade agreement several days later.

Gorbachev was well aware that this "horizontal" strategy of the republics, as it was dubbed in the Soviet press, threatened to render the proposed union treaty moot through the development of a web of horizontal ties between the union republics themselves. Lest there be any doubt about their intent in this regard, Yeltsin made the threat explicit by suggesting that he would get together with the leaders of other union republics and negotiate the text of a new union treaty without Gorbachev's participation. Khasbulatov explained the approach in a speech to the USSR CPD in late December as follows: "The new center should emerge as [a] result of a process of concluding agreements among the republics and should be a complex resultant [sic] of forces that will create Union bodies of power and administration on a scale and with powers determined by the republics."[20]

Gorbachev's "tilt to the right" in late 1990 took a more sinister turn in early January. On 7 January 1991, elite paratroop units were sent to the Baltics, Armenia, Georgia, Moldova, and parts of Ukraine. That same day, the market-oriented Lithuanian government made the mistake of ordering price increases in the republic, which served as an excuse for conservative enterprise managers to "persuade" their employees to march on the Lithuanian parliament and demand the resignation of the government. The government was forced to use water cannons to break up the increasingly threatening demonstrations the next day.

That evening, Lithuanian's prime minister, Kazimiera Prunskiene, announced that the government was resigning and that she was rescinding the price increases.

Nevertheless, the pressure on Lithuania intensified. On 10 January, Gorbachev signed a decree instructing the republic to repeal all "previously adopted unconstitutional acts" and condemned it for implementing "a policy aimed at the restoration of a bourgeois system and customs that are at variance with the people's interests."[21] Soviet troops began occupying buildings in the republic's capital the next day, which prompted clashes between Lithuania's informal militia, the "home guard," and Soviet Interior Ministry troops. A large crowd of Lithuanian citizens and members of the home guard gathered in and around the parliament building, central television station, and other key sites to deter an attack. The crisis atmosphere deepened after Soviet newspapers reported that a hard-line pro-Union "National Salvation Committee" had formed and was preparing to seize power in Vilnius. When the Federation Council met the next day in Moscow, Gorbachev took the opportunity to call on all parties involved to use "political methods" to resolve their differences. He did not, however, order the Soviet Interior Ministry troops to withdraw.

The crisis came to a head on the night of 12–13 January 1991 after the National Salvation Committee announced that it had taken control of the republic. Soviet OMON troops attempted to seize control of the central television station but were met by demonstrators who attempted to block their way. The Soviet troops then opened fire on the civilian protesters, killing fourteen and wounding many more. A similar sequence of events unfolded in Latvia the following week. Again, a self-described "National Salvation Committee" attempted to seize control of the capital. Five Latvians were killed by OMON forces who were trying to seize a government ministry building on the night of 20 January. The situation remained extremely tense in both republics until local military commanders announced later that month that the "state of emergency for the army" had ended (in fact, no formal state of emergency had been declared by legal authorities either in Moscow or in Vilnius and Riga), at which point the Soviet army and Interior Ministry troops began to return to their barracks.

Baltic nationalists had long suspected that, when push came to shove, Yeltsin's "Russian-ness" would ultimately prevail over his anticommunism, and that he would support the use of force to preserve Moscow's rule in the Baltics. They were mistaken. On 13 January, the day after the violence in Vilnius, Yeltsin took the risky step of flying to Tallinn, the Estonian capital, to meet with the leaders of Estonia and Latvia and a Lithuanian representative. The four of them agreed to send an appeal to the United Nations proposing an international conference to resolve the crisis in Vilnius. A separate statement was also issued (this one was signed by Lithuania's leader, Vytautas Landsbergis, by fax) that called upon citizens of the four republics serving in the Soviet army not to participate in armed actions that violated the republics' sovereignty. Yeltsin then reiterated the appeal in an address covered by local television and radio, and he signed several agreements that affirmed the sovereignty of Russia and the Baltic states and that specified that the four republics would construct their relations "on the basis of international law."[22]

Yeltsin returned to Moscow that same day and held a press conference in which he announced publicly that Russia, Ukraine, Belorussia, and Kazakhstan were considering negotiating a union treaty on their own. In response to a question on the impact of the violence in Vilnius on the union treaty, Yeltsin said the treaty had been dealt a "serious blow" because "you won't find anyone among the republic leaders who wants to sign a treaty with a noose around his neck." He expressed astonishment at the fact that Defense Minister Yazov did not even know that the RSFSR had passed a law prohibiting the use of conscripts from the RSFSR from participating in actions directed against Soviet civilians or from serving outside the borders of the RSFSR. (He would suggest to the RSFSR Supreme Soviet later that month that Yazov be prosecuted for his failure to comply with these laws.) Finally Yeltsin suggested that Russia might consider establishing its own army.[23] The statement outraged conservatives—as the CPRF leadership put it in a formal statement, Yeltsin had lost "all sense of political responsibility" and had entered into "a virtual collusion with neo-fascists" in cooperating with the Baltic nationalists.[24]

Gorbachev's credibility as a leader suffered a profound setback as a result of the bloodshed in Vilnius and Riga. He spoke briefly to reporters two days after the crackdown during a recess of the USSR Supreme Soviet, calling for a dialogue with Lithuania's leaders but blaming them and the price increases for the violence. He asserted that the National Salvation Council had tried to send representatives to Lithuania's parliament to discuss a compromise but that they had been beaten up, a claim that was rejected by credible journalists in Vilnius. In remarks to the Supreme Soviet that day, he condemned Yeltsin in particular for his suggestion that Russia might need its own army, calling his statement "a very flagrant violation of the USSR Constitution."[25]

He waited to make a formal statement on the crackdown in the Baltics until 23 January. While he asserted, rather elliptically, that the crackdown was "in no way an expression of the way presidential power operates," he again blamed the Baltic governments for provoking the violence and attacked Yeltsin for "irresponsible statements that are fraught with serious dangers." In a reference to the appeal to the United Nations from Yeltsin and the Baltic leaders, he caustically argued: "Going on bended knee to foreign countries and to the United Nations, inviting them to deal with matters that we ourselves can and must deal with, is strange and absurd, to put it mildly."[26]

Gorbachev's denial that he had given the order to use force and did not know who had suggested that he was either a liar or incompetent. His handling of the crisis thus managed to alienate both conservatives and reformers. For the former, he had failed to follow through by ordering Soviet troops to dissolve the parliaments and governments in the Baltics. For the latter, he failed to distance himself from the tragedy by firing or otherwise disciplining Pugo, Kryuchkov, or Yazov. Moreover, many reformers suspected that, his denials notwithstanding, Gorbachev had either explicitly ordered or implicitly encouraged the crackdown himself.[27] The "Founding Council" of the liberal newspaper, *Moskovskiye novosti,* issued a statement claiming that Gorbachev had "essentially justified the tactics used in the actions in Lithuania" and asserted that "almost nothing is left" of the president's reform program.[28] Calls were made at a demonstration the next day in Moscow attended by some 100,000 protestors for the resignation not only of Kryuchkov, Pugo, Yazov, and Kravchenko, but for the first time of Gorbachev himself. Even firm critics of Lithuania's secessionist campaign among Moscow's democrats criticized the crackdown as illegal and ill-considered—as Otto Latsis, a well-known *Izvestiia* commentator and former editor of the leading Communist journal, *Kommunist,* argued:

> Lawlessness must not be answered with lawlessness. If the response to the Lithuanian Supreme Soviet's illegal acts had been its removal from power through the introduction of presidential rule, no one could have denied that a legally empowered official was taking a step provided for by law. Of course, it would have been an extreme and undesirable step, and one could question its timeliness and its political advisability under the given circumstances. But no one could question its legality."[29]

Thus, the hapless resort to force in the Baltics, regardless of whether it had been ordered directly by Gorbachev, highlighted the extent to which he was increasingly unable to control his own government, impose central writ in the Baltics, or rein in Yeltsin. The USSR, it was clear, was suffering an acute crisis of multiple sovereignty. The crackdown also led to a rapid deterioration in relations with the West, despite the fact the United States was still very much interested in Moscow's support for its bombing campaign against Iraq, launched on 16 January in preparation for what would prove a decisive ground offensive in February. A summit with Bush scheduled for February was called off, and Western governments condemned the violence and indicated it would inevitably threaten their improving relations with Moscow.[30] Personal relations between Gorbachev and Yeltsin, already very bad, worsened, especially after Yeltsin called publicly for Gorbachev's resignation in a nationally televised speech on 19 February.[31] And finally, the antiunion opposition remained in power in all three Baltic republics, while the Baltic peoples were now even more hostile to Moscow.

To demonstrate its resolve to defy pressure from Moscow, the Lithuania Supreme Soviet voted on 16 January (the same day that the USSR approved Gorbachev's proposed referendum on the union—see below) to hold it own referendum in February (i.e., five weeks before the referendum on the union) in which voters would be asked whether they were in favor of a "democratic and independent state of Lithuania." The referendum took place on 10 February, with 90.5 percent of those voting in favor and turnout at 84.4 percent.[32] The results suggested that Lithuania's (mostly Russian and Polish) minority population supported the Lithuanian government and undermined Gorbachev's frequent claim that he was being implored to introduce presidential rule in the country by the significant portion of the Lithuanian electorate that opposed the Lithuania independence campaign. Lithuania's referendum was followed on 3 March by similar referendums in Estonia and Latvia. In Estonia, 83 percent of eligible voters turned out, with 77.7 percent voting in favor of Estonia's independence. In Latvia, where ethnic Latvians constituted a bare majority of the population, turnout was 87.6 percent, with 73.7 percent in favor.[33]

Nevertheless, Gorbachev continued to adhere to a hard line. On 16 January, he suggested to the Supreme Soviet that the "Law on the Press," which had brought a genuinely free press to the Soviet Union, be suspended unless the media show greater "objectivity." The Supreme Soviet followed by charging one of its committees with studying how to ensure a more "objective" media. Gorbachev then issued a series of decrees providing for joint patrols by the police and the military to "strengthen the safeguarding of public order" in Moscow, the capitals of the union republics and autonomies, and cities with significant enterprises or military installations within their confines. That same month, the new Soviet prime minister, the bumbling Valentin Pavlov, signed a decree granting the KGB authority to search the premises of enterprises suspected of black marketeering or other illegal economic activities. In early February, Pavlov gave a bizarre newspaper interview in which he accused Western banks of trying to undermine the Soviet economy by flooding the country with rubles, which he characterized as a "financial war" that was somehow linked to the conflict in the Persian Gulf. Later that month, Gorbachev publicly denounced the "democrats" for their "furious attacks" on the center and "attempts to cast aspersions on the union," and he asserted that they were using "neo-Bolshevik tactics" in an attempt to seize power.[34]

* * * * *

On 16 January 1991, the USSR Supreme Soviet finally agreed to schedule Gorbachev's union referendum for 17 March. After considerable controversy, it was agreed that voters would be asked the following: "Do you consider necessary the preservation of the Union of Soviet Socialist Republics as a renewed federation of equal sovereign republics, in which the rights and freedoms of an individual of any nationality will be fully (*v polnoi mere*) guaranteed?"

As many Soviet commentators complained, this formulation asked several questions at once. Should the union be preserved? Should it be a union of Soviet and socialist republics? Should the rights and freedoms of individuals be guaranteed regardless of nationality? Nor was it was clear what a "renewed federation" would look like. Would the autonomies have equal status with the union republics? Would the union republics retain a politically meaningful right of secession? And what was meant by the terms "Soviet" and "socialist"?[35] Further complicating the referendum's political significance were decisions by Russia, Ukraine, Kyrgyzia, and Uzbekistan to add supplemental questions—in the former case, voters in the RSFSR would be asked to endorse the establishment of a directly elected RSFSR president, while in the other three instances voters were asked whether they supported their republic's sovereignty within a new union.[36]

Kazakhstan also modified the wording of the question on the preservation of the union, substituting "equal sovereign *states*" for "equal sovereign *republics*." Finally, Armenia, Estonia, Georgia, Latvia, Lithuania, and Moldova refused to allow the referendum to proceed on their territory.

As the date for the referendum approached, Gorbachev concluded that its prospects would be improved if the draft union treaty were endorsed by the leaders of at least some of the union republics. As noted earlier, most of the union republics had already made clear their objections to the terms of the November draft. Moreover, Yeltsin and his Ukrainian and Kazakh counterparts, Leonid Kravchuk and Nursultan Nazarbayev, were by then engaged in direct discussions about drafting a union treaty on their own. They nevertheless agreed to send representatives to the Gorbachev-hosted negotiations, as did all other union republics except the so-called six intransigents—Armenia, Estonia, Georgia, Latvia, Lithuania, and Moldova (Azerbaijan agreed to send a representative as an "observer" only).

These "9+1" talks, as they were called (i.e., the nine participating republics plus the union), revealed disagreements in particular over the status and powers of the autonomies. As a result, two versions of a revised draft were prepared. In one, only the union republics would be represented in the upper house of parliament, the Council of Nationalities, while in the other there would be representation from both the union republics and the autonomies. There was also disagreement over whether the autonomies would be signatories to the treaty. Nevertheless, leaders of the nine participating republics initialed the two versions on 3 March, and three days later both versions were discussed by the Council of the Federation. Agreement was reportedly reached on all outstanding issues except of the degree of representation of the autonomies in the federal legislature.

A week before the referendum, Soviet newspapers published a new version of the proposed treaty.[37] There were a number of significant differences from the November draft, most of which strengthened the republics at the expense of the center. Again, the first "basic principle" of the draft asserted that each republic "is a sovereign state," although the USSR was now described not only as "sovereign" but also as a "federal democratic state that is formed as a result of the voluntary association of equal republics." Article 1 restored the traditional right of secession, asserting that "the parties to the treaty have the right to leave the union in accordance with procedures established by the parties to the treaty," which suggested that the union republics would have the right to negotiate a revised law on secession. The preamble affirmed "the right of nations and peoples to self-determination (*samoopredelenie*)" and added that "the sovereign states that are parties to the treaty" were "proceeding from the declarations of state sovereignty proclaimed by the republics." Basic Principle 7 stated:

> The republics are full (*polnopravnye*) members of the international community. They have a right to establish direct diplomatic, consular, trade, and other ties with foreign states, to exchange authorized representatives (*polnomochnye*

predstavitel'stva) with them, to conclude international treaties, and to participate directly in the activity of international organizations that does not infringe on the interests of the parties to this treaty or their common interests and does not violate the USSR's international commitments.

The powers assigned to the union were further reduced. The union would now have responsibility only for "implementing" (*osushchestvlenie*), not "working out" (*vyrabotka*), foreign policy and foreign economic activity; for "drawing up" (*sostavlenie*), not "confirming" (*utverzhdenie*) and "fulfilling" (*ispolnenie*), the union budget; and for "monitoring" (*rassmatrivaet*), not "resolving" (*razreshaet*), disagreements among republics or between the union and the republics over the compatibility of federal and republic laws with the union constitution. Adopting the new union constitution, as well as "determining" (*opredelenie*) foreign policy, the "strategy of state security," military policy, and the "strategy for the country's social and economic development," inter alia, now fell within the joint jurisdiction of union and republic governments. In effect, the only power reserved for the union alone was "declaring war and concluding peace" (Article 5), although even here the republics were expected to cooperate in determining "military policy." As in the previous draft, all-union legislation on matters of joint jurisdiction would only take effect in individual republics "if the republic whose interests are affected by the given laws does not object." Again, the signatories to the treaty were not identified, although this time language was added that made clear what had been implied in the previous draft: "Relations between the Union and republics that do not sign the Union Treaty are subject to regulation on the basis of existing USSR legislation and mutual commitments and agreements."

The most important change from the November draft, however, related to the autonomies. There was now no explicit distinction between union republics and the autonomies—instead, the term "republic" was used exclusively. The fact that the signatories were not identified left it unclear as to whether this referred to the union republics, to the union republics and the autonomous republics, or to the union republics and all the autonomies (by then, many of the autonomous oblasts and autonomous okrugs had unilaterally defined themselves as "republics"). Again, the draft specified that "republics that are parties to the treaty enter the Union directly or as part of other republics," which implied that the autonomies would be treated as signatory republics. And again, the draft specified that "the republics that are parties to the treaty possess equal rights and have equal duties" (Article 1), which some commentators interpreted to mean that there would be no difference in the powers of the union republics and the autonomies. Finally, as noted earlier, the only provision upon which there had been no agreement dealt with whether the autonomies would be represented in the "Council of the Republics," one of two houses of the new legislature (Article 12). As a result, two versions of the provision were published.

Because the new draft was published so soon before the referendum, there was little opportunity for the public to discuss it or become familiar with its terms. Nevertheless, the referendum took place as scheduled on 17 March 1991. Overall, 80 percent of the Soviet electorate (147 million out of 184 million on the voting lists) turned out for the vote, including some 1.3 million who managed to vote in the republics and autonomies (e.g., Nagorno-Karabakh and Adzharia in Georgia) that refused to participate.[38] Of those participating in the USSR as a whole, 76.4 percent voted "yes." In none of the nine participating republics did support for the union fall below 70 percent (see table 5.1), while in the five Central Asian republics and Azerbaijan (all with traditionally Muslim titulars), the "yes" vote was well over 90 percent.[39] Turnout in Ukraine for the USSR referendum was 83.5 percent, with 70.2 percent voting for the union. On the other hand, 80.2 percent also voted "yes" to the separate question about Ukraine's participation in "a union of sovereign states" in accordance with the republic's sovereignty declaration.[40]

The returns in the RSFSR were also ambiguous. Turnout in the republic for the union referendum was 75.4 percent, with 71.3 percent voting "yes." Turnout for the question on the Russian presidency was 75.1 percent (not including the electorate in four autonomies that refused to include the question on the ballot—Checheno-Ingushetia, North Ossetia, Tatarstan, and Tuva), with 69.9 percent of those voting in favor of an RSFSR presidency, almost exactly the same return as the 71.3 percent voting for the union.

On the other hand, returns in the RSFSR's autonomous republics and autonomous oblasts showed greater support for the union (82.6 percent) than the overall RSFSR return. In another indication that the electorate in the autonomies was more suspicious of RSFSR than union authorities, support for the RSFSR presidency in the autonomies (62.2 percent) was substantially below the average in the RSFSR overall. Moreover, the fact that four autonomous republics refused to include the RSFSR presidency question on the ballot was interpreted in Moscow as an indication of their pro-union, pro-Communist, and anti-RSFSR sentiments. It was also clear that Yeltsin remained less popular in the autonomies than in the rest of the Russia. In contrast, 77.8 percent of Muscovites and 78.5 percent of Leningraders voted "yes" on the RSFSR presidency.[41]

The referendum was interpreted in the Soviet press as a victory for Gorbachev, a victory for Yeltsin, or both. In the long term, it would leave a bitter legacy of postindependence resentment in the union republics where the electorate voted to preserve the union, including in Russia. But in the short term the extent of support for the union meant little politically because it was not clear what kind of union was being supported—opponents of a strong union could always argue that the voters were supporting the kind of weak "federation" that Yeltsin had in mind. The Russian electorate's support for a new RSFSR presidency, on the other hand, proved extremely important. Russia's new president (and it was correctly assumed that Yeltsin would win a presidential election) could deal with Gorbachev on more equal terms, and indeed he would have an advantage over Gorbachev in that he would be popularly and directly elected.

Gorbachev had thus painted himself into a corner. He still needed the leaders of the union republics to sign the union treaty and the all-union and union

Table 5.1. Results of Referendum on the Preservation of the Union

Union Republic	Yes Preserve Union	Turnout
Azerbaijan SSR	93%	75%
Belarus SSR	83%	83%
Kazakhstan SSR	94%	89%
Kyrgyzstan SSR	95%	93%
Russian SFSR	71%	75%
Tajik SSR	96%	94%
Turkmen SSR	98%	98%
Ukrainian SSR	70%	83%
Uzbek SSR	94%	95%
Total	76%	80%

republic legislatures to ratify it. Indeed, he might even need the approval of all political elites of the autonomies as well. But they were becoming increasingly assertive and less inclined to accept that the referendum results substantially constrained them. Gorbachev therefore faced the almost impossible task of trying to negotiate the terms of treaty with too many executives who were concerned about ratification by too many legislatures, and who were also increasingly convinced that Gorbachev lacked the means to force them to accept his authority or the authority of the union government.

Meanwhile, Yeltsin found himself in a difficult political position as well, despite the fact that the RSFSR electorate had supported his proposed presidency. Late that same month, he was confronted by a serious challenge to his leadership from the Communist opposition in the RSFSR parliament. Ivan Polozkov, the conservative leader of the newly formed Communist Party of the Russian Federation (CPRF), announced that his party and its allies would attempt to remove Yeltsin as Supreme Soviet Chairman at the upcoming session of the RSFSR Congress of Peoples' Deputies. DemRossiia responded by calling for a march by Yeltsin's supporters on the Russian parliament on 28 March, the day the vote in the Congress was to take place. Gorbachev, who later claimed that he was being fed considerable misinformation at the time by Kryuchkov, Pugo, and his chief of staff, Valerii Boldin (all of whom would be key figures in the attempted coup in August), was told that the demonstrators planned to storm the Kremlin.[42] He therefore instructed the Council of Ministers to ban all demonstrations in Moscow between 26 March and 16 April. Despite the ban and the presence of an estimated 50,000 policemen and special riot police, the demonstration proceeded as planned, with an estimated 250,000 taking part. While the march was not marred by violence, the atmosphere in Moscow was extremely tense, as many feared that Soviet Interior Ministry troops would use force against the demonstrators or that "provocations" by conservatives would lead to a massive bloodletting. The crisis atmosphere finally abated when, in a decisive victory for Yeltsin, the RSFSR Congress voted 532–286 to reject the governmental decree banning demonstrations in Moscow.

The failure to prevent the protest, let alone to remove Yeltsin from office, further weakened Gorbachev's political standing. The Soviet president, it seemed to many, was inclined to issue orders and publish decrees that he could not or would not enforce, and with each such incident both his own authority and that of the center were undermined. While he may well have been supportive of a crackdown to restore "constitutional order," he was at the same time clearly unwilling to accept the massive bloodshed that a successful crackdown would almost certainly require. In the wake of Gorbachev's "turn to the right," the January violence in the Baltics, and his unsuccessful efforts to undermine Yeltsin politically, his popular support continued to plummet, and Yeltsin became the undisputed champion of the democratic reform movement and the Russian people—a poll taken at the time gave Yeltsin a 70 percent approval rating, compared to 14 percent for Gorbachev.[43]

The show of support for Yeltsin led his opponents on the RSFSR CPD to announce that they were giving up their effort to unseat him. Instead, the Congress approved Yeltsin's proposal to establish a directly elected RSFSR presidency, and it scheduled presidential elections for 12 June 1991, the anniversary of Russia's declaration of sovereignty. In the interim, Yeltsin was given special powers to issue emergency decrees similar to those granted Gorbachev by the USSR CPD. Yeltsin made perfectly clear that he intended to use these new powers to countermand any decrees by Gorbachev that he considered inimical to Russia's interests or a violation of Russia's sovereignty. A "war of decrees," Moscow newspapers noted, was now accompanying the "war of laws."

In his speech to the RSFSR Congress on 30 March, Yeltsin had indicated that he was confident that an agreement on the union treaty would soon be reached because the union republics would realize that doing so was in their interest, not because they were being forced into it. He also indicated a new willingness to work with Gorbachev on a compromise draft. Nevertheless, on 18 April 1991 representatives of the "Big Five"—Russia, Ukraine, Kazakhstan, Belarus, and Uzbekistan—met in Kiev. The meeting led to an agreement that the Big Five would, if necessary, negotiate a treaty among themselves for the establishment of a new union without the participation of representatives of the center. They also agreed that they would not allow the autonomies to be treated as signatories to the new treaty or to permit their status and powers to be equalized with their own.[44]

Late that March, Gorbachev began once again to reposition himself politically. It had become clear after the January violence in Lithuania that imposing central writ on the republics would require massive force. It had become equally clear that there could be no union treaty without Russia, and that Russia's participation would require Yeltsin's cooperation. So Gorbachev "tilted back to the left." Although in private he continued to complain of Yeltin's "scandalously insulting, increasingly brazen public attacks" on him,[45] he began to signal that he was interested in a compromise. He also renewed his contacts with reform-minded allies of the early perestroika era, including Aleksandr Yakovlev.

The willingness of Gorbachev and Yeltsin to cooperate resulted in an important breakthrough. On 23 April 1991, Gorbachev and the leaders of nine of the union republics met at a government dacha (country home) in Novo-Ogarevo, a village outside Moscow. The meeting lasted for over nine hours, but after heated debate Gorbachev, Yeltsin, and the other participants finally agreed to the wording of a joint statement, which was published the next day. The statement affirmed the need for "a new treaty among sovereign states" and stipulated that within six months after the treaty was ratified, a new union constitution would be presented to the Congress of Peoples' Deputies for ratification. Elections would then be held for new union "bodies of power." If Gorbachev wanted to remain president, he would have to win a popular election for the first time in his career.

The statement went on to acknowledge that Latvia, Lithuania, Estonia, Moldova, Georgia, and Armenia had the right not to join the new union but that nonsignatories would not receive "most favored nation status." What exactly was meant by "most favored nation status" was not specified. Nor did the statement provide that the independence of nonsignatories would be recognized— Gorbachev was still unwilling to accept that some of the republics might secede, and it was therefore possible for him to continue to insist that the 1922 Union Treaty, the USSR constitution, and Union laws remain binding for nonsignatories. Finally, the statement indicated that agreement had been reached on a program of economic reform and that the Novo-Ogarevo republics would fulfill their obligations to the all-union budget and cooperate on various "anti-crisis measures."[46]

The 23 April statement was an agreement on basic principles, not on the text of a draft treaty. Negotiations continued on the text, with the status of the autonomies remaining the key sticking point. Meanwhile, the autonomies continued to insist on a voice at the negotiating table and demanded that they be recognized as full signatories to the treaty. Tatarstan went even further, insisting that it be recognized as a full republic with a status equal to that of the RSFSR and the other union republics.

Of the nine republics involved in the "Novo-Ogarevo process," as the Soviet press referred to it, only four had autonomies located within their borders: the RSFSR (thirty-one autonomies), Uzbekistan (one autonomy), Tajikistan (one autonomy), and Azerbaijan (two autonomies). Predictably, these four resisted any arrangement that would equalize the status and powers of "their" autonomies. The other union republics were equally adamant, however, in their opposition to the autonomies' demands. Had the status and powers of the autonomies been equalized, the union republics' political weight in the union would have been greatly reduced. Rather than being one of nine (or possibly fifteen) constituent units of the new entity, they would be one of as many as fifty-three. They thus objected to any scheme that would dilute their voice in central legislative or executive bodies. The leaders of the non-Russian republics were also concerned about the political weight of Russia in the new union even without the autonomies (particularly a new union without the six intransigents, not to speak of Ukraine). Treating the RSFSR's thirty-one autonomies, which they felt the Russian government would be able to dominate, as constituent members of a new union would make Russia's influence even more disproportionate.

Shortly after the 23 April Novo-Ogarevo meeting, Gorbachev announced that only the federal government and the union republics, and not the autonomies, would be parties to the treaty. At the initiative of Murtaza Rakhimov, the chairman of the Supreme Soviet of Bashkortostan, the autonomies responded by organizing a meeting in Moscow on 7 May. The result was a statement protesting their exclusion from the 23 April Novo-Ogarevo meeting. Gorbachev, Yeltsin, and the leaders of fourteen of the RSFSR's sixteen autonomous republics (Dagestan and Karelia were represented by lower-ranking officials, while the heads of the autonomous oblasts and okrugs were not invited) then held a meeting on 12 May 1991. After some six hours of discussions, they announced that they had agreed to a compromise whereby the RSFSR's autonomies would sign as constituent units of *both* the USSR and the RSFSR.[47] Only Tatarstan's leader, Mintimir Shaimiev, refused to endorse the agreement, indicating that his republic would sign the treaty as a member of the USSR, not the RSFSR. Only then would Tatarstan be willing to negotiate a separate bilateral treaty with the RSFSR that would define its relationship with the Russian federation.[48]

Meanwhile, the Soviet economy was collapsing. In March, the nation's coal miners had gone on strike, crippling much of the country's industry. On 1 April, the Soviet government had freed prices on approximately 30 percent of consumer goods, mostly luxury items, a decision that had been preceded by panic buying and the disappearance of many goods from store shelves. More price increases were expected in the future. That same day, the exchange rate for dollars for foreign tourists was raised to 27 rubles to the dollar in an effort curb the rapid growth of the black market and the dollarization of the economy—the commercial rate for most transactions remained at 1.75 rubles to the dollar, with the "official" rate of 0.57 rubles to the dollar now virtually irrelevant. Several days later, the head of the Supreme Soviet's budget committee announced that the republics had provided only 18 billion of the anticipated 54 billion rubles for the federal treasury, and he warned that if the republics, particularly Russia, continued to refuse to meet their obligations to the USSR budget, there would be "devastating consequences."[49]

The government's "anti-crisis" program was submitted to the USSR Supreme Soviet in mid-April. Described by Prime Minister Pavlov as a "third way" between the traditional Soviet "command administrative system" and the free market, the program was widely regarded as conservative and ill considered. Indeed, it led the IMF to refuse additional financial support for the USSR until the Soviet government committed to a serious reform program. Official statistics showed a net decline in material product for the Soviet economy of some 10 percent in the first quarter of 1991, while government officials were warning that production would fall by some 15 percent for the year as a whole.

Gorbachev reacted to the deteriorating economic situation by stating at a meeting of the Council of the Federation that the mounting crisis was due to the unwillingness of the republics to adhere to the laws and economic program of the central government. As he put it: "A threat is hanging over our country. It is a danger to our statehood, to the Soviet federation, for whose preservation a majority has expressed its support. It is the threat that the economy will collapse, with all the ensuing consequences for people's interests and the country's defense capability."[50] Indeed, one of the reasons that Gorbachev brought the leaders of the union republics together for the Novo-Ogarevo "summit" on 23 April was his need for their support in keeping the Soviet economy from collapsing. Thus the joint statement of 23 April had included a number of provisions on the economy, including a call to the country's coal miners, who had gone out on strike in March, to go back to work, as well as an agreement to end "the war of budgets." Additional intergovernmental negotiations followed, and on 16 May the Soviet press announced that the federal government and thirteen of the union republics agreed to emergency measures that included budget cuts, a ban on strikes, and an accelerated program for converting military industries to the production of civilian goods.

By mid-May, there were signs that Gorbachev was again considering more radical economic reforms. Late that month, he asked Grigorii Yavlinsky, one of the drafters of the 500-day program, to draw up a plan for radical economic measures. With the help of Graham Allison, a political economist at Harvard's Kennedy School of Government, Yavlinsky drafted a program that became known as the "Grand Bargain." The plan called for the West to provide the Soviet Union with substantial economic assistance in return for a reduction in Soviet defense spending, further democratization, and a transition to a genuine market economy. Gorbachev refused to endorse the Grand Bargain publicly or to make clear to Western governments that it had his full support (he would say that he supported "90 percent" of it, but which 90 percent was unclear). Moreover, President Bush was about to embark on his ultimately unsuccessful reelection campaign just as the U.S. economy was entering into a recession, and he was particularly reluctant to support what was being billed as a new Marshall Plan for the USSR. Western Europe, meanwhile, was preoccupied by plans for "Europe 1992" as well as by the crisis in Yugoslavia, while the Japanese remained adamant that the Kuril Islands, which the USSR had seized at the end of World War II, be returned to Japan before they would consider significant aid. Gorbachev thus returned from the G-7 summit in London in early July with no promise of significant financial support. His high hopes dashed, he was now even more vulnerable to charges that he was humiliating the Soviet state by his fruitless begging for a rescue package from the West.

Negotiations over the text of the union treaty continued in late April and May, and on 7 June Grigorii Revenko, the Soviet president's representative and chair of the Preparatory Committee that was working on the revised text, reported in an interview in *Izvestiia* that considerable progress had been made in the negotiations and that a draft would soon be sent to the respective legislatures for approval. There were, however, still significant disagreements over the demarcation of powers between the center and the republics, the status of the autonomies under the treaty and their powers, the powers of the central executive and legislative in the transitional period before a new union constitution was adopted and their role in drafting the treaty, and the name of the new union. With regard to the critical question of taxation and burden sharing, Revenko stated:

> But in Novo-Ogarevo, except for the Russian SFSR's final word, in principle all the rest of the republics spoke out in favor of federal taxes. There is understanding of the fact that a two-or-three-channel tax system of taxes can only strengthen the state. A citizen who has no involvement in the state in which he lives, who is not a partner in it, is not a citizen. I am not talking about percentages here, but also the principle of the state's existence.[51]

Revenko expected debate over all these issues in the USSR and republic legislatures to be heated, but he was optimistic that a final version of the treaty would be signed by the end of the summer. His optimism seemed justified when on 18 June he announced that the draft text had been sent to the legislatures of the signatories. His hope that Russia and the other republics would eventually agree to an independent taxing authority for the union government would, however, be disappointed.

On 12 June 1991, the RSFSR's presidential elections, the first in Russia's 1,000-year history, took place as scheduled. The result was a decisive political victory for Yeltsin, who avoided a runoff by winning 57.3 percent of the vote. Nikolai Ryzhkov, the former USSR prime minister, placed second with 17.3 percent of the vote. The still little-known nationalist and head of the mislabeled Liberal Democratic Party of Russia (LDPR), Vladimir Zhirinovsky, came in third with 7.9 percent, while Aman Tuleev, the chairman of the Supreme Soviet of the Kemerovo oblast in Siberia, came in fourth with 6.1 percent. Tellingly, the hard-line Communist candidate, General Albert Makashov, received only 3.7 percent of the vote, while Vadim Bakatin, Gorbachev's former interior minister and the candidate who was generally (although perhaps incorrectly) viewed as the Soviet president's favorite, came in last with 3.2 percent. The returns confirmed that support in Russia for both moderates and hard-liners associated with the CPSU was minimal.

As might have been expected by the disagreements at Novo-Ogarevo over the status of the autonomies, Yeltsin did less well in the autonomous republics, oblasts, and okrugs than in the rest of the RSFSR—50.6 percent compared to 58.4 percent, respectively. His support was particularly low in Tuva (15.2 percent, by far his lowest support throughout the RSFSR), Gorno-Altai (22.4 percent), North Ossetia (27.3 percent), Kalmykia (31 percent), and Buriatia (34.5 percent). Interestingly, Yeltsin's best showing in the autonomies was in Checheno-Ingushetia, which he had visited in March and which gave him 76.7 percent of its vote. Tatarstan's leadership refused to endorse Yeltsin or to accept the legitimacy of the RSFSR presidential elections on its territory. It allowed the vote to take place but called on Tatarstan's electorate not to turn out in the RSFSR vote. Presidential elections were organized for the republic that same day. Tatarstan's electorate (which included only slightly fewer ethnic Russians than ethnic Tatars) responded with a below threshold turnout in the RSFSR elections (36.6 percent), while over two-thirds of eligible voters participated in Tatarstan's presidential elections. Shaimiev, the only candidate, won an overwhelming victory.[52]

Yeltsin's election as Russia's president was a major blow to the CPSU's already tumbling prestige. The intense concerns of conservatives, and their distress at what they felt was Gorbachev's inability to act decisively to "restore order," was made clear five days later when Prime Minister Pavlov appealed to the USSR Supreme Soviet to afford him powers that legally rested with the Soviet president. The prime minister's attempt at a "constitutional coup" was rebuffed when Gorbachev gave a resolute speech to the Supreme Soviet on 21 June. After threatening to resign, Gorbachev received a vote of confidence when the Soviet legislature rejected Pavlov's appeal, 262 to 24.

The following week, Soviet newspapers published a third version of the proposed union treaty.[53] The constituent units of the proposed union, which previously had been referred to as "republics," were now called "states" (*gosudarstva*). The new draft also provided for a somewhat stronger federal center compared to the March version. Article 4 specified that relations between the signatory states were to be governed not only by the union treaty and other treaties between the signatory states, but by the "USSR Constitution." Article 6 affirmed that the constitutional system was to be founded on *both* the union treaty and the USSR constitution (Article 9 of the previous draft had stated that the union constitution would be based on the union treaty alone). The center was also now charged with "issuing currency" and adopting the constitution (Article 5). Finally, Article 7 limited the union republics' ability to ignore federal legislation on matters of joint jurisdiction:

> Questions that fall under joint jurisdiction are decided by bodies of power and administration of the Union and the states that form it through consultations (*soglasovaniia*), special agreements, and the adoption of foundational legislation (*priniatiia osnov zakonodatel'stva*) of the Union and the republics and of republic laws that are in conformity with them.

No longer would the republics have a right to suspend the USSR's law dealing with matters of joint jurisdiction merely on the grounds that they objected to it. Instead, they would have to reach agreement with union authorities through "consultations" and "special agreements." A republic could suspend a union law on its territory and appeal to the Constitutional Court only if the law "violates this treaty or contradicts the republic's constitution or republic laws that are within the limits of its [the republic's] powers" (Article 11).

The RSFSR Supreme Soviet provisionally approved the draft treaty on 5 July 1991 on the condition that it be revised to allow the union republics to control taxation and foreign trade on their territory. In asking for parliamentary approval, Yeltsin defended the treaty in unequivocal terms: "The union treaty is an act of huge political importance, and just to reject it would mean political collapse and the destabilization of the country." When Yeltsin was sworn in as Russia's first president five days later, he again endorsed the treaty and confirmed that "Russia will actively participate, together with the other republics, in the very complex work of fundamentally transforming the Union."[54] Invited to attend the swearing-in ceremony, Gorbachev too gave a positive appraisal of the "9 plus 1" talks. He took the opportunity to remind Yeltsin that the Russian Federation, like the USSR, was "made up of dozens of peoples united in a multinational state" and that "the interests of the peoples of the Russian Federation, like those of all the republics joined in our Union, are met not by scattering to their own areas, not by self-isolation, but rather by cooperation and concord in the renewal of the multinational state."[55]

The draft treaty was approved by the USSR Congress of Peoples' Deputies the next day. However, the Ukrainian Supreme Soviet voted several days later to put off consideration of the treaty until the fall to give its legislature time to decide whether it conformed to Ukraine's proposed new constitution. At that point, it would make recommendations on amendments and negotiate with the other parties to adopt those amendments. The result would have been yet another revised text, which would have to be ratified by the legislatures of all signatory states. In the meantime, Ukraine would continue to assert its right to annul laws that violated its sovereignty. As if to emphasize the point, on 20 July 1991 Kiev announced plans to introduce its own currency, despite provisions in the draft treaty for a single unionwide currency. Kravchuk would explain Ukraine's strategy on 29 March 1991 as follows:

> We are proceeding in stages [and] affirming Ukraine's sovereignty in all spheres—economic, social, international, cultural—in all aspects of our life. . . . These are the first steps to independent statehood. Some people may not understand this, but this is for real. It is such a pleasure to watch those deputies who are conscious of the fact that they are the creators of an independent state, a state which does not look submissively to the center, and which is not a colony.[56]

On 24 July 1991, Gorbachev announced that the revised draft had been initialed by most of the Novo-Ogarevo leaders after agreement had finally been reached on taxation provisions.[57] It soon became clear, however, that the precise language of the provision was still a subject of contention, as were the contributions of the republics to the federal treasury for the coming year, and as a result the new text would not be published for another three weeks. To resolve the impasse, Gorbachev, Yeltsin, and Nazarbayev reconvened on 29 July, at which point they agreed on the final wording of the taxation provision. It was also agreed that a new union government would be formed after the treaty was signed. The taxation provision (Article 9) (the revised draft was finally published on 15 August 1991) read as follows:

> Unified (*edinye*) taxes and revenues (*sbory*) set at fixed percentage rates, which are determined by agreement with the republics on the basis of a list of expenditures presented by the Union, are established for the financing of union budget expenditures associated with the exercise of the powers assigned to the Union. The monitoring of expenditures in the union budget is carried out by the parties to the Treaty.
>
> All-Union programs are financed by *pro rata* payments made by the republics affected by the programs, and by the Union budget. The scope and purpose of all-Union programs are regulated by agreements between the Union and republics, taking into consideration the indices of their social and economic development.[58]

Thus, the federal government would have to negotiate its cut of taxes raised by the republics and reach agreement with the union republics on a common percentage contribution, presumably as part of the annual budget process. Special federal "programs" would be funded in part out of the federal budget and in part by "*pro rata*" payments from the republics "affected" by the program, which would require a determination of which republics were "affected" by each program. Moscow would presumably negotiate contributions with each affected republic on a bilateral basis. How to decide which republics were "affected" by a particular program, however, and how to work out a "*pro rata*" share from each republic, was entirely unclear. (The fact that the federal government was contributing to the program from the federal budget would mean that all republics, at least indirectly, would be paying for these programs and would thus be "affected" by them.) Even less clear was how the federal government would accomplish this while "taking into account the indices of their social and economic development." The language had all the earmarks of negotiated compromise that in effect postponed the difficult task of reaching consensus on burden sharing among the republics.

Several days after his meeting with Yeltsin and Nazarbayev, Gorbachev conceded that the treaty's formal adoption by Kiev would have to wait for the Ukrainian referendum later that year. He announced that the treaty would be "ready for signing" on 20 August and that he expected the RSFSR, Kazakhstan, and Uzbekistan to sign it then and to ratify it promptly. He hoped the Novo-Ogarevo republics other than Ukraine would sign and ratify it shortly thereafter. On 4 August 1991, the Soviet president left for a vacation at his new dacha in Foros in the Crimea, expecting to return to Moscow for the signing ceremony on the 20th.

Meanwhile, Gorbachev had been continuing to receive political support from Western governments that, while they were reluctant to bankroll the faltering Soviet economy, continued to express hope that the Novo-Ogarevo process would succeed. As President Bush put it to Gorbachev in a meeting in London on 17 July,

> We want [the Soviet Union] to become a democratic country, a market economy, dynamically integrated into the Western economy . . . and we want the federative problem between the center and the republics to be successfully resolved. . . . We don't want economic catastrophe for the Soviet Union, we are not gloating over your problems. . . . The decline of the Soviet Union isn't in our interests. You deserve our respect.[59]

Bush had made these same points to the president of Lithuania and the prime ministers of Estonia and Latvia in a meeting in Washington on 8 May 1991. Responding to a reporter's question prior to the meeting, he indicated that he would tell the Baltic leaders "that we have a strong and, I think good relationship with President Gorbachev. . . . When you look at the accomplishments of Mikhail Gorbachev, they are enormous."[60] In his private meeting, Bush urged the Baltic leaders to negotiate with Gorbachev rather than deepen the already acute conflict between the Baltic states and Moscow. Ambassador Matlock later recalled, "Bush's words, in the context of this meeting, seemed almost an insult."[61]

The extent of U.S. support for the preservation of the union was highlighted even more dramatically by a speech given by the American president to the Ukrainian parliament in early August 1991. Warning that the costs of independence could be substantial and that independence was not a panacea for Ukraine, he asserted: "Americans will not support those who seek independence in order to replace a far-off tyranny with a local despotism. They will not aid those who promote a suicidal nationalism based upon ethnic hatred." This was apparently intended primarily as a warning to Georgia's recently elected president, Zviad Gamsarkhurdia, who was sounding increasingly intolerant of Georgia's national minorities.[62] Nevertheless, it was poorly received by his listeners, who interpreted it as criticism of the Ukrainian government and Ukrainian nationalism. Bush also referred to his audience as "Soviet citizens," specifically endorsed the union treaty, and gave Gorbachev a ringing personal endorsement, claiming that he had "achieved astonishing things." And he avoided criticizing the Soviet president or government for the bloodshed in Lithuania or elsewhere. His address, which the conservative American columnist William Safire would refer to memorably as the "Chicken Kiev" speech, caused Bush considerable political embarrassment at home, but it accurately reflected the concerns shared by most Western governments at the time about the risks of a conservative coup or the violent breakup of the USSR.

Western concerns about a possible anti-Gorbachev coup were well founded. Late in the evening of Sunday, 18 August 1991, two days before the scheduled signing ceremony and with Gorbachev still on vacation at his "dacha" in Foros, pro-union conservatives launched their long-anticipated but ultimately abortive coup. The public was first alerted to the turn of events early Monday morning when TASS, the state news agency, announced over the radio that a "State Committee for the State of Emergency" had been established to restore order and was now in control of the country. Gorbachev, it went on, was unable to perform his duties as president due to "health reasons" and was stepping down, to be replaced by his vice-president, Gennadii Yanaev. Joining Yanaev on the Emergency Committee were most of the key figures of the Soviet government, including the prime minister and the ministers of defense, state security (the former KGB), and interior. Some of Gorbachev's closest political associates, most notably Anatolii Lukyanov, the chairman of the USSR Supreme Soviet, and Gorbachev's chief of staff, Valerii Boldin, were also among the putschists.[63] Gorbachev, his family, and several of his key aides were placed under effective house arrest in Foros.

As Lukyanov suggested in a statement Monday morning and subsequent testimony by the plotters confirmed, the coup had been timed to take place before the signing ceremony for the union treaty on Tuesday, 20 August. The decision to proceed with the putsch was also influenced by a Yeltsin decree of 20 July that prohibited political parties from organizing cells in places of work— the primary Party organizations that were the most important vestige of the CPSU's erstwhile monopoly of power. And finally, the Soviet media reported that an agreement had been reached by Gorbachev, Yeltsin, and Nazarbayev to form a new government after the union treaty had been signed, which would have meant that the putschists would very likely have lost their jobs in the very near future, indeed conceivably before the end of the week.[64] Any attempt to resist the union treaty would thereafter have had to come from outside the halls of power.

The incompetence of the coup leaders, their unwillingness to use the amount of force needed to repress the opposition, Yeltsin's success in rallying Muscovites to the defense of the "White House," as the Russian parliament building was known, where he and other leading reformers managed to establish a base of resistance, and the Soviet military's confusion over where its loyalties rested ultimately led to the failure of the coup. The drama would come to head on the evening of 20 August, when three anticoup resisters were killed outside the Russian parliament building as Soviet tanks and armored personnel carriers tried, in the face of opposition from Yeltsin supporters wielding Molotov cocktails, to break through barricades that had been set up by thousands of demonstrators outside the White House. The half-hearted assault ended almost immediately, and that morning troops in the vicinity of the White House began to withdraw. Confronted with a divided military that was extremely reluctant to fire upon civilians, it was clear that the putschists had lost their nerve. Gorbachev was escorted back to Moscow from the Crimea by a delegation of Russian parliamentarians late in the afternoon of August 21. Within days, the coup plotters would be in jail or, in two cases, dead at their own hands.

It has become commonplace to argue in the period since that the coup dealt a deathblow to the USSR.[65] In one sense, at least, this was certainly true—the coup brought a decisive end to Communist power in the Soviet Union. It also ended any hope that country could remain entirely intact—almost immediately afterwards the independence of the Baltic republics was formally recognized by the international community. Nevertheless, it was still far from clear whether some kind of unified state that included some, or even all, of the other republics could be salvaged from the wreckage of the regime. But it is certainly not the case, as some have suggested, that in the absence of the attempted coup the signing of the new union treaty would have significantly ameliorated the USSR's acute crisis of multiple sovereignty.[66] On the contrary, the new order provided for in the treaty, even assuming that the treaty was actually ratified by all or some of the union republics, would have been overwhelmed by its extremely impractical design as well as by the myriad economic and political difficulties the country was facing by the summer of 1991.

The treaty's weaknesses were manifold. To begin with, six of the fifteen union republics (Latvia, Lithuanian, Estonia, Georgia, Moldova, and Armenia) had made perfectly clear that they would not be signatories. Each of those six had either declared independence outright by the time the coup occurred or had announced that they were in "transition" to independence. While Gorbachev had agreed that the six intransigents would not be forced to join the union, he never indicated that he would accept a unilateral declaration of independence or would stop pressuring them to join the union except in the highly unlikely circumstance that they followed the all-but-impossible procedures provided for in the law on secession.[67]

Yet another problem was that the draft specified that the 1922 Union Treaty would become null and void only for the parties to the treaty (Article 23) and that nonsignatories would be "subject to regulation on the basis of USSR legislation and mutual commitments and agreements." As this suggested, Gorbachev seemed to believe that a new union treaty and the economic and political costs of de facto but not de jure independence would eventually draw the intransigents back into the union. This would have been unlikely under the best of circumstances, but the economic problems the Soviet Union was facing and the certainty that those problems would get much worse made them unrealistic in the extreme. Moreover, Yeltsin had signed a friendship treaty with Lithuania in late July that formally recognized Lithuania's independence, and he likely would have done the same with some or all of the others regardless of the provisions in the treaty. Even if Gorbachev and the union center were unwilling to recognize the intransigents' independence, Yeltsin and the RSFSR government probably would have, which meant that the "war of sovereignties" with Armenia, Estonia, Georgia, Latvia, Lithuania, and Moldova would almost certainly have continued.

As for the nine signatories, only the five Central Asian republics and Belorussia seemed likely to accept the treaty without amendment.[68] Azerbaijan had participated as an "observer" only, and its leadership would probably have acceded to the treaty only on the condition that Moscow restored Baku's authority over Karabakh, an outcome that the Soviet government was in no position to bring about. Ukraine, on the other hand, had made clear that it would consider signing the treaty only after its planned referendum and after its parliament had adopted a new constitution.[69] Given that it would be many years (1996) before Ukraine would adopt a new constitution, it seems very unlikely that the Ukrainian legislature would have ratified the 15 August draft at all, but at the least it would have demanded substantial changes in the text, which would have meant more wrangling over its terms. As for Russia, its parliament would probably have concluded that ratification of the union treaty required a constitutional amendment, which would have needed the approval of two-thirds of the total number of delegates to the RSFSR CPD. This level of support, particularly given both conservative and liberal opposition to the treaty, was by no means guaranteed, particularly without Ukraine's participation. Indeed, the RSFSR parliament would probably have waited for the Ukrainian parliament to make clear its position before considering ratification.[70]

Finally, the relationship of the autonomies to the new union was a guaranteed source of future conflict. Tatarstan and the RSFSR government had yet to reach an agreement on Tatarstan's status, and the autonomous republic had made clear that it would refuse to sign the treaty as a member of the RSFSR. Likewise the desire of Abkhazia, North Ossetia, and the self-proclaimed Transdniestr and Gagauz republics to join the union would have raised serious problems given that their host republics, Georgia and Moldova, had made clear that they would not become part of Gorbachev's renewed union.

Beyond these problems with ratification, the Soviet government faced a host of profound challenges in mid-1991 that would have undermined the stability of the union even if the treaty had come into force. By August 1991, ethnoterritorial conflicts had turned violent in Karabakh (February 1988), Abkhazia (July 1989), South Ossetia (January-February 1991), and Transdniestra (November 1990). Nonterritorial interethnic violence had also broken out in Osh and in the Fergana Valley in Central Asia, while widespread disorder in Tajikistan had led to the declaration of a state of emergency in the republic that lasted from February 1990 to June 1991. Georgia's internal situation was deteriorating rapidly under Gamsarkhurdia's erratic rule, and the republic would experience a civil war by year's end. The only conflicts to turn violent *after* the USSR's dissolution were a territorial conflict between North Ossetia and Ingushetia over the disputed Prigorodnyi raion and the war between Chechnya and Russia that began in December 1994. It was not, in other words, the dissolution of the Soviet Union that led to the violent conflicts in the region. Rather, those conflicts contributed to the USSR's collapse by making it even more difficult for the Soviet government to deal with its rapidly accumulating political problems.

Equally importantly, the Soviet Union was at the beginning of a long and tortuous process of economic restructuring and an acute economic depression from which there was no prospect of rapid recovery. Even with a well-designed reform program, and even if the reform process had begun with the Soviet economy in reasonable macroeconomic balance, the transformation of a planned economy into a reasonably well-functioning market system is extremely painful and costly, entailing the dismantling of entire industries and the need to create new jobs for a majority of the work force. In the Soviet case, however, macro-economic imbalances were large and growing by mid-1991. Most notably, a growing "monetary overhang" in the form of forced savings due to wage increases in excess of the supply of goods and services sold at fixed prices was aggravating the country's already serious shortages and distribution problems. Foreign reserves had been depleted—unmet payments to foreign exporters were estimated at between \$3 and \$5 billion—and the federal government was running out of money. By late March, the federal budget deficit already exceeded the level approved by the Supreme Soviet for the entire year. A report prepared by Yavlinsky's Center for Economic and Political Research for Gorbachev and published in late May summarized the situation as follows:

> In the past year the state has lost the main levers for controlling the economy, reserves have been "eaten up," and the very structures of control are collapsing. The economy, which entered a phase of crisis, is hanging on for the time being through inertia and force of habit of millions of people who continue to go to work every day and to receive in exchange pieces of varicolored paper that, again because of inertia, are known as money.[71]

The notion that, as Deputy Prime Minister Vitalii Shcherbakov claimed in a speech to the Supreme Soviet on 16 May, the economy would stabilize by the end of the year and begin to show positive growth in 1992 was entirely unrealistic and reflected the government's failure to appreciate both the depth of the country's crisis and the difficulty of overcoming it.

Even with a coherent reform program, the differences between the federal government and the republics, and among the republics themselves, would have remained intense.[72] The distributional effects of reform and proceeds from privatization were certain to have generated acute intergovernmental conflict, and each republic would have continued to claim that it was being exploited by the others. Disagreements over burden sharing would also have been aggravated by the serious differences that had already emerged over the optimal pace and character of reform.

In short, even a well-designed federation would have been under an enormous strain had the treaty been ratified. But the new union was *not* well designed. On the contrary, it provided for an entirely unique organizational form with a federal government that was at least as weak and unstable as the American Continental government under the Articles of Confederation. The new union government would have lacked independent powers of taxation, with all the instability and conflict that would have resulted from the need to reach agreement on a federal budget each year. (The Continental Congress at least had the power to determine its own budget, although it needed the consent of the states to raise revenues.) Moreover, the union's weak federal government would have had to function at a time when, unlike the Continental Confederacy, national governments typically consume and redistribute a far greater share of national income and play a far more important and technically demanding role in the economy than was the case in the late eighteenth century.

The treaty would also have failed to resolve many of the other centrifugal pressures on the union. It would not have prevented the republics from debasing the national currency by issuing ruble credits that would have to be made good by transfers from the federal government. (The Russian Federation's hyperinflation in the first few years after independence was aggravated by just these sorts of transfers to other successor states that were freely issuing ruble credits.)[73] A new law on secession would also have had to be drafted with input from the republics. Not only would this have served as another source of controversy, but the law that finally emerged from the process would likely have made secession relatively easy to effect. Given the USSR's economic difficulties and other sources of tension, some of the republics would doubtless have attempted to use the law to withdraw from the union and establish their independence.

Perhaps most importantly, the treaty failed to reconcile the "sovereignty" of the national government with the "sovereignty" of the union's constituent members. This would inevitably have led to very different understandings of the respective powers of the treaty's signatories. As seven well-known reform intellectuals put it in an appeal to Yeltsin not to sign the treaty, the treaty made sovereignty "purely something said for effect, and it makes the Union itself a purposely unviable formation doomed to uninterrupted and perhaps bloody conflicts."[74] Yeltsin confirmed their point by responding that in signing the treaty "we aren't losing the slightest bit of the sovereignty we have gained." On the contrary, he went on, "we are acquiring real rights to conduct an independent domestic and foreign policy." The treaty, he asserted, would allow the transfer of control from the USSR to the RSFSR over "all enterprises and organizations operating on Russian territory." And what if Gorbachev did not agree? "Well, then the decree [transferring control] will be signed by the President of the RSFSR. The new Union Treaty makes this step perfectly legal."[75] Gorbachev, one suspects, would hardly have agreed.

In short, the treaty provided for a union that was no less utopian and impractical than the economic reform programs that had been considered or adopted in the Soviet Union since the launching of perestroika in 1987. Like those economic reforms, it too was an untried "third way" that was very different from federal systems elsewhere in the world.

Notes

1. TASS, 13 June 1990, FBIS-SOV-115, 50–51.

2. Chernyaev 2000, 190. According to Chernyaev, Georgii Shakhnazarov, another key Gorbachev advisor who was more directly involved with domestic politics and nationality issues than Chernyaev (he would later play a key role, along with Grigorii Revenko, Vladimir Kudryatsev, and Boris Topornin, as a leading advisor to Gorbachev in the effort to negotiate a new union treaty for the USSR), also seems to have been telling

Gorbachev in this period that he needed to be more proactive on the nationality question in general and conciliatory with the Baltic states in particular (Chernyaev 2000, 188, 251, and 285).

3. Chernyaev 2000, 265.

4. Chernyaev 2000, 187.

5. Chernyaev 2000, 189, 253.

6. Chernyaev 2000, 227.

7. *Pravda,* 14 January 1990, *CDSP,* vol. 42, no. 2, 5.

8. Matlock 1995, 374.

9. Furtado and Chandler 1992, 442.

10. *Izvestiia,* 4 November 1990, 1.

11. *Pravda,* 12 December 1990, *CDSP,* vol. 42, no. 50, 12. Gorbachev claimed that treating the autonomies as constituent units of the new federation was required by a "recent law." Doubtless he was referring to the 26 April 1990 law on the delineation of powers and its designation of the autonomous republics as "subjects of the federation." It is worth noting, however, that not only the Supreme Soviets of the autonomous republics but also those of the autonomous oblasts and okrugs were being asked to ratify the treaty.

12. Archie Brown, *The Gorbachev Factor* (New York: Oxford University Press, 1996), 271.

13. Brown 1996, 283.

14. Chernyaev 2000, 302.

15. Chernyaev 2000, 303.

16. Chernyaev 2000, 303.

17. Chernyaev 2000, 314.

18. *Izvestiia,* 21 December 1990, *CDSP,* vol. 42, no. 52, 8. He was replaced on 12 January by Aleksandr Bessmertnykh.

19. Gorbachev 1995, 581.

20. *Izvestiia,* 22 December 1990, *CDSP,* vol. 43, no. 1, 6.

21. *Izvestiia,* 10 January 1990, *CDSP,* vol. 43, no. 2, 2.

22. Moscow Domestic Service in Russian, 14 January 1991, FBIS-SOV-91-010, 90.

23. *Izvestiia,* 15 January 1991, *CDSP,* vol. 43, no. 2, 9.

24. *Pravda,* 18 January 1991, 3.

25. *Izvestiia,* 16 January 1991, *CDSP,* vol. 43, no. 3, 8.

26. *Izvestiia,* 23 January 1991, *CDSP,* vol. 43, no. 4, 11.

27. Whether Gorbachev ordered the use of force on the evening of 12–13 January is a matter of some controversy among Western analysts. Some, such as John Dunlop (1993, 151–54), suggest that he was at least indirectly complicit in the bloodshed, while others, such as Archie Brown (1996, 280–82), argue that information about developments in the Baltics was deliberately withheld from Gorbachev and that Gorbachev was unaware that a violent crackdown was imminent.

28. *Moskovskiye Novosti,* 20 January 1991, *CDSP,* vol. 43, no. 3, 11.

29. *Izvestiia,* 15 January 1991, *CDSP,* vol. 43, no. 3, 12.

30. In his memoirs, Bush makes clear that he was convinced that Gorbachev had not given the order to use violence against the opposition in Lithuania (Bush and Scowcroft 1998, 496). With regard to the postponed meeting with Gorbachev, Bush would write in his diary in 17 March 1991, "While we needed to get arms control straightened out, I would go in a minute if there was some way that he could announce that the Baltic states were being set free. Nothing would have done more for his standing in the West than if Gorbachev cut them loose. But I knew that was asking a great deal of him" (Bush and Scowcroft 1998, 501).

31. In a meeting on 24 January 1991 with Ambassador Matlock in which Matlock conveyed Washington's dismay with the bloodshed in the Baltics, Gorbachev would say the following of Yeltsin: "The destructive element comes from the infatuation with sovereignty, especially on the part of Russia, of Boris Nikolaevich. . . . When we talk one on one, everything is normal and we seem to understand each other. But when he leaves and goes back to those surroundings, he becomes a different person. He's like a vessel, one that you can drink from if it's good wine that you pour into it. But if something filthy's poured in, then that's what comes out. He's very illogical" (Chernyaev 2000, 328).

32. Henry E. Brady and Cynthia S. Kaplan, "Eastern Europe and the Former Soviet Union," in *Referendums around the World: The Growing Use of Direct Democracy,* ed. David Butler and Austin Ranney (Washington, D.C.: The AEI Press, 1994), 193.

33. Brady and Kaplan 1994, 193.

34. *Izvestiia,* 1 March 1991, *CDSP,* vol. 43, no. 9, 11.

35. There was also a question as to whether the referendum was legal, since a recently adopted law on referendums had specifically banned referendums on border changes or changes in the status of the republics.

36. Brady and Kaplan 1994, 187–88. An additional question was added in Galicia (western Ukraine), where voters were asked if they supported full independence for Ukraine.

37. *Izvestiia,* 9 March 1991, 2.

38. *Izvestiia,* 21 March 1991, *CDSP,* vol. 43, no. 11, 4.

39. *Izvestiia,* 27 March 1991.

40. Brady and Kaplan 1994, 194. In Galicia, 88 percent voted in favor of full independence for Ukraine, testimony to the strength of nationalism in western Ukraine.

41. "Results of the Vote on the USSR Referendum 17 March 1991" and "Results of the Vote of the RSFSR Referendum 17 March 1991," Central Election Commission, Moscow, 1991.

42. Gorbachev 1995, 587.

43. *U.S. News and World Report,* 8 April 1991, 38–39.

44. Roman Solchanyk, "The Draft Union Treaty and the 'Big Five,'" *Report on the USSR* (1991), 16–18.

45. Chernyaev 2000, 341.

46. *Izvestiia,* 24 April 1991, *CDSP,* vol. 43, no. 17, 1.

47. *Izvestiia,* 13 May 1991, *CDSP,* vol. 43, no. 19, 1.

48. *Pravda,* 18 May 1991, *CDSP,* vol. 43, no. 20, 26.

49. *New York Times,* 5 April 1991.

50. *Izvestiia,* 10 April 1991, *CDSP,* vol. 43, no. 15, 20.

51. *Izvestiia,* 7 June 1991, *CDSP,* vol. 43, no. 23, 20.

52. *Izvestiia,* 13 June 1991, 2.

53. *Izvestiia,* 27 June 1991, 2.

54. *Izvestiia,* 10 July 1991, *CDSP,* vol. 43, no. 28, 3.

55. *Izvestiia,* 10 July 1991, *CDSP,* vol. 43, no. 28, 4.

56. Quoted in Alexander J. Motyl and Bohdan Krawchenko, "Ukraine: From Empire to Statehood," in *New States, New Politics: Building the Post-Soviet Nations,* ed. Ian Bremmer and Ray Taras (New York: Cambridge University Press, 1997), 255.

57. It was later reported that agreement had been reached that the union republics would turn over a uniform 10 percent of all taxes collected on their territory (*Financial Times,* 5 August 1991, 2).

58. *Izvestiia,* 15 August 1991, 2.

59. Chernyaev 2000, 357.

60. Michael R. Beschloss and Strobe Talbott, *At the Highest Levels: The Inside Story of the End of the Cold War* (New York: Back Bay Books, 1994 [1993]), 379–80.

61. Matlock 1995, 528.

62. Beschloss and Talbott 1994, 418.

63. Boldin, who had begun working for Gorbachev in 1981 shortly after the future Soviet leader came to Moscow from the provincial city of Stavropol', would later justify his participation in the failed coup in his memoirs, published in English as *Ten Years That Shook the World: The Gorbachev Era as Witnessed by His Chief of Staff,* trans. Evelyn Rossiter (New York: Basic Books, 1994), where he makes clear that the coup plotters felt that proposed union treaty would destroy the country.

64. In his memoirs, Yeltsin recalls telling Gorbachev at the 29 July meeting that the republics would join the new union only if Gorbachev first rid himself of some members of his "odious entourage," naming Kryuchkov and Yazov specifically. He argues that Nazarbayev backed him up, adding Pugo and Kravchenko of Gosteleradio to the list. Kryuchkov, Pugo, and Yazov would be key figures in the August coup.

65. See, for example, Matlock 1995, 665–67.

66. See, for example, Gorbachev 1995, 626–30, and Brown 1996, 288–89.

67. The only republic that was even paying lip service to the law on secession was Armenia, which was also the most homogenous of the union republics—its population was over 93 percent Armenian in 1989. This homogeneity, which had only increased after the exodus of many Azeris pursuant to the Karabakh conflict, meant that the republic had little to fear from the law's provision on autonomies and minority settlements. Even Armenia, however, was insisting on the primacy of its laws over those of the center during the transition period, which suggested that its willingness to comply with the law on secession would last only as long as its leaders felt it was in the republic's interest to do so.

68. Indeed, it was not even clear which parties would attend the signing ceremony on 20 August. In early August, Gorbachev's spokesman had indicated that delegates from the RSFSR, Kazakhstan, Uzbekistan, and some of the RSFSR's autonomies would put their signatures to the document at the signing ceremony. Belorussia and Tajikistan were expected to sign in early September after their parliaments had reviewed recent revisions in the text. This, he hoped, would induce other republics to follow their lead within the following two months (*Izvestiia,* 7 August 1991, *CDSP,* vol. 43, no. 32, 5).

69. In his memoirs, Gorbachev recalls it had been agreed that the signing of the treaty would take place in two stages, with the leaders of Azerbaijan and Ukraine hopefully adding their signatures at the beginning of October (Gorbachev 1995, 629).

70. Nor can it be assumed that, even if Yeltsin had signed on 20 August as planned, he would have continued to support the treaty and expended any political capital on convincing the Russian legislature to ratify it. Gorbachev, who had placed such high hopes in the political consequences of the treaty, would later admit that he was unsure of the extent of Yeltsin's support for the treaty after a telephone conversation with the Russian president on 14 August. He writes, "On the whole we parted on good terms. However, I could not get rid of the feeling that Yeltsin was holding something back. I did my utmost to warn him against wavering at this crucial and historic moment. As I was to learn later, Yeltsin was under pressure from his associates to attach some conditions to his signature of the treaty" (Gorbachev 1995, 629–30).

71. *Izvestiia,* 20 May 1991, *CDSP,* vol. 43, no. 20, 2.

72. It is worth noting in this regard that the Yugoslav crisis intensified despite, and indeed some would argue as a result of, a reasonable economic reform program adopted by the federal center (see, for example, Woodward 1995).

73. Richard E. Ericson, "The Russian Economy since Independence," in *The New Russia: Troubled Transformation,* ed. Gail W. Lapidus (Boulder, Colo.: Westview Press, 1995), 49–50.

74. *Nezavisimaia gazeta,* 8 August 1991, *CDSP,* vol. 43, no. 32, 5.

75. *Nezavisimaia gazeta,* 16 August 1991, *CDSP,* vol. 43, no. 32, 6.

Chapter 6

Sovereignty as Independence

To our great sorrow, leaders of a number of former Soviet republics equated sovereignty with autarchy. (Nursultan Nazarbayev, President of Kazakhstan, commenting on the Belovezhskaia agreement establishing the Commonwealth of Independent States, December 1991)

While the union treaty that had been scheduled for signing on 20 August 1991 would not have solved the Soviet Union's federation crisis, the failure of the August coup dramatically accelerated the process of disintegration. From the coup's collapse until the final dissolution of the USSR in December, Yeltsin and the RSFSR government would gradually assert jurisdiction over almost all central ministries other than the military. In large part, Gorbachev acquiesced to this step-by-step process of stripping away the central government's formal powers. Chastened by the betrayal of many of his longtime colleagues and humiliated by his treatment at the hands of Yeltsin afterwards, the Soviet president apparently concluded that he no longer had the power to enforce the central government's writ by force and that attempting to do so might provoke a civil war. Rather than calling on the military and forcing the power ministries to reconcile their conflicting loyalties in a show of force with the Russian government, he persisted in his ultimately futile attempt to convince the republics to sign yet another version of his ever-elusive treaty, even as he wasted time and energy trying to convince Western leaders to bankroll the Soviet economy.[1]

When Gorbachev returned to Moscow on 22 August 1991, he once again failed to capture the mood of the country or to seize the political opportunity to position himself as a champion of reform rather than as an obstacle to genuine democratization and liberalization. He was initially reluctant to order the arrest or even fire some of those who had taken part in the coup or sided with the putschists. And instead of taking to the streets to join in the victory celebrations or going directly to the Russian parliament to congratulate Yeltsin, he made a brief televised statement in which he characterized the defeat of the putsch as a victory for perestroika. He then reaffirmed his seemingly unshakable confidence in the prospects for the union treaty, which he claimed would be signed in the near future.[2] This was followed by an emotional but long-winded account of his four days of house arrest at a hastily convened press conference, where he again took the opportunity to defend the Party. The CPSU, he insisted, contained many genuine democrats, and he would "fight to the end" for the Party's renewal. Defending the October Revolution against those who claimed it was a catastrophe, he asserted, "Socialism is the vital creativity of the masses, this is the model that we have to implement, this is something that Lenin said, that we have to develop the process of democratization."[3] The Soviet leader had been repeating these platitudes endlessly since his arrival in power, and he persisted despite the fact that the public had long since grown weary of them.

Having failed to take advantage of the opportunity to restore some of his lost credibility, Gorbachev met the next day with the leaders of the nine Novo-Ogarevo republics to agree to a new date for signing the draft treaty. Soviet newspapers reported the next day that agreement had been reached only on the vague notion that the treaty should be signed at the earliest possible date. That same day, Gorbachev made his first appearance before the RSFSR Supreme Soviet, an event that would prove a public relations disaster for him and, to a lesser extent, for Yeltsin as well. The Soviet president once again spoke out in defense of the Party, but on this occasion he was brusquely interrupted by Yeltsin and forced to watch as the Russian president signed a decree ordering an investigation into the CPRF's "unconstitutional activities" and suspending its operations on RSFSR territory. Yeltsin then instructed Gorbachev "like a naughty schoolboy" (as *Izvestiia* put it the next day) to read aloud the notes of a Council of Ministers meeting held at the beginning of the coup at which all but two of the ministers present disavowed the Soviet president and his policies. Finally, Gorbachev was forced to rescind three appointments he had made the previous day for defense minister, KGB head, and interior minister (Yeltsin claimed that his appointees had supported the coup), replacing them with candidates who had been vetted first by Yeltsin and then by the other republic leaders at their earlier meeting.

Despite his hopes for a "renewed" Party, Gorbachev was finally persuaded that the CPSU had been thoroughly discredited during the coup and had to be abandoned. Yakovlev, it was later reported, told him that calling for a "renewal" of the Party now was "like offering first aid to a corpse." On 24 August 1991, Gorbachev announced his resignation as CPSU general secretary, and he went on to sign decrees instructing local Soviets to place guards over CPSU property and banning political parties from the armed forces, interior ministry, KGB, and other government agencies. Nevertheless, he refused to resign as a Party member. Once again, Yeltsin trumped him, issuing a decree the next day that asserted RSFSR jurisdiction over all Party assets, including its cash holdings in both rubles and foreign currency, and banning the publication of *Pravda* and other Party papers and journals on RSFSR territory.

Prospects for an early signing of the draft union treaty were further dimmed by the behavior of the leaders of the other union republics. In the aftermath of the coup, a majority of union republics declared independence (see tables 6.1 and 6.2). The Estonian and Latvian parliaments had done so even before the coup collapsed. The RSFSR immediately recognized Estonia's and Latvia's independence, having done so already, as noted earlier, for Lithuania in July 1991. Most Western governments, including Washington, likewise quickly rec- . ognized the independence of the Baltic states. Stung by criticism of his "Chicken Kiev" speech in the United States, Bush apparently did not want to appear excessively pro-Gorbachev and pro-Union by lagging behind in recognizing the Baltic states. Nevertheless, his loyalty to Gorbachev induced him to write the Soviet president in late August to the effect that he would wait briefly for the Soviet government to recognize the independence of the Baltic states before Washington did so. However, Gorbachev failed to move quickly enough. With over thirty states having already done so, Washington formally recognized the independence of Estonia, Latvia, and Lithuania on 2 September. Four days later, the newly established USSR Gossoviet (State Council, see below) followed suit, despite Gorbachev's protests that "secession" had to be validated by the USSR Congress of Peoples' Deputies.[4] Responding to domestic criticism that he had waited too long for the U.S. delay, Bush would remark, "When history is written, no one will remember that we took forty-eight hours more than Iceland or whoever else it is."[5] On 17 September 1991, the Baltic states were admitted into the UN General Assembly.

With the exception of Russia and Kazakhstan, all union republics that had not yet done so declared independence by the end of October. This was true even of republics like Belorussia (which renamed itself Belarus), Uzbekistan, and Turkmenistan, each of which had decidedly pro-unionist electorates and conservative leaders who had tilted toward the putschists during the coup. With support from both moderate nationalists and the "national Communists" led by its chairman, Leonid Kravchuk, the Ukrainian parliament voted for independence on 24 August, although it made its declaration contingent upon endorsement by the referendum that was to be held simultaneously with presidential elections later that year. Georgia, which had declared its independence in April, announced on 6 September that it was breaking all ties with the USSR. Armenia waited to declare independence until 22 September, the day after a referendum in which 94.3 percent voted for independence. The other republics simply declared independence—Belarus on 25 August; Moldova on 27 August; and Azerbaijan, Uzbekistan, and Kyrgyzstan on 31 August. In most cases, independence

Table 6.1. Independence Referendums

Republic	Date	Turnout	Voted Yes
Lithuania	2/9/91	85%	90%
Latvia	3/3/91	87%	74%
Estonia	3/3/91	83%	78%
Georgia	3/31/91	91%	99%
Armenia	9/21/91	95%	94%
Ukraine	12/1/91	84%	90%

Table 6.2. Independence Declarations

Lithuania	11/03/90	(conditional moratorium declared on 30/06/90)
Estonia	30/03/90	(transition)
Latvia	04/05/90	(restoration of pre-1941 constitution)
Armenia	23/08/90	(transition to independence)
Georgia	09/04/91	
Estonia	20/08/91	
Latvia	21/08/91	
Ukraine	24/08/91	(contingent on 12/1/91 referendum)
Belarus	25/08/91	
Moldova	27/08/91	
Azerbaijan	30/08/91	
Kyrgyzstan	31/08/91	
Uzbekistan	31/08/91	
Tajikistan	09/09/91	
Turkmenistan	26/10/91	
Russia	12/12/91	
Kazakhstan	17/12/91	

declarations were accompanied by decrees banning or severely curtailing Communist Party activities on the republic's territory, transferring control of enterprises and organizations that had been under USSR jurisdiction to republic governments, and asserting jurisdiction over export licensing and other foreign trade activities. Fearful of provoking violence by subjecting the armed forces to even greater uncertainty about the chain of command, however, the union republics exempted the military from their unilateral assertions of jurisdiction over Soviet assets.

As with the sovereignty declarations that preceded them, the meaning of the "independence" declarations issued in August and September was sometimes unclear.[6] For Georgia and Moldova—two of the six intransigents—it seemed that full independence and a seat in the General Assembly were being demanded, although Moldova's accession to the Commonwealth of Independent States at the end of the year suggested that it might have settled for some kind of "associated status" with a new union possessing a very weak central government. Armenia, on the other hand, which had been an intransigent before the coup, announced an independence referendum for late September but in the meantime agreed to participate in the newly formed USSR State Council. It also participated in the process of negotiating a new union treaty. On the other hand, republics with pro-union leaderships and electorates—Belorussia, Kyrgyzstan, Turkmenistan, and Uzbekistan—clearly were *not* pushing for immediate international recognition. All four continued to support Gorbachev's efforts to create a new union, and they agreed that the new entity should have its own executive, legislative, and judicial bodies and competencies. Given the international community's unwillingness to recognize at the same time both the new union as well as its individual members as states, the implication was that these four would have been willing to accept something less than full independence. Finally, the significance of the Azerbaijani and Ukrainian independence declarations was the most uncertain of all. Both republics still seemed willing to accede to a new union, although it was unclear whether they would agree to a union that had the legal status of an independent state. Reflecting the uncertainty of the time, an *Izvestiia* correspondent would write that Ukraine's deputies dispersed after their historic decision on 24 August (the vote was 346 to 1) to declare independence pending an endorsement through a referendum "without fully realizing what had been done."[7]

In part, the "independence parade" of August and September was the result of the same kind of bandwagon effects that had contributed to the earlier parade of sovereignties. In many cases, the traditional *nomenklatura* in the republics was scrambling to preserve its position and curry favor with an increasingly empowered public. By championing "independence," political elites in the union republics could show their new electorates that they were aggressively representing their interests while resisting Gorbachev's attempts to define their status and limit their prerogatives. Republic governments were entirely unwilling to accept a status that was lower than that of their former peers, particularly when it came to negotiating over economic policy and the division of powers in a new union.

There was, however, another consideration as well. Even before the coup, Yeltsin had been making important decisions about the terms of the union treaty, economic policy, and control of USSR assets without consulting the other republics' leaders. This tendency became more apparent during the coup when the Russian president issued a series of decrees asserting RSFSR control over the armed forces, the KGB, and interior ministry without regard to the claims of the other republics. Gorbachev, for example, revealed in his speech before the RSFSR Supreme Soviet on 23 August that he and Yeltsin had agreed that the president and prime minister of the new union should both "represent" Russia (presumably meaning citizens of the RSFSR, not necessarily ethnic Russians, although that was left unclear). At the same time, he went on, the vice-president (who presumably would have very limited powers) could be from Central Asia (Gorbachev and Yeltsin reportedly had Nazarbayev in mind for the post). Rather than being reassured by these signs of cooperation between the Russian and Soviet presidents, the leaders of the other union republics were alarmed by what they considered high-handed decisions made unilaterally by Yeltsin and Gorbachev, and they feared that an alliance was forming that might well lead to the re-imposition of Moscow's will on the non-Russian republics, albeit in a new form. They therefore had an even greater incentive to declare independence—doing so, it seemed, would make it impossible for the RSFSR to dominate the non-Russian republics and would give the latter greater leverage in resisting any attempt to create an unbalanced union that favored Russia.

These concerns about Russian bullying reached a high point on 27 August when Yeltsin's press spokesman, Pavel Voshchanov, issued a statement on behalf of Yeltsin that suggested that Russia would consider questioning the validity of its borders with its neighbors if the other union republics refused to participate in a new union:

> The Russian Federation does not question the constitutional right of every state and people to self-determination. However, there is the problem of borders, a problem that can and may remain unsettled only given the existence of relations of alliance codified in an appropriate treaty. In the event that these relations are broken off, the RSFSR reserves the right to raise the question of reviewing its borders.[8]

Nazarbayev responded that if Russia began questioning its borders with its neighbors, there was a "possibility of inter-republican war."[9] Indeed, Voshchanov's statement flatly contradicted the 19 November 1990 RSFSR-Ukraine and the 21 November 1990 RSFSR-Kazakhstan treaties affirming the territorial integrity of the signatory republics—agreements that Yeltsin had strongly endorsed at the time. But Yeltsin and his advisors were alarmed by the independence declarations of the other republics, and the Russian president was increasingly worried that the USSR would fragment. Accordingly, the statement reflected the Russian government's desire to remind the other union republics that pressing for full independence and international recognition could prove costly to all parties. Regardless of whether the Voshchanov statement was approved in advance by Yeltsin, it cost the Russian president support from political elites in the non-Russian republics, particularly Kazakhstan and Ukraine, each of which had large Russian minority populations and was extremely sensitive about the risk of Russian irredentism.

Two days after Voshchanov made his statement, a joint USSR-RSFSR delegation headed by Russian vice president Aleksandr Rutskoi, and Anatolii Sobchak, the pro-democracy mayor of Leningrad (which would formally restore its prerevolutionary name of St. Petersburg in September), left for Ukraine and Kazakhstan on a mission to reassure Kiev and Alma Ata about Russia's commitment to existing borders.[10] After making clear that they did not share the views of the Russian president on the matter (a harbinger of the opposition that Yeltsin would face from some of his erstwhile allies in the coming months), they signed statements reaffirming Russia's intention to build relations with its two largest neighbors on the basis of equality and respect for existing borders.[11]

Gorbachev and the leaders of ten of the former union republics (Georgia, Moldova, and the now internationally recognized Baltic states refused to send representatives) agreed at a joint meeting on 1 September that a transition government should be provided for pending the adoption of the union treaty and a new USSR constitution. Their proposals were presented the next day to the USSR Congress of Peoples' Deputies, which convened for what would prove to be its final session. After voting in favor of the formation of a "Union of Sovereign States (USS)," the Congress approved the formation of a new executive body for the USS to be called the State Council, which would be chaired by Gorbachev and would include the leaders of each republic that wished to participate. The Congress provided for the establishment of an Interrepublic Committee for Operational Economic Management, which would report to the State Council and oversee economic and social policies and the drafting of a treaty on economic relations between the republics. Gorbachev, again apparently with Yeltsin's approval, appointed Ivan Silayev, the RSFSR prime minister, to be its chair, with Yavlinsky and Moscow Deputy Mayor Luzhkov and Gorbachev representative Arkadii Volsky as his deputies. The Congress agreed that a restructured Supreme Soviet would serve as the interim USSR legislature pending the adoption of a new union treaty. It would consist of twenty representatives from each union republic and one from each autonomous republic. On 5 September, the Congress adjourned, never to reconvene. Four days later, Yeltsin formally rescinded his assertion of authority over the power ministries.

When the State Council convened for the first time in early September, the Baltic republics, Georgia, and Moldova again refused to send representatives. Those leaders who did attend agreed that the federal government's first priority should be to adopt a treaty on interrepublic economic relations that would help stabilize the deteriorating economy. A comprehensive treaty defining the political structure for the new union would have to wait until this more pressing matter was attended to. Yavlinsky was charged with drawing up a treaty for a new economic union, which was presented to the State Council for preliminary approval on 22 September 1991. The union was to be open to all the USSR's former republics, including the Baltic states. There would be a central bank under the control of the USSR, a single currency, a floating exchange rate, a common market, pluralism in forms of property, sharing of the USSR's debt obligation among the republics, and the "coordination" of tax and budgetary policy by the federal government.

The draft received the endorsement of the State Council and was then sent to the republics for comments. Predictably, legislators in the union republics had many objections. Ukraine rejected provisions granting the federal government the right to coordinate fiscal policy, while the RSFSR refused to extend the ruble zone to member-states that would not participate in the not-yet-defined political union (thereby suggesting once again that Yeltsin was committed to the preservation of the union). The Central Asian republics, which remained particularly conservative on economic reforms, objected to provisions providing for pluralism in forms of property. Nevertheless, Gorbachev and the leaders of eight of the republics endorsed the "Treaty on the Economic Community of Sovereign States," as it was called, signing it formally on 18 October.[12] Ukraine, Georgia, Moldova, and Azerbaijan refused to participate in the new "Community." Only after Western governments, for reasons discussed below, made clear that any republic that rejected the economic union would receive less aid and investment, did Ukraine and Moldova agree to sign, which they finally did in early November. Azerbaijan's president, Ayaz Mutalibov, announced that his representative would sign in due course.

The formation of the economic union was treated by Gorbachev and defenders of the union as a considerable victory and an important step toward the adoption of a political union. The institutionalization of economic cooperation between the former union republics, he repeatedly told his advisors, was similar to what was under way between the member states of the European Community (EC), which would become the European Union (EU) after the signing of the "Maastricht Treaty" on 7 February 1992.[13] He had regained the political initiative, he was sure, after the political setback in the wake of the coup. As he confidently explained to King Juan Carlos of Spain, Felipe Gonzales, the Spanish prime minister, and President Bush at a dinner during a summit in Madrid on the Palestinian conflict later that month:

> I am going to do everything in my power to preserve the union, a renewed union, with greater rights of sovereignty for the republics and, at the same time, with a strong center to serve the unified economic space and to provide a coordinated foreign policy and a joint system of defense via combined armed forces. This union would keep everything intact that cannot be broken up: energy, transportation, communication, ecology.[14]

In fact, the treaty was, as Ambassador Matlock later put it, "little more than a promise to continue negotiating."[15] It required some two dozen additional agreements for implementation and failed to specify how the federal government would "coordinate" the tax and budgetary policies of the republics, how revenue would be provided to the federal center, how the central bank would control the money supply by restricting the ability of the union republics to issue credits, how federal ministries would share jurisdiction with republic ministries, or how the servicing of the USSR's external debt would be shared.

It was increasingly clear that Yeltsin intended to have the RSFSR go its own way on economic reform. On 23 August, he made good on his threats from before the coup to place all union enterprises and organizations on RSFSR soil, other than those specifically assigned to the USSR by Russian legislation, under the jurisdiction of the Russian government. He also established a "Committee for Protecting the Economic Interests of the RSFSR," and instructed the Council of Ministers, in conjunction with the RSFSR central bank, to prepare proposals by 1 October on a host of financial matters, including taxation of foreign currency earnings and the RSFSR's share of both the USSR's external debt and foreign obligations to the USSR. The Council of Ministers was charged with submitting proposals by the end of the year on the licensing of foreign investment in all mining and commercial fishing enterprises on RSFSR territory and with creating a customs regime by 1 October. While the Council of Ministers was instructed to work with the other union republics to coordinate its proposals, no mention was made of coordination with USSR officials.

Yeltsin left Moscow on 18 September for three weeks, paying a brief visit to the Caucasus to try to broker a settlement between the Armenians and Azeris over Karabakh and then flying for an extended vacation to the resort town of Sochi on Russia's Black Sea coast. His prolonged absence, which reportedly was made in part on the advice of his doctors, contributed to a rapid split in the political coalition that had helped Yeltsin survive the showdown with conservatives in the Russian parliament on 28 March as well as the attempted coup. One faction, led by Oleg Lobov, first deputy RSFSR prime minister, and Yurii Petrov, head of the RSFSR presidential administration, was committed to the preservation of the union and opposed to rapid and radical economic reform. Lobov and Petrov were supported by the RSFSR's prime minister, Ivan Silayev, by many of the RSFSR's ministers of branch industries and financial affairs, by a number of prominent economists, including Yavlinsky, and by Yeltsin's vice president, Aleksandr Rutskoi. The other faction was led by Gennadii Burbulis, a senior advisor to the Russian president who was particularly close to Yeltsin at the time. Burbulis believed that the RSFSR had to move decisively on economic reform and that it should do so on its own, a position supported by many heads of Russia's noneconomic ministries, particularly the pro-Western minister of foreign affairs, Andrei Kozyrev, as well as Sergei Shakhrai, Yeltsin's legal advisor, and two as yet little-known economists who would play a critical role in Russian economic policy in the coming years, Yegor Gaidar and Aleksandr Shokhin. Because the members of this radical faction were mostly young, they were referred to in the Russian press as "the Young Turks."

Yeltsin, the Young Turks were convinced, had only a brief window to launch a program of radical economic reform. The Russian economy was already in crisis, and they feared that, like Gorbachev before him, Yeltsin would quickly lose popular support if he failed to move immediately on the economy. They also believed that the inevitable pain of rapid marketization could be eased if Russia were to charge world prices for oil, gas, and other commodities that it was selling to the other republics. Burbulis was particularly insistent that radical economic reform required that the RSFSR make a clean break with the union.[16] Not only would Russia then be in a position to benefit from more "normal" economic relations and trade at world prices with other republics, but independence would mean that union authorities would not be able to thwart Russia's economic reform program. Nor would the RSFSR need to coordinate these reforms with the other union republics that were still reluctant to embrace marketization. As a result, Burbulis came to the conclusion that the USSR should be dissolved.[17]

It has been suggested that Yeltsin came to share Burbulis's position by September or even earlier, and that his subsequent participation in the negotiations over a new union was disingenuous. Others have argued that Yeltsin's actions during the months leading to the USSR's final dissolution were driven principally by self-interest and a desire to humiliate Gorbachev.[18] As the British political scientist Archie Brown put it, Yeltsin's "pursuit of personal power took precedence over construction of a new federation or confederation."[19]

Yeltsin has denied both these assertions. In his 1994 memoirs, he recalls that both Burbulis and Silayev visited him in Sochi and that he was struck by the contrast between "the cautious compromising older Silayev" and the "young Burbulis, who was full of vitality and energy."[20] It was only then, he claims, that he decided in favor of Burbulis's program of radical economic reform. He does not, however, suggest that he decided to press for full independence or the dissolution of the union at that time. On the contrary, he asserts in his memoirs that he continued to negotiate in good faith over a new union treaty after the coup, and only when it became clear that other republics—above all Ukraine—were no longer willing to accept the sort of union being advocated by Gorbachev did he change his mind.[21]

While it is impossible to know with certainty what Yeltsin believed or when he believed it, there is substantial corroborating evidence to support his contention that he did not deliberately set about destroying the union in the months between the coup and December 1991, when the final decisions on the dissolution were made. As we shall see, Yeltsin was still publicly defending the need for a "union state" with a unified military and a single foreign policy directed by a head of state at least until 4 November 1991. Gorbachev's press secretary at the time, Andrei Grachev, who is otherwise extremely critical of Yeltsin, would later write, "Yeltsin's statements on the single army for the future state and the need to maintain a central structure for foreign affairs confirm that only one month before the encounter in Belovezhskaya Forest, he had no deliberate intention of destroying the structures of the union or refusing to sign the new union treaty.[22] Nor did Yeltsin at any point publicly advocate a declaration of independence by the RSFSR, despite the fact that independence declarations had been issued by the majority of republics still engaged in the Novo-Ogarevo process. Had he been eager to bring about the dissolution of the USSR, it is difficult to see why he would not have asked the RSFSR legislature to follow the lead of other republics and declare independence.

Despite what appears to be an instinctive preference for the preservation of some kind of union, albeit without the Baltic republics as members, Yeltsin's actions in the coming months were also influenced by economic considerations. The Russian president was not an economist, and he was at least as ignorant as Gorbachev about the mechanics of market economies. He was therefore in no position to assess the validity of the arguments of the pro-unionists or the Young

Turks on economic grounds. But he had relentlessly criticized Gorbachev for being too conservative and irresolute on marketization, and he was determined not to repeat what he perceived to be Gorbachev's mistakes on the economy. His decision in Sochi to side with the Young Turks and to press for a program of radical and rapid marketization was thus understandable, and it does not suggest that he anticipated or wanted a dissolution of the union. But, whether he realized it or not, moving ahead decisively with radical economic reform made agreement on a renewed union much more difficult. Radical economic reform meant that the RSFSR would have to press for control of the USSR's branch ministries, of monetary and credit emissions, and of production facilities on its territory, and also to assert its right to liberalize prices. No longer could Gosplan be allowed to issue state orders to producers; no longer could Soviet central planners set prices for most goods and services; no longer could the Soviet central bank control the money supply or make good on the debts incurred by other republics; no longer could Gorbachev or Soviet bureaucrats be allowed to block reforms; and no longer could Russia, which would have to try to keep its own fiscal house in order, cover the Soviet government's budget deficits. Above all, Yeltsin could not allow his reform program to be held hostage to negotiations over the union treaty or to the policy preferences of the other republics, most of which remained vigorously opposed to marketization—of those still involved in the Novo-Ogarevo process, only Armenia appeared as committed to marketization as Russia.

The first indication that Yeltsin had decided in favor of the Young Turks on economic policy was the resignation of Silayev as Russian prime minister on 27 September (Silayev remained head of the unionwide Interrepublic Economic Council). Yeltsin returned to Moscow from vacation on 10 October and attended a State Council meeting the next day at which Yavlinsky's proposed economic treaty was approved. (It would prove to be the last State Council meeting attended by Ukraine's leader, Leonid Kravchuk). Four days later, the RSFSR Supreme Soviet adopted a law that rendered the decisions of any interrepublic agency (e.g., the State Council) nonbinding on RSFSR territory. Yeltsin followed with a decree stipulating that Gosplan, which was continuing to issue state orders for a substantial portion of the USSR's economic output, no longer had any legal authority on RSFSR territory.

Yeltsin presented his program for a rapid marketization of the Russian economy to the RSFSR Congress of Peoples' Deputies on 28 October. After outlining the program's substance, he asked for emergency powers to rule by decree for one year, predicting that if his plan were adhered to, the Russian economy would begin to improve within six months. Doubtless he believed this prediction, or at least hoped for a reasonably rapid recovery. Certainly he could not have anticipated that Russia was in for years of declining growth, and accordingly the excessive optimism he shared with many of his advisors about the benefits of rapid marketization and the prospects for a rapid economic recovery contributed to his willingness to embrace economic "shock therapy." Yeltsin indicated that Russia would begin to charge world prices for exports to other republics. The Congress approved both the reform program and his request for emergency powers. It also elected Khasbulatov as chairman of the Presidium of the Supreme Soviet (he had been acting chair since the previous session in July, when he had been unable to secure sufficient votes). While the media portrayed this as a victory for Yeltsin, Khasbulatov, a professional economist who would soon be Yeltsin's principal adversary in the RSFSR legislature, was already expressing his opposition to Gaidar's reform program.

The State Council convened once again on 4 November. It was agreed that thirty-six USSR ministries would be abolished on 15 November—all that would remain of the center thereafter would be the Soviet president and the ministries of defense, foreign affairs, interior, electric power, railroads, nuclear power, and civil aviation. An Interstate Economic Committee, which was to be the executive body of the Council of the Heads of Government in the new Economic Union with a staff of only 1,500, would carry out many of the functions previously fulfilled by the far larger USSR branch ministries. Yeltsin used the opportunity to reaffirm his commitment to the union and his opposition to a separate military for Russia.[23] He was still of the opinion that a union government would be established that would control a unionwide military, including the USSR's nuclear forces, as well as those ministries under USSR jurisdiction as envisaged in the State Council agreement. Indeed, as noted earlier, he specifically referred to the new union as a "state" in a press conference after the meeting: "Since we are trying, despite all difficulties, to create a new state, the Union of Sovereign States, it unquestionably should have a unified army, unified armed forces."[24] The implication was that the new union would retain the USSR's seat at the UN, would have at least some kind of central executive organs, and would conduct a collective military and foreign policy with a directly elected president as chief executive. Yeltsin reassured the new foreign minister, Boris Pankin, that the RSFSR was not insisting on the dissolution of the Soviet foreign ministry or seeking to establish its own diplomatic missions abroad.[25] All that Russia would insist on, he asserted, was representation in the USSR's foreign missions. And for the time being, the RSFSR would not try to establish official diplomatic relations with other states.[26]

By the time the State Council reconvened at Novo-Ogarevo on 14 November in what would prove a dramatic and contentious meeting, Yeltsin seems to have changed his mind. He now objected to the use of the term "union state," preferring instead "union of states."[27] Gorbachev and Nazarbayev, on the other hand, continued to argue in favor of the term "confederated state." In another blow to Gorbachev, Ukraine refused to send a representative to the meeting, unlike the previous session on 4 November when the Ukrainian prime minister, Vitaly Fokin, had been present. In the ten days between the two meetings, the Ukrainian parliament had decided that neither its chairman nor the prime minister should attend meetings of union bodies at least until after the referendum.

Gorbachev recalls in his memoirs that three different options were considered at the meeting: a union of sovereign states with no suprastate "state structures" (i.e., the union would not have its own executive, legislative, and judicial organs); a union *with* a supranational state structure that would be "either federal or confederal" (what, exactly, was meant by those imprecise terms was never made clear, however, and the participants may well have had very different understandings of their meaning); and a union "that carried out a number of state functions, albeit without the status of a state and without a specific name."[28]

The meeting, which was attended by two legal experts, Vladimir Kudryavtsev, head of the Institute of State of Law, and Veniamin Yakovlev, a university professor and member of the USSR Academy of Sciences, was witness to an extended discussion of the meaning of the terms "union" and "federation."[29] The results of the discussion were apparently less than conclusive—the terms "union," "commonwealth," "federation," and "confederation" were not used any more consistently by the participants either during the meeting or after.[30] Shushkevich, for example, stated at one point, "Let's start with a confederation, and then later on move to a federation," as if those terms fully captured the extraordinary complexity and variety in the separation of powers in federal states, or as if there was a clear difference in meaning between the terms "federation" and "confederation."[31] While Gorbachev would resist describing the union as a confederation during the meeting, he would reportedly tell his aides several days later, "You see, I am willing to build any kind of union—federal, confederal, whatever—but not destroy it."[32] That he would object to the phrase "confederative state" with considerable determination during the meeting but then later indicate that he would happily create "any kind of union" testifies less to his inconsistency than to the extent of the semantic confusion prevailing at the time, as well as the tendency of the participants to argue over abstractions. Indeed, there was similar contentious debate, and confusion, over whether the union would be a "subject of international law."[33] Finally, there was a more politically meaningful disagreement over whether the new union would have its own constitution, with Yeltsin arguing that the union treaty should serve as the "basic law," and Gorbachev and Nazarbayev holding out for a separate constitution.

Gorbachev was deeply angered by what he took to be Yeltsin's renewed obstructionism at the meeting. At one point, he acidly asked his colleagues: "If there are no effective state structures, what good are a president and a parliament? If that's your decision, I'm prepared to resign."[34] Yeltsin, it seems, had by then decided that a final settlement should await the outcome of the Ukrainian referendum scheduled for 1 December.[35] Despite the sharp language and four hours of heated debate, a compromise was finally worked out whereby the union would be described as a "confederative state" but without a constitution—the "basic law" of the new entity would be the union treaty itself. In a press conference after the meeting, Yeltsin predicted that the union would survive: "It is difficult to say how many states will join in the union, but I am firmly convinced that there will be a union."[36] And he again referred to the new union as a "state"—it would be, he asserted, "a union of sovereign states—a confederative state, fulfilling the functions delineated by the state participants in the treaty."[37] Nazarbayev likewise confidently asserted that "a union of sovereign states that are independent and equal" was being created, but he made clear that the powers of the new union had yet to be worked out: "The future will show what this union will be like in the final analysis—confederal or something else."[38]

Yeltsin continued to take steps to wrest full control of the Russian economy from the union government. On 6 November, he announced the formation of a new government, naming himself prime minister. Burbulis was appointed deputy prime minister, Gaidar first deputy prime minister for the economy, and Shokhin first deputy prime minister for social policy. He followed this up on 15–17 November with ten decrees that, inter alia, placed the central bank under RSFSR jurisdiction, allowed the value of the ruble to float, and asserted control of all licenses for oil, gas, gold, and diamonds produced in the RSFSR.[39]

Meanwhile, Russia's refusal to contribute its allotted share of revenue to the USSR treasury was starving the union government of resources. On 29 November, Viktor Gerashchenko, chairman of the USSR State Bank, announced that the union treasury had enough money to last for two more days. Yeltsin and Gorbachev met the next day to address the central state's fiscal crisis, whereupon Yeltsin announced that the RSFSR would provide the USSR with an emergency allocation of 92 billion rubles in order to avert bankruptcy and a default on the USSR's foreign debt obligations. The appropriation was a temporary measure that was not expected to cover the center's expenditures for more than a few weeks. The episode resulted in another setback for the center when the RSFSR, which had already been appointing its own representatives to Soviet embassies abroad and had even appointed some "dual" RSFSR/USSR ambassadors, asserted financial control over the Soviet Union's foreign missions.

The text of the draft treaty (the fifth to be published) that provided for the establishment of a new "union state" as agreed to in principle on 14 November was published on 26 November.[40] It provided for a "Union of Sovereign States" (USS) that would be a "sovereign state, a subject of international law, and the legal successor of the Union of Soviet Socialist Republics." Signatory states would agree to share the USSR's foreign debts. The USS would retain the Soviet seat on the UN Security Council, but it would not have its own constitution—the treaty and the Declaration of Human Rights ratified by the last Congress of Peoples' Deputies in September would be the USS's foundational documents. The treaty would be open for signing by the USSR's former union republics only, which meant that the autonomies would not be constituent members. The new union would have its own president elected by "the citizens of the union" (whether directly or indirectly would be determined by a future electoral law) and a vice president; a bicameral legislature; a government headed by a prime minister; a constitutional court, supreme court and subsidiary courts, and a court of arbitration; a procuracy; and a common currency. The Interrepublic Economic Committee of the Economic Union would become a government "macroministry" responsible for coordinating economic policy. The acceding states would have the right to form their own militias, the size and function of which was left for a future interstate agreement, but there would be a "unified armed forces and centralized command of strategic forces, including nuclear missiles."

Gorbachev's hopes for a successful resolution of the Novo-Ogarevo process had soared after the 14 November meeting of the State Council and its endorsement of the draft treaty, however weak the union government might be under the terms of that treaty. As he put it in his memoirs, "[T]here was one more river to cross in this three year marathon: the 25 November session of the State Council."[41] The meeting, he hoped and expected, would witness a formal signing ceremony that would help with parliamentary ratification and make it difficult for Yeltsin or others to insist on still more changes. Five days before the meeting, in a gesture of goodwill to his Novo-Ogarevo negotiating partners, he announced that Shevardnadze would return to his former position as Soviet foreign minister, apparently in the belief that the former CPSU first secretary in Georgia would be an effective interlocutor with Yeltsin and the other union republic leaders.[42]

Once again Gorbachev's hopes would be bitterly disappointed. In what he later described as a "perfidious move," Yeltsin announced at the meeting that he would not, in fact, sign the treaty, despite his apparent commitment to do so at the tumultuous 14 November session. And he again expressed his objection to the term "union state" and reiterated that signing the treaty should await the results of the Ukrainian referendum, after which Kiev could participate in negotiations over its terms and be an original signatory. Yeltsin claimed that the RSFSR Supreme Soviet was opposed to some of the text's key provisions, and he accordingly felt obliged to wait for the Russian legislature to endorse it before signing it himself. In fact, this latter justification for his refusal appears to have been disingenuous—heads of state typically initial treaties pending ratification by legislatures. The real reason behind his obduracy, it seems, was his unwillingness to commit to a union without Ukraine. Yeltsin's call for a postponement was supported by Stanislav Shushkevich, who had become the leader of Belarus after the coup, and by Islam Karimov, the leader of Uzbekistan.

Gorbachev was furious. A large number of reporters had gathered downstairs at the Novo-Ogarevo residence expecting to witness a "historic" signing ceremony and to attend a press conference with the signatories. After arguing to no avail that the treaty should be signed immediately because Ukraine's voters should understand that a new Union would be established regardless of the outcome of their referendum, Gorbachev angrily asserted: "When you set up your shantytown instead of a united state, you will put your people through torture. We are strangling in shit as it is. . . . If you reject the confederated state version, then you can just go on without me."[43] He then walked out.

Yeltsin and Shushkevich would later claim that they were shocked by Gorbachev's outburst. "We were left alone in the room," Yeltsin recalled, "and precisely then, as a heavy oppressive silence hung over the room, we suddenly realized that it was over. We were meeting here for the last time. The Novo-Ogarevo stage had drawn to a close."[44] Several months later, Shushkevich would tell Ambassador Matlock that he and Yeltsin had been negotiating in good faith and believed that the negotiations were making genuine progress, but that Gorbachev had simply refused to appreciate their need to consider the political consequences of signing the treaty in their respective republics.

Despite Gorbachev's theatrical departure, the other participants in the meeting felt that some kind of statement had to be given to the reporters waiting downstairs. They therefore appointed Yeltsin and Shushkevich to find Gorbachev and persuade him to sign some kind of compromise statement. At the urging of Yeltsin and Shushkevich, the Soviet president agreed to return to the meeting, and a compromise was worked out whereby the assembled leaders agreed to submit the treaty to their legislatures for approval but without signing it first themselves. They also agreed to a joint statement indicating that they expected a formal signing by the end of the year. They were, however, unwilling even to present the joint statement to the press collectively, which meant that Gorbachev had to do so, and to answer reporters' questions, alone. In doing so, he attempted to characterize the session as a success, and he took the opportunity to announce a date for the anticipated signing—20 December 1991. But the refusal of the leaders of the republic to initial the treaty or to participate in a joint press conference made it perfectly clear that the meeting had gone badly.

With Gorbachev's failure to obtain a public expression of support for the treaty from the State Council on 25 November, the main front of the intensifying drama became Ukraine and its impending referendum and presidential elections. Antiunion mobilization had come relatively late to Ukraine—until late 1989, the republic had been governed by the Brezhnev-era Party first secretary, Vladimir Sheherbitsky, who did his best to resist glasnost and political and economic reforms in his republic. It was not until 8 September 1989 that a Ukrainian popular front, Rukh (which means "Movement" in Ukrainian) held its first congress. Some two weeks later, Sheherbitsky was forced to leave office after Gorbachev flew to Kiev to oversee his removal personally. Nationalist mobilization proceeded rapidly in the republic thereafter, and Rukh and its allies won approximately one-third of the seats in the republic's parliamentary elections in the spring. On 6 July 1990, the new legislature passed a sovereignty declaration with almost no dissenting votes, and shortly thereafter Leonid Kravchuk, a former CPU Central Committee secretary for ideology, was elected parliamentary chair.

Kravchuk was initially regarded as an able defender of the Party's prerogatives and a relative conservative by the rapidly changing standards of the time, particularly after the hard-line policies embraced by the central leadership in Moscow during Gorbachev's "turn to the right" were efficiently implemented in the republic. Unexpectedly, however, the leadership's ban on demonstrations, restrictions on the opposition's access to television and radio, and the arrest of leading nationalist Stepan Khmara provoked a counterreaction from below. In October, mass demonstrations, which were led for the most part by students, took place in Kiev, including a protest on 16 October that was attended by 150,000 people. The demonstrations began to draw support from workers, with strikes breaking out around the republic, which prompted the resignation of the Ukrainian prime minister.

At that moment Kravchuk changed course and committed unequivocally to a political program stressing "sovereignty" for his republic. As Alexander Motyl and Bohdan Krawchenko have noted, championing sovereignty was "the only position, as he no doubt realized, that permitted him to retain power, keep the conservatives and Gorbachev at bay, and continue to court the nationalists."[45] Kravchuk began to cooperate with Rukh, emphasizing that Ukrainian citizenship should be defined in civic, not ethnic, terms, thereby rejecting the xenophobic anti-Semitism and intolerance that had traditionally been associated with Ukrainian nationalism.[46] Kravchuk's strategy was soon rewarded by a spectacular rise in approval ratings—whereas in November 1990 he had not made it onto a list of the top twenty most popular politicians in the republic, by June 1991 polls indicated he was the most popular choice for Ukrainian president with support from 54 percent of respondents.[47]

As described earlier, the Ukrainian parliament had declared independence on 24 August, but it made independence contingent upon endorsement in a referendum, which was eventually scheduled for 1 December 1991. In late October, the Ukrainian parliament voted to create an independent defense force 400,000–450,000 strong, as well as a national guard of 30,000. A month later, however, Kravchuk announced that the Ukrainian army would be significantly smaller—around 90,000. He also indicated that an agreement had been reached that, although each republic could have its own militia, there would be a collective defense force under the joint control of the republics and the union government. Kravchuk's announcements seemed to suggest that, once the referendum had been approved (and polls indicated it would pass by a wide margin), he would support the formation of some kind of central authority, albeit one with limited powers.

In fact, the political significance of the referendum was entirely unclear. After a brief preamble referring to "the mortal danger" presented by the attempted coup, the referendum asked, "Do you support the declaration of independence of Ukraine?" Ukraine's voters were not, in other words, being asked bluntly if they favored secession from the union. As noted earlier, most of the other republics had already declared independence but were still involved in the Novo-Ogarevo process. It was therefore perfectly possible for a Ukrainian voter to be in favor of both the independence declaration and Ukrainian participation in some kind of union. The ambiguous significance of the referendum was nicely captured by a telephone exchange several days later between Gorbachev, who was convinced that the Ukrainian electorate preferred remaining within the union but was being led astray by an irresponsible Ukrainian leadership, and Kravchuk.[48] As Gorbachev later recalled:

> I asked Kravchuk: You've heard what I've said about independence. Why have you decided to interpret it as meaning you have to leave the union? Other republics declared their independence before you did and are still taking part in the building of a new union.

> There is nothing strange about the fact that the majority of the Ukrainian
> population voted for independence. Who would have wanted to vote against it?
> Last March, however, roughly as many people said they were in favor of pre-
> serving the union with Ukraine's participation. That means that if the question
> had been worded differently, "independence outside of or inside the union," the
> results would have been different.[49]

Indeed, lack of clarity about the meaning of the referendum, agreement
from Ukrainian conservatives not to oppose it, virtually universal media support,
and Kravchuk's promises of huge economic benefits from a "yes" vote combined to produce overwhelming support for the independence declaration on 1
December.[50] As Gorbachev had pointed out, 70 percent of the Ukrainian electorate had voted in favor of the union in March, but now 90.3 percent approved a
declaration of independence, with turnout at 84.1 percent. A majority even voted
"yes" in Crimea, which was heavily populated with ethnic Russians, as did other
predominately Russian regions in the eastern part of the country.[51] In the presidential election, Kravchuk received 61.6 percent of the vote, thereby avoiding a
runoff and handily beating several opponents, including Vyacheslav Chornovyl,
a well-known dissident and the candidate of Rukh, who received only 23.3 percent of the vote. Notably, Chornovyl had been considerably more assertive
about Ukrainian independence than Kravchuk.

When the returns were reported on 3 December, Yeltsin immediately announced that the "Russian leadership" recognized Ukraine's independence.
Canada, with its large Ukrainian diaspora, and Poland indicated they would
likely do so as well. The United States, however, would prove more cautious.

In fact, while the Western position on recognition of the independence of
the Baltic republics had changed immediately after the failure of the August
coup, the independence declarations of the other republics had been effectively
ignored by foreign governments, again reflecting the confusion over their meaning and significance. Western governments, fearful of the potential for violence
that might accompany a further fragmentation of the USSR, continued to make
clear that they still very much preferred that the union remain intact and that
Gorbachev's effort to create a "renewed" union succeed. As the vice-president
of the European Community (soon to become the European Union) put it in a
statement during a trip to Moscow in early October, "The West would like to see
the advent in the USSR of a real political structure that would define the framework for economic reform. We feel that a union will provide such a framework."[52] Similarly, the German foreign minister, Hans-Dietrich Genscher,
whose visits to Ukraine and Central Asia after the coup without passing through
Moscow were interpreted by Gorbachev as a subtle challenge to his authority
and the integrity of the union, tried to reassure Gorbachev in Moscow later that
month: "In Kiev, I persuaded them not to turn back. We in the European Community are trying to make one market out of twelve, and the same goes for our
currencies."[53] Michel Camdessus, head of the International Monetary Fund,
made it clear that the union, not the individual republics, would be afforded as-

sociate membership in IMF, while Ukraine and Moldova were pressured by Western officials to accede to the Treaty on Economic Union. As the Soviet foreign minister from late August until mid-November would later put it, "I am quite certain that right up to the moment when the thunderclap sounded from Belovezhskaia Pusha, the West continued to support Gorbachev: all its bets were on him and on the renewed democratic Union. . . . Western leaders in all our diplomatic contacts made no bones about their wish to see the Soviet Union continue."[54]

Nevertheless, as evidence mounted in the fall of 1991 that the Soviet Union was on the brink of collapse, President Bush found himself under increasing political pressure at home to hedge his bets on Gorbachev and the union, despite his personal loyalty to the former. With a presidential election approaching in 1992, he was being urged by his political advisors, mindful of the political costs of the Chicken Kiev speech, to make a gesture to Ukraine on the eve of its referendum. Accordingly, on 28 November Bush informed a delegation of visiting Ukrainian-Americans that the United States would recognize Ukraine "expeditiously" if the republic decided to secede after the referendum, a statement that was leaked to the press the next day.[55] Already beleaguered, Gorbachev felt betrayed by Bush's statement, and he expressed his surprise and disappointment in a conversation with the American president on 30 November, warning that Ukrainian independence would "bring matters to a catastrophe for the union, for the Ukraine itself and for Russia, Europe, and the world." Indeed, many of Bush's foreign policy advisors felt that his 27 November statement had been a mistake because it established a dangerous precedent of American support for unilateral secession.[56] Whereas the annexation of the Baltic states had been treated as illegal by Washington from the beginning, the United States had never challenged Soviet claims to Ukraine. Affording Ukraine diplomatic recognition before the Soviet government did so would be tantamount to recognition of unilateral secession, a major break with traditional U.S. policy. As a result, despite Bush's leaked statement of 28 November, Washington did not offer to recognize Ukraine after the referendum but instead waited to see how events would unfold.

As noted earlier, when Gorbachev telephoned his congratulations to Kravchuk, he argued that the vote meant that the republic was now free to enter the new union voluntarily, and he angrily questioned Kravchuk's interpretation of the results as necessarily entailing full separation from the union. Kravchuk, however, made it perfectly clear that he interpreted the results as an endorsement of precisely that. He went on to issue a public statement asserting that, rather than a new union, the four republics with nuclear weapons on their territory—Russia, Ukraine, Belarus, and Kazakhstan—should form a group to control the USSR's nuclear arsenal and supervise the destruction of its nuclear weapons. He made no mention of the union treaty or the need for union central executive organs, a legislature, a judiciary, or a post of union president for Gorbachev. He indicated that while Ukraine would not demand a right to control unilaterally any of the USSR's nuclear weapons or even to participate in the decision to use them, it would insist on a launching veto.

Kravchuk was sworn in as Ukraine's president on 5 December. In his acceptance speech, he stated that the main goal of his presidency would be to strengthen Ukraine's statehood, a theme that he would repeat incessantly in the coming years. He asserted that Ukraine would defend the borders it had inherited from its Soviet past. Then, in his first press conference as president, Kravchuk announced that he would refuse to sign any treaty that provided for a central government. That same day, Ukraine's parliament voted to nullify the 1922 Union Treaty and "all subsequent constitutional acts of the USSR."[57] A day later, it passed a resolution against joining any union that compromised Ukraine's independence.

The referendum results, Kravchuk's interpretation of them, and the parliamentary resolutions were decisive setbacks for the Novo-Ogarevo process—the Soviet state, it was clear, was in extremis. Its financial woes, despite the emergency appropriation from the RSFSR, were acute and the Soviet economy appeared headed for a meltdown. To cover the center's cash obligations, the central bank was printing money, which meant that inflation was accelerating and the exchange rate of the ruble was falling rapidly on the black market. In early December, Vneshekonombank was forced to lower the tourist rate for rubles from 47 to 90 rubles to the dollar. It informed Western banks several days later that it would have to halt payments on the principal for all loans made before 1 January 1991.[58] Tellingly, no effort was being made to prepare a budget for the USSR for the coming fiscal year.[59]

Gorbachev made a television appearance on 3 December and issued a grim warning about the consequences of dissolution of the union. The next day, he revealed that the Moscow mayor's office had told him that the city was not receiving adequate supplies of meat, milk, butter, and other goods because other republics were not fulfilling their contractual obligations to the city and that a food crisis was imminent. He issued an appeal to Ukraine, Belorussia, Kazakhstan, and Moldova, all important suppliers of agricultural products to Moscow, to deliver additional food to the city, warning that reserves of meat, butter, and sugar would last but a few days. The reports of dwindling food stocks served to aggravate already serious shortages by inducing more hoarding, which was already under way because of plans for full price liberalization by the RSFSR government scheduled for 16 December, a move that many feared would trigger a popular revolt.

With the crisis atmosphere in Moscow deepening, rumors began to spread of a possible military coup, with Rutskoi in particular identified as the most likely leader of a military revolt. As a former air force general, Rutskoi had close ties to managers of defense industries and the uniformed military, and he had become increasingly outspoken in his opposition to the Russian government's economic reform plans. In late October, he had threatened to resign if the Russian government proceeded with its shock therapy program, and on a trip to the Urals in late November he derisively referred to the Young Turks as "young boys in pink shorts, red shirts, and yellow boots."[60] He repeatedly expressed his support for the preservation of the union, a unified defense, and a common economic space.

There was also growing concern in Russia about the consequences of Ukrainian independence. Russians have strong emotional ties to Ukraine, the homeland of Kievian Rus' to which Russians trace their origins as a people. Most Russians refused to believe that their "little brothers," the Slavic Ukrainians (and especially those in the more russified eastern part of the republic), would want to separate from their "elder brothers" the way the Baltic peoples had. There was also the question of Crimea, which had been given by Khrushchev as a "birthday gift" to Ukraine in 1954 on the 300th anniversary of the union of Ukraine and Russia, and whose population of 2.4 million was 67 percent Russian and only 25.8 percent Ukrainian in 1989. Many Russians believed that Crimea, and indeed other parts of eastern Ukraine, properly belonged to Russia, and there were fears that Ukrainian independence might mean war between Moscow and Kiev. Nor did many Russians wish to be part of a union with the Central Asian republics and Belarus but without Ukraine. Many Russians were convinced that Russia had been subsidizing the Central Asian economies and would continue to do so in a new union, while others worried that the higher birthrates of the Central Asians would mean that the "burden" of subsidizing Central Asia would increase and even that Orthodox Slavs would eventually be outnumbered by the Turkic-speaking Muslims of Central Asia. There were other practical concerns as well. Russian economists feared that the introduction of a separate Ukrainian currency would flood Russia with rubles, which would lead to hyperinflation. A failure to coordinate price liberalization might cause goods to pour into republics that liberalized first, draining those republics that had not liberalized consumer products, which might provoke increased popular enmity and even lead to war.

In view of these concerns, Yeltsin held a meeting with Gorbachev on 5 December to discuss the implications of the Ukrainian referendum. Once again, Gorbachev insisted that, despite the evidence, Ukraine could yet be persuaded to join the proposed union. Yeltsin clearly disagreed, and after the meeting the Russian president revealed that Kravchuk would be joining him and Shushkevich in Belarus on 8 December. The meeting had been scheduled several weeks earlier to serve as the forum for signing an economic agreement between Russia and Belorussia. When Yeltsin announced that Kravchuk would also attend, the Soviet press began speculating about a "Slavic Summit" at which the three leaders, whose republics made up 80 percent of the USSR's territory, had three-quarters of its population, and produced three-quarters of its goods and services, would sign a political treaty that would mean the USSR's dissolution.

Shortly before leaving for Minsk on 7 December, Yeltsin gave further fuel to these speculations by informing the press that the old idea that the republics would delegate authority to a new union government was no longer viable: "Today, we see the failure of the idea of a half-federation, half-confederation, that would implicitly bind each state under a system of dual power."[61] Kravchuk, meanwhile, made clear that he would agree to nothing that provided for a union state. Upon his arrival in Minsk, he informed the press: "You can persuade Kravchuk, but you cannot persuade the Ukrainian people. The old Soviet Union is doomed."[62]

Concerned that Gorbachev might order their arrest by Soviet security forces, Yeltsin, Kravchuk, and Shushkevich decided not to hold their meeting in Minsk, as the press had expected, but at a lodge in a hunting preserve several miles north of Brest known as Belovezhskaia Pushcha. The three leaders would later insist that no agreement had been worked out before the meeting.[63] As Burbulis explained, "We came to Minsk without a text and without any carefully weighed idea of a commonwealth. It was born right there."[64] Yeltsin would recall that the atmosphere at the meeting had been extremely tense. A number of different variants of a treaty of union were discussed, but Kravchuk remained adamant that nothing with a "center" was acceptable and that a new association could have none of the attributes of a sovereign state. He also refused to use Gorbachev's draft treaty as a basis for discussion. Kravchuk would later recall: "I made it very clear at that time: Ukraine will never take part [in a new union]. And that was the decisive factor in the dissolution of the Union."[65] Only then did the three leaders turn to several draft agreements that, according to Yeltsin, had been "labored over" earlier by Burbulis, Shakhrai, and Ilyushin (he does not reveal, however, when these "labors" had begun).[66]

The result was a dramatic agreement that effectively brought the seventy-four-year history of the USSR to an end. Entitled "Agreement on the Creation of a Commonwealth (*Sodruzhestvo*) of Independent States (CIS)," the text unequivocally stated that the USSR no longer had legal writ on the territory of the three signatories: "From the moment this Agreement is signed, the norms of third states, including the former USSR, may not be applied on the territory of the states signing the Agreement." The new Commonwealth would be open to all former republics as well as to other states that shared the goals and principles of the agreement.[67] A separate statement explained that the agreement was necessary because "talks on the drafting of a new union treaty have reached an impasse and that the objective process of the secession of republics from the USSR and the formation of independent states has become a real fact." It blamed the "shortsighted" policies of the center for the political and economic crisis and asserted that there was an urgent need for radical political and economic reform.[68]

The attempt to form a union with a separate state structure and the status of an independent state under international law was over—there would be no central executive organs, legislature, judiciary, or procuracy. Each member state would have the right to withdraw from the Commonwealth merely with twelve months' notice. The Commonwealth would have neither independent taxing authority nor the right to declare war. "Common coordinating bodies," with headquarters in Minsk, would be established to coordinate foreign policy and promote cooperation in the formation and development of a common economic space and customs policy, transportation and communications, environmental protection, migration, and crime prevention. The signatory states would assume the USSR's international treaty obligations, accept their current borders, and respect each other's territorial integrity, and they would maintain open borders with full freedom of movement for their citizens. A common military-strategic space would be maintained under a joint command, and there would be unified joint control of nuclear weapons (it was later explained that this meant that all three parties would have a veto over launching any nuclear weapons). Just how all of this "cooperation" and "coordination" would be effected, however, was not specified. Nor were enforcement mechanisms provided for. The only mention of funding was a provision specifying that the parties to the agreement "guaranteed" that there would be adequate support for the armed forces.

A third document was signed at the Belovezhskaia Pushcha by the heads of government (Burbulis for Russia, Prime Minister Viktor Kebich for Belarus, and Prime Minister Vitol'd Fokin for Ukraine). The agreement repeated most of the provisions in the economic treaty signed in October. In addition, the signatory governments agreed to proceed with radical economic reforms on a coordinated basis.[69] They would use the ruble as a common currency for the time being, and they agreed to introduce national currencies only on the basis of special agreements with each other. Finally, they agreed to coordinate price liberalization (all three states would liberalize most prices on 2 January 1992) and to persuade their legislatures to adopt a uniform value added tax. Gaidar revealed the next day that the uniform rate would be 28 percent and that they had agreed to put a ceiling on budget deficits.

At the end of the meeting, Yeltsin called President Bush to inform him about the formation of the Commonwealth of Independent States (CIS). Shushkevich followed with a call to Gorbachev. In the course of their conversation, Shushkevich informed the Soviet president that Yeltsin had already spoken with Bush, which enraged Gorbachev as a breach of protocol and propriety. Gorbachev, who insisted on speaking directly with Yeltsin, recalls telling him, "What you have done behind my back with the consent of the U.S. president is a crying shame, a disgrace!"[70]

Yeltsin returned to Moscow that night and met with Gorbachev the next day to explain the agreement's details. To Yeltsin's surprise, Nazarbayev attended the meeting as well. Gorbachev's reaction to the agreement was expressed publicly in a statement issued immediately after the meeting. The agreement had its "positive aspects," he conceded, but he insisted that Yeltsin, Kravchuk, and Shushkevich did not have the right to put an end to the Soviet Union unilaterally: "Of course, every republic has the right to leave the union, but the fate of a multinational state cannot be decided by the will of the leaders of three republics. This question can only be resolved through constitutional means with the participation of all the sovereign states and accounting for the will of their peoples." He then suggested that the Congress of Peoples' Deputies reconvene to consider the Belovezhskaia Agreement and his draft union treaty simultaneously.[71] Despite Gorbachev's protestations, the Ukrainian and Belorussian parliament ratified the CIS treaty on 10 December, while the Russian Supreme Soviet did so on 12 December. Each republic made clear that it would no longer

send representatives to the USSR Supreme Soviet or the State Council, and neither would Yeltsin, Kravchuk, or Shushkevich participate any longer in the
Novo-Ogarevo process.

Gorbachev's appeal to convene the Congress of Peoples' Deputies fell on
deaf ears. It had been Gorbachev himself who had urged the Congress to dissolve itself after the coup, and it was only after the deputies refused that a provision was included allowing the Congress to reconvene if a petition was signed
by one-fifth of the delegates. Arguing that the Congress should be the ultimate
arbiter of the union's fate therefore appeared hypocritical—why disband it in the
first place if was still a legitimate body with a right to make such a momentous
decision? Regardless, Ukraine, Belarus, Russia, and the six intransigents would
have refused to send representatives to the session, which meant that a reconvened Congress would have lacked a quorum.

Nor did Gorbachev have the moral authority or political base to resist the
accord by political means, despite the fact that many prominent Russian democrats, not to speak of Russia's "statists," imperialists, Communist conservatives,
and nationalists, were opposed to dissolution of the union. Gorbachev had effectively abdicated on the legal supremacy of the union by committing to the Novo-
Ogarevo process, which implied that the powers of center would be derived
"from below"—i.e., through negotiations with the leaders of the union republics.
Claiming that they did not have the right to reject his proposed treaty or to adopt
their own would therefore have appeared inconsistent—had he not earlier implied that the union republics would themselves decide how much authority to
delegate to the union center? Gorbachev had also asserted as late as 25 November 1991 that he "could not imagine a union treaty without Ukraine,"[72] and he
had repeatedly offered to resign if his union treaty was rejected. It was therefore
very difficult for him to refuse to do so now that his offer of resignation was in
effect being accepted. Indeed, his only real choice at that point was to accept the
fait accompli or declare presidential rule in the hope that the military would
support him.

There were, in fact, widespread rumors of an intervention by the military to
oppose the Belovezhskaia Agreement as well as signs of unrest within the armed
forces. The day before the meeting in the Belovezhskaia Pushcha, the head of
the general staff of the USSR Armed Forces, who was known for his hard-line
pro-unionist views, was relieved of his command. Three days later, two deputy
defense ministers were fired, as was the commander of the Kremlin's security
forces. That same day, Gorbachev held a previously planned meeting with senior military officials at the defense ministry at which he again defended the
Novo-Ogarevo process and claimed that the disintegration of the USSR would
be extremely dangerous. Then, in what some observers would later argue was a
call to resist the Belovezhskaia Agreement by force if necessary, he informed
the gathered officers that they had a responsibility before their 1,000-year history (just what history he had in mind was not specified—presumably Russia's)
to defend the union.[73]

Yeltsin met with senior officers the next morning to respond to Gorbachev's appeal. Arguing that the establishment of the CIS was the best way to preserve stability, Yeltsin stressed the importance of the defense union provided for in the Belovezhskaia Accord. He reiterated a promise he had made on 5 December, two days before leaving for the Belovezhskaia meeting, to raise the salaries of all the USSR military officers by 90 percent, and he promised that the RSFSR would pay their salaries even if they were stationed outside the RSFSR. The Russian government, he was suggesting, controlled the purse strings of the military and, unless it was prepared to seize power, it would need Yeltsin's support.

There were other deterrents to military intervention in support of Gorbachev and the preservation of the union as well. The Soviet defense minister and his colleagues were doubtless wary that Gorbachev would encourage them to seize power and then disavow their actions, as many suspected had been the case with the August coup and the crackdowns in Lithuania, Georgia, and Baku. Nor was there a tradition of military intervention in politics in Soviet or Russian history, and Soviet military culture put great emphasis on the supremacy of civilian authorities and inadmissibility of using the army against the population. Gorbachev had also repeatedly disavowed the use of force to preserve the union, arguing that any attempt to do so could lead to civil war. Indeed, the union had already lost Ukraine and the six intransigents, and there would have been no way to force them back into the fold except through massive violence. Finally, and perhaps most importantly, even if the military had managed to arrest Yeltsin, dissolve the RSFSR parliament and government, and convince Belarus and the Central Asian republics to join a new Union, the new regime would still have had to deal with the USSR's profound economic and social crisis with no vision of how to govern.

All these considerations made a military intervention unlikely and help account for Shaposhnikov's statement the day of the Belovezhskaia meeting welcoming the accord's provisions on a single strategic space. Whether the military gave serious consideration to opposing the Belovezhskaia Agreement by force is not known, but it seems unlikely. Regardless, when U.S. Secretary of State James Baker met with Yeltsin at the Kremlin on 16 December, Shaposhnikov was at his side. The struggle over the fate of the union, it now appeared clear, would be resolved by civilians, not by men on horseback.

With the military apparently unwilling to rescue Gorbachev, attention shifted to the Central Asian republics, particularly to Kazakhstan and the prounionist Nazarbayev, who had been elected Kazakh president on 1 December with over 98 percent of the vote (he had been the only candidate). Yeltsin, Kravchuk, and Shushkevich were concerned that the CIS would be received as an exclusive "Slavic" club and that the Central Asians would be unwilling to join what had been created by others. To counter this impression, the three leaders had argued (rather unpersuasively) that the RSFSR, Ukraine, and Belarus were the only surviving founding members of the USSR (the Transcaucasian Federation had been disbanded) and that they therefore had the right to act unilaterally to dissolve it. They had tried to convince Nazarbayev, who was on his way to Moscow by plane, to join them at the Belovezhskaia Pushcha at the last minute. Unable to contact him in the air (Yeltsin would later claim that the Soviet Ministry of Aviation had refused to put them through), they reached him by telephone at the airport in Moscow. Nazarbayev at first agreed to join them in the Belovezhskaia Pushcha but then changed his mind after talking to Gorbachev.

As noted earlier, Nazarbayev attended Yeltsin's meeting with Gorbachev on 9 December. Afterwards, the Kazakh president made clear his resentment at the way the CIS had been formed by remarking irritably that basing the new union on "national-ethnic [i.e., Slavic] principles is a vestige of the Middle Ages."[74] But there was even less he could do to resist the agreement than Gorbachev, particularly given that Kazakhstan, with its large Russian minority, economic ties to Russia, and fears of Russian irredentism, could not afford to be left out of the Commonwealth. Rather than rejecting the CIS, Nazarbayev organized a meeting of the five Central Asian leaders in Ashkhabad, Turkmenistan, on 17 December. The day before the meeting, he had Kazakhstan declare independence so that it would be on an equal footing with the other republics. It was thus the last republic to do so.

The Ashkhabad summit resulted in a commitment by the Central Asian states to join the CIS on the condition that they have equal status as founding members with Russia, Ukraine, and Belarus. Four days later, the leaders of eleven of the fifteen former republics met in Alma Ata and formally constituted the CIS—only the three Baltic states and Georgia demurred. The founding treaty provided for a Council of State made up of the leaders of the signatory states and "committees" of foreign, defense, and economic ministers. There was, indeed, no "state structure," just as Kravchuk had insisted.

While the United States and its Western allies were taken by surprise and initially confused by the Belovezhskaia Agreement and the founding of the CIS, it quickly became clear that as long as the dissolution of the Soviet state was peaceful, they would not stand in its way. The day after the Belovezhskaia meeting, U.S. Secretary of State Baker once again articulated the Bush administration's fears about the impending breakup of the USSR in a television interview stressing in particular its implications for the control of nuclear weapons. Nor was it clear just what had been agreed to at the Belovezhskaia Pushcha—a new union state or fifteen successor states? The Bush administration accordingly issued a statement on 10 December saying that it was prepared to work with the CIS but that it would not break relations with the Soviet government. When Baker arrived in Moscow several days later, the Russian foreign minister, Andrei Kozyrev, pointedly asked that the United States recognize Russia, Belarus, and Ukraine, but Baker made no promises. Later that week, administration officials indicated Washington would not consider recognizing any of the successor states until they agreed to honor the USSR's international obligations, particularly in regard to arms control agreements and debt servicing. Not all of the U.S. allies agreed, however—Germany's foreign minister, Hans Dietrich Genscher, who had been a strong advocate of early recognition for the Yugoslav splinter states, argued that it would be wrong to delay recognition.

The same day that the Central Asian leaders were meeting in Ashkhabad, Gorbachev signaled that he had accepted his final defeat. He agreed that all Soviet agencies would either be abolished or come under Russian control by the end of the year. The next day, he announced that he would resign when the CIS formally came into existence. Then, on 23 December, he held a contentious and painful eight-hour meeting with Yeltsin on the procedures for transferring power.

At 7 P.M. on 25 December 1991, the Soviet president formally resigned in a televised speech. After defending perestroika and acknowledging "some mistakes," he once again tried to square the circle of sovereignty and union:

> I have firmly advocated the independence of peoples and sovereignty of the republics. But at the same time I have favored the preservation of the [union] state and the integrity of the country.
>
> Events have taken a different path. A policy line aimed at dismembering the country and disuniting [*sic*] the state has prevailed, something that I cannot agree with.[75]

The red flag of the Soviet Union, with its famous hammer and sickle, was lowered over the Kremlin, to be replaced by the tricolor flag of the Russian Federation. Gorbachev handed the launch codes for the Soviet nuclear arsenal to Defense Minister Shaposhnikov, who passed them on to Yeltsin, who was waiting in a nearby Kremlin office. Six days later—at midnight on 31 December 1991—the USSR passed into history.

With the signing of the Alma Ata Accord and Gorbachev's resignation as Soviet president, the international community had no choice but to recognize the independence of the fifteen former union republics. There was no longer a Soviet government to do business with, and no Soviet state for foreign governments to exchange diplomatic representatives with because all Soviet embassies and diplomatic personnel were now under the jurisdiction of the Russian government. The CIS, on the other hand, lacked even the most minimal attributes of a state, and its member states had made perfectly clear that it was an interstate association that would prove to have even less authority than the European Community.

Fortunately, the disappearance of the federal center meant that the independence of the union republics could be recognized without endorsing secession. The successor states, it could be argued, had attained their independence through the dissolution of a national government, not through secession from an internationally recognized state. Accordingly, Russia was given a seat in the UN General Assembly as well as the USSR's seat on the Security Council on 24 December 1991. Two days later, President Bush announced that the United States would grant all the former republics diplomatic recognition on condition that they agree to ratify the Nuclear Non-Proliferation Treaty and abide by the terms of the nuclear and conventional arms agreements previously signed by the USSR.

* * * * *

There was an additional matter of principle that the international community, to its further consternation, would be forced to confront—a problem that received limited attention in the heady months of late 1991 but that would prove a source of political conflict and international instability in the coming years. By the time the Soviet Union formally dissolved, independence declarations had been issued by six subnational governments located within the boundaries of the new successor states: Nagorno-Karabakh, South Ossetia, Transdniestra, Gagauzia, Crimea, and Chechnya (see table 6.3).[76] Abkhazia effectively would do so on 23 July 1992 through a parliamentary vote to restore its 1925 constitution.

Chechnya's declaration of independence in early November presented a particularly serious problem for Yeltsin and the leadership of the soon-to-be independent Russian Federation. In early September, Chechen nationalists had seized power in Grozny, then the capital of the Chechen-Ingush ASSR (the separation of Chechnya and Ingushetia was recognized by the Russian legislature in early 1992). Led by a former Soviet air force general, Dzhokhar Dudayev, the new government announced that the republic would hold presidential and parliamentary elections in late October. At the same time, Dudayev announced his candidacy for the presidency, stating that if elected he would declare Chechen independence from Russia. The elections took place on 27 October, and Dudayev was elected president with what Chechen officials claimed was 90.1 percent of the vote.[77] As promised, the new Chechen president issued a decree on 1 November that formally declared the republic independent, and the decree was ratified by the new Chechen parliament the next day.[78] Fearing that separatism would spread throughout Russia if the Russian government failed to restore its legal writ in the republic, Yeltsin responded on 7 November with a decree declaring a state of emergency in the republic. Gorbachev, who had long argued that the secession of any of the union republics would be a disaster for nontitular minorities, refused to allow the Russian government to use all-union defense or interior ministry troops to implement the state of emergency, which forced the Russian government to send RSFSR interior ministry troops to the republic instead. When the Russian forces landed at a military air base outside Grozny, armed detachments loyal to Dudayev surrounded them and prevented them from entering the city, where a huge crowd had gathered to defend Chechnya from a "foreign invasion." Humiliated, the Russian troops were forced to leave the republic by bus on 9 November. That same day, the RSFSR Supreme Soviet adopted a resolution declaring Yeltsin's declaration of a state of emergency illegal and ordering Russian troops to leave the republic, thereby providing Yeltsin with a face-saving excuse for a "withdrawal" on the grounds that he was complying with the will of the Russian legislature. The incident helped unite Chechens around Dudayev (albeit only briefly—the republic would

Table 6.3. Independence Declarations by Subnational Governments in the Successor States

---

Gagauzia (sovereignty within USSR, not Moldova): 19 August 1990
Transdniestra (sovereignty within USSR, not Moldova): 2 September 1990
Transdniestra: 26 August 1991 (endorsed by referendum on 1 December 1991)
Nagorno-Karabakh: 2 September 1991 (from Azerbaijan and USSR)
Gagauzia: 2 September 1991 (from Moldova and USSR)
Chechnya: 1 November 1991 (from Russia and USSR)
South Ossetia: 21 December 1991 (from Georgia and USSR)
Crimea: 5 May 1992 (from Ukraine)
Abkhazia: 23 July 1992 (from Georgia)

---

soon be riven by internal divisions) and solidified popular support for Chechen independence. Ironically, then, Yeltsin discovered, like Gorbachev before him, that a half-hearted effort to suppress separatists was entirely counterproductive. Yeltsin's eventual decision to resort to full-scale war would prove an even greater disaster, as would become clear after Russian federal forces were sent into Chechnya to defend Russia's "territorial integrity" in December 1994 and again in September 1999.

In short, the successor states that confronted challenges to their territorial integrity in the wake of the Soviet dissolution were prepared, like the states that attained independence in the wake of decolonization in the 1950s and 1960s as ardent champions of "the right of national self-determination" but that then denied that "right" to minority peoples within their borders, to use force if necessary to defend the borders that they had inherited from the Soviet past. The result would be a series of "sovereignty wars" in Abkhazia, Chechnya, Karabakh, South Ossetia, and Transdniestra, wars that in the coming decade would cause tens of thousands of deaths.

There was an important difference between the independence declarations of the autonomies and those of the union republics, a difference that helps explain why the great bulk of the violence that accompanied the Soviet breakup resulted from struggles over the territorial integrity of the former union republics rather than the USSR. As we have seen, the autonomies (as well as Transdniestra and Crimea, which did not have autonomous status as of 1991) could not rely on any formal right of secession under the Soviet constitution.[79] Their assertion of independence had to rely instead on the general principle of "national self-determination" and its putative endorsement under international law.

There were two partial exceptions to this general rule. Abkhazia and Karabakh not only insisted on their right to national self-determination, but they also claimed that their refusal to remain within Georgia and Azerbaijan, respectively, was justified by Soviet-era law. In the first instance, the Abkhaz held that the restitution of the Abkhaz constitution of 1925 was legal because the Georgian constitution of 1921, which Tbilisi reinstated late in the Gorbachev era as Georgia's basic law, did not identify Abkhazia as a constituent unit of Georgia. The Karabakh Armenians, on the other hand, argued that they were acting "on the basis of the USSR constitution and laws which extend to the peoples of the autonomous entities and ethnic groups the right to independent decision making on their state-legal status in the event of a union republic's secession from the USSR."[80] More specifically, they claimed that, under the April 1990 USSR law on secession, Azerbaijan's attempt to secede from the USSR gave Karabakh the legal right in turn to declare independence from Azerbaijan.[81]

In fact, the legal basis for the independence declarations of the nonunion republics was very weak. Neither the Soviet constitution nor the constitutions of the union republics afford them a right of secession. As for the April 1990 USSR law on secession, it specified an elaborate series of steps that had to be taken before an autonomy or a "compactly settled" ethnic community could separate from a union republic, steps that the autonomies (notably Karabakh) did not, and indeed could not, take.[82] Moreover, the law made clear that the option of separating from a union republic (which meant not full independence but rather remaining a part of the USSR) was only available to the autonomies when, and if, the union republic of which they were a part moved to secede from the USSR in accordance with the procedures specified by the law. As we have seen, the only union republic that even paid lip service to the provisions of the April 1990 law in asserting independence was Armenia, and the USSR's dissolution took place long before Armenia had the opportunity to comply with the prolonged process of seceding in accordance with the law's provisions.[83]

The political leverage of the autonomies in Moscow was likewise limited. The autonomies had less formal representation in the USSR's central institutions than the union republics, and they represented a far smaller share of the Soviet population, economy, and territory—only the Tatar and Bashkir ASSRs were partial exceptions. Their political weight had been momentarily enhanced in late 1990 and early 1991 when Gorbachev attempted to elicit their support in his political struggle with Yeltsin and the antiunion opposition in the union republics. As the Novo-Ogarevo process appeared to be reaching a successful conclusion in the late spring of 1991, however, it became clear that Gorbachev was prepared to abandon his alliance with the autonomies in exchange for an agreement by the union republics, above all Russia, to ratify his precious union treaty. With the failure of the August coup, the political influence of the autonomies all but evaporated. This was true in the first place because many of their leaders had appeared to support the putschists during the critical days of 19–23 August 1991.[84] Reformers in the capitals of the union republics, particularly Moscow, became convinced that the autonomies had become bastions of pro-Communist and pro-union sentiments where the traditional *nomenklatura* was using demands for "sovereignty" to curry public favor while resisting genuine democratization and marketization. In addition, the greatly diminished authority of the USSR's central institutions after August meant that there was no longer any opportunity for Gorbachev to form an alliance with the autonomies in opposition to the union republics. The legal status and powers of the autonomies, it was now clear, would be decided not by federal law but directly through negotiation or coercion between the autonomies and their host republics. Thus the autonomies were not afforded representation on the newly constituted State Council; they were completely shut out of the Novo-Ogarevo process; and the 26 November draft treaty did not identify them as subjects of the union, define their status, or indeed refer to them in any way.

Understandably, then, political elites in the more assertive autonomies felt abandoned by the center and resentful at being politically marginalized after August 1991. Regional separatists were at the same time encouraged by the success of the antiunion opposition in the union republics and were convinced that national self-determination and full independence could likewise be realized by the autonomies, which after all confronted not the seemingly all-powerful Soviet central government but the comparatively weak governments of the union republics. Many also feared that the weakening and imminent demise of the Soviet center would leave the ethnic minorities at the mercy of nationalist governments committed to ethnic definitions of their newly won statehood ("Russia for the Russians") and thus disinclined to respect the collective rights and privileges the autonomies had enjoyed in the Soviet period. The result was the rapid proliferation of independence declarations by subnational governments after August described in table 6.3.

The ultimate arbiter of the independence claims of the autonomies was the international community. As the separatist leaders in Abkhazia, Chechnya, Crimea, Gagauzia, Karabakh, South Ossetia, and Transdniestra quickly learned, however, foreign governments were even more opposed to the fragmentation of the successor states than to the breakup of the USSR. None of the autonomies could claim, like the Baltic republics, that their incorporation into either the USSR or their particular union republic had been treated as illegal by the international community. In addition, whereas the breakup of the USSR may have been illegal under Soviet law—the procedures provided for in the law on secession were ignored, while the USSR constitution was not amended to allow the USSR to dissolve itself—the international community could still argue that it was a voluntary "dissolution" in which the central government simply ceased to exist. This was clearly not the case for the former union republics, which were still very much extant and were entirely unwilling to recognize the independence of any of the autonomies. Nor did the international community have any criteria for adjudicating which autonomies, or which "compactly settled nationalities," had a right to independence and which did not. Again, unlike the union republics, the autonomies were not "sovereign states" under Soviet law, and they lacked a formal right to secede. The international community, with lessons of the Yugoslav debacle very much in mind, was by then all-the-more fearful of the risks of violence that might accompany the fragmentation of the USSR. That some or all the former union republics would also splinter risked even greater instability, disruption, and violent conflict.

Rather than formal independence, then, there would be a different but strikingly similar outcome in five of the seven cases of subnational separatism. Separatists would triumph on the battlefield in Abkhazia, Karabakh, South Ossetia, Transdniestra, and Chechnya (in the latter case, the Chechen victory would come after the 1994–1996 Russo-Chechen war—as of the date of this writing, a second war is under way in Chechnya, the outcome of which has yet to be determined). In no case, however, would the militarily victorious separatists be recognized as independent by the international community. Only in the case of Crimea and Gagauzia would negotiated compromises over sovereignty be reached. Abkhazia, Karabakh, South Ossetia, and Transdniestra would find themselves in a condition of "no peace, no war," in control of their territory but legally in limbo, while Chechnya would find itself involved in a prolonged and devastating conflict with Moscow. Formally, then, the fragmentation of the USSR would end with the independence of the fifteen union republics.

* * * * *

In response to critics' claims that he had single-handedly and arbitrarily engineered the destruction of the great Soviet state, Yeltsin would defend the Belovezhskaia Agreement by arguing that it had in fact been the only possible mechanism for preserving any kind of association of the former republics that would include Ukraine. As Gaidar would explain at a press conference on 9 December 1991: "We decided that it was much more important and much more useful to devise some formula for ties between republics than to preserve the old name, a single parliament, or the capital in Moscow but cut off Ukraine from Russia in the process."[85] By this reckoning, the agreement was the result, not the cause, of the Soviet Union's collapse.

In one sense, at least, this was true. It would have been difficult for Yeltsin to sell a federal government with significant powers to the Russian elite or electorate by late 1991 even with Ukraine as a member. But once Ukraine made clear that it would not join Gorbachev's union under any circumstances, his task would have been all but impossible—for the majority of Russians, a loose association with Ukraine was far preferable to a tighter union without it.

On the other hand, it is not true, as the argument suggests, that Yeltsin was simply accepting a fait accompli that had been crafted by others. Even though it was not directed at destroying the Soviet state, Yeltsin's campaign to weaken the authority of the center had been under way since early 1990 and was a critical factor in the USSR's demise. Had Gorbachev's efforts to negotiate a new Union with significant central authority been supported, rather than undermined, by the Russian government, some kind of Soviet state, albeit a weakened and truncated one, might have survived. But it is also true that under those circumstances the risks of a major bloodletting in defense of Soviet sovereignty would have been considerably greater as well. Unlike the Serbs under Milosevic, the Russians under Yeltsin, to their credit, refused to take up arms in defense of "their" federal government.

Moreover, the argument that the Belovezhskaia Agreement saved what could be saved implies that the "commonwealth" that emerged from the Belovezhskaia meeting was meaningful and that an entity had been created with significant and autonomous political authority. Doubtless its creators believed at the time that a common defense, coordinated foreign policies and economic reforms, and even a common currency could be preserved by the CIS's member states. In fact, as many commentators recognized at the time, the CIS proved an arrangement for effecting a peaceful divorce, not saving the marriage. Its most meaningful provisions—the defense union and commitment to a common currency—fell apart almost immediately. Rather than "a common military-strategic space," "joint command of military-strategic forces," or "unified control of nuclear weapons," Ukraine, Kazakhstan, and Belarus would agree to give up their nuclear weapons in a CIS agreement signed in Minsk on 30 December 1991 and then again as part of the Lisbon Protocol, to which the United States was a signatory, in May 1992. Each successor state would also proceed to create its own independent defense forces. Nor would there be meaningful coordination of foreign policies—on the contrary, all the Soviet successor states except Belarus, Armenia, and Tajikistan would come to view Russia as the principal threat to their sovereignty and security and would begin to look elsewhere for diplomatic and material support. Nor would the successor states make significant efforts to coordinate their economic reform programs—rather, the tempo and character of their subsequent marketization efforts would vary dramatically. And while hundreds of CIS agreements would be signed in the coming years, very few would be implemented. The post-Soviet Commonwealth, like the British Commonwealth, helped ease the psychological pain of imperial collapse, but it too proved to be an extremely weak institution. Soon it would amount to little more than an agreement to hold periodic meetings of heads of state and government ministers.

Defenders of the Belovezhskaia Agreement would also argue that the creation of the CIS and dissolution of the Soviet Union had been effected perfectly legally. This claim, too, is untenable—the agreement was certainly illegal under Soviet law. While the union republics had a constitutional right to secede, the Soviet constitution did not specify how that right could be realized. Neither did it indicate that the union republics had a *unilateral* right of secession. Like many constitutional rights, it required enabling legislation to become meaningful. When that legislation was finally adopted in April 1990, it took effect before any of the founding members of the CIS had issued sovereignty declarations or asserted the primacy of their laws over those of the center. Regardless, the Soviet constitution made perfectly clear that it had priority over the constitutions of the union republics and that federal laws that were consistent with the USSR constitution had priority over laws passed by the republics.

Legally, then, Gorbachev was correct in arguing that under Soviet law only the Congress of Peoples' Deputies had the right to nullify the Soviet constitution and dissolve the union. The fact that this was impossible was a political, not a legal, matter. Like most sociopolitical revolutions, the dissolution of the Soviet Union violated the legal norms of the ancien régime—indeed, what was unusual about the Soviet revolution was that so much of it was effected in accordance with Soviet law.

On the other hand, the Belovezhskaia Agreement was perfectly legal under the laws of the three signatory republics. By late 1991, the Soviet Union was suffering from an acute case of multiple sovereignty—central authorities and the union republics disagreed fundamentally about the locus of legitimate legal and political authority. The republics had asserted the primacy of their laws over those of the federal government, and as long as the agreement was ratified by the three parliaments, *their* laws were being observed. Thus the argument that the creation of the CIS was a unilateral act by three willful leaders acting entirely outside the law is also incorrect—the issue was *which* law, Soviet or republic.

The Belovezhskaia Agreement was fundamentally a political act and should be judged accordingly. It has been fervently attacked on these grounds as well, not only within the former Soviet Union (particularly in Russia) but by many Western specialists. The agreement brought about the dissolution of the Soviet Union, the argument goes, and the dissolution of the Soviet Union has been a disaster for the Soviet people. This tragic outcome was primarily the result of the willful and self-interested behavior of a limited number of political actors, above all Yeltsin. As Archie Brown put it, "It was still the case in the last months of the Soviet Union's existence, as it had been earlier, that cooperation and a willingness to compromise between Gorbachev and Yeltsin, for the sake of preserving as much of an economic political union as could be achieved voluntarily, would have been in the interests of a majority of Soviet citizens."[86]

This argument rests on a number of dubious assumptions. To begin with, it suggests a compatibility of interests among the former republics that did not exist. Russia, to cite but one example, had a powerful economic incentive to begin charging the other republics world prices for its commodities, while the other republics had an interest in preventing it from doing so. Clearly, the distributional effects of preserving or changing existing trade patterns and terms of trade were very considerable. But it is certainly not obvious that a majority of Soviet citizens would have benefited from keeping them unchanged—after all, Russia had a substantial majority of the population of the republics still involved in the Novo-Ogarevo process.

More importantly, the argument implies that there would have been net welfare gains from the preservation of the union, either because interrepublic trade would have been less disrupted or because of reduced political instability and violence. In fact, the contrary was more likely. The long-term prospects for economic recovery in the republics were primarily a function of well-designed and resolutely implemented economic reforms—hence the relatively rapid improvement in living standards in the Baltic states, where market reforms were embraced with vigor, and the profound recession in Ukraine after independence, where they were long delayed. But there is no reason to believe that the preservation of the union would have meant a more coherent economic policy. On the contrary, the November draft afforded the central government almost no autonomous powers over the economy, which suggests that the republics' economic programs would not have been significantly different had Gorbachev's new union come into being.

To the extent that the treaty did have an impact on economic policy, it most likely would have been to confound efforts by those republic governments that were intent upon radical reforms. This was particularly true for Russia. Had Yeltsin signed the treaty and then moved to implement a radical reform program, he would have been vulnerable to criticism from a union president (whether Gorbachev or someone else) who would not be responsible for the economy and thus would not have borne the burden of blame for the inevitable pain of marketization. The union president would have had a powerful incentive to mobilize popular opposition to Russia's reforms, which would have made Russia's internal politics even more complicated, confused, and disorderly than they would prove after independence. And political chaos would in turn have made successful economic reform even less likely. Indeed, it is closer to the mark to argue that the dissolution of the union was a necessary, albeit hardly sufficient, condition for a coherent program of economic reform for Russia and the other republics.

Nor is it clear that preserving existing trade patterns through the creation of a "common economic space" made economic sense for many or even most of the republics. Both interrepublic and intrarepublic production links were being profoundly disrupted by the dissolution of Gosplan and marketization in any case, and it cannot be assumed that preserving those links was economically beneficial. The preservation of the union would likely have had limited impact on trade given the weakness of the central government. Nor was the economic rationale for the preservation of a common union currency obvious—benefits from the preservation of the ruble zone would have required a sound currency, but the ruble was rapidly losing purchasing power by late 1991 (it fell from 50 to 200 rubles per dollar in limited exchange auctions over the course of the year, with inflation running at approximately 20 percent per month by the end of 1991).[87] Nor was the Soviet Union in late 1991 "an optimal currency area" in which the benefits of separate monetary policies were clearly outweighed by the savings in transaction costs and the elimination of exchange rate risks associated with a common currency. Indeed, it was not the formation of the CIS that led to separate currencies for the successor states in 1992–1993—rather, it was the desire of the many republics to continue to print money and issue credits that induced Russia to force the other republics out of the ruble zone.[88]

Finally, it is highly unlikely that a new union would have promoted political stability or prevented conflict. The Belovezhskaia Agreement and the formation of the CIS had the decided advantage of putting an end to the endless wrangling over "sovereignty" between the center and the union republics. Even more importantly, it committed the High Contracting Parties to respect each others' territorial integrity and existing borders. With the exception of the undeclared war between Azerbaijan and Armenia over Karabakh, there would be no armed conflicts between any of the Soviet successor states. Had the union treaty of 26 November 1991 been adopted, this might not have been the case. The Novo-

Ogarevo drama would have continued, albeit in different form, with Gorbachev and other defenders of the union struggling to convince additional republics to accede to the treaty even as different political groups campaigned for the all-union parliamentary and presidential elections. Nor were the respective competencies of the union government and the republics resolved by the vaguely worded treaty, which would have guaranteed a continuing struggle between the center and the republics over "sovereignty," yet another distraction for already overloaded political systems. Most dangerous, however, was the risk of a turn in Russia toward neo-imperialism and a policy of intimidation of other union members (as indeed occurred in Moscow beginning in late 1992 with respect to the "Near Abroad") under conditions where unionwide institutions were still being contested. Non-Russian members of the union would have lacked the legal and political protections afforded independent states by the international community, and Russian efforts to impose central writ on the other republics would have been treated as an internal affair of the new union. Under those circumstances, the Soviet Union might very well have followed the Yugoslav path.

Notes

1. For a description of Gorbachev's extensive involvement in foreign policy in the months between the failure of the coup and the USSR's formal dissolution in December 1991, see Boris Pankin, *The Last Hundred Days of the Soviet Union* (New York: I. B. Tauris, 1996). Pankin, who replaced Bessmertnykh as Soviet foreign minister immediately after the coup, would argue that Gorbachev "needed to be active—perhaps even hyperactive—on the foreign affairs front. . . . Because of the dynamics of his relationship with Yeltsin, Gorbachev was no longer able to control the domestic affairs of the country during the last three months of its life, and this virtual isolation on the home front caused him to look to foreign affairs for opportunities to assert himself. This exclusion from domestic affairs also left him with plenty of time on his hands to receive foreign visitors. . . . For my part, I found myself the captive audience of an increasingly desperate man expounding his ideas and explaining the events of the coup over and over again to each of these visitors. Gorbachev's monologues took up so much time that the visitors seldom had time to get to their own points" (Pankin 1996, 117).

2. *Izvestiia,* 23 August 1991, *CDSP,* vol. 43, no. 34, 20.

3. *New York Times,* 23 August 1991.

4. Pankin would later recall that Gorbachev was initially reluctant even to put the issue of the recognition of the independence of the Baltic republics on the agenda of the first State Council meeting. Pankin was able to convince Gorbachev to agree to support their recognition by arguing that it would not set a precedent for full independence for the other union republics because of the "very specific historical and political circumstances of their joining the Soviet Union" (Pankin 1996, 239).

5. Beschloss and Talbott 1994, 444.

6. Postcoup independence declarations by the republics posed a particular problem for the Soviet foreign minister, who after all was supposedly the legal representative of a single internationally recognized state. As Pankin would put it, "But what was I to make of the series of republics that proclaimed their independence? Almost each one of the last

ten days of August brought a new declaration of independence. Before the coup, there had been a 'parade of sovereignties'. . . . Now came a 'parade of independences'" (Pankin 1996, 79).

7. *Izvestiia*, 27 August 1991, *CDSP*, vol. 43, no. 35, 12.

8. *Rossiiskaia gazeta*, 27 August 1991, *CDSP*, vol. 43, no. 35, 15.

9. *Washington Post*, National Edition, 2–8 September 1991, 7.

10. Yeltsin had chosen Rutskoi as his vice president in the spring after the latter had supported him during the showdown with Yeltsin's conservative critics in the RSFSR parliament in late March. Yeltsin selected Rutskoi, an air force general and a former Afghan war hero who had recently formed a reformist faction of the CPRF, "Communists for Democracy," as his vice-presidential running mate because he balanced his ticket in June with a military hero and a Party member who had supported the RSFSR's sovereignty campaign. Rutskoi would lead the Communists for Democracy faction into a formal split with the staunchly conservative rump CPRF in the summer.

11. Sobchak, like other leaders of the Russian democratic movements such as Gavriil Popov, the mayor of Moscow, was a supporter of a preserved union state, as he would make clear in a speech at the Extraordinary Congress of Peoples' Deputies on 2 September (McFaul 2001, 131–32). Sobchak would take a tough line later in the year on Russian relations with Ukraine. In an interview to *Le Figaro* on 4 December 1991, three days after the Ukrainian referendum on independence (see below), he claimed that if Ukraine embarked on "forced Ukrainianization in Crimea, with its Russian majority," Russia would "immediately raise territorial claims on Ukraine if Ukraine refused to join in a political union, *Report on the USSR*, 13 December 1991, quoted in George W. Breslauer and Catherine Dale, "Boris Yel'tsin and the Invention of a Russian Nation-State," *Post-Soviet Affairs* 13, no. 4 (1997): 317. The statement speaks to the ambivalence that many liberals and democrats in Russia felt at the time about the breakup of the USSR, an ambivalence that at least in part was due to fear that successor states formed on the basis of the "nationality" principle would be both intolerant of ethnic minorities and undemocratic.

12. *Pravda*, 21 October 1991, FBIS-SOV-91-204, 31.

13. Andrei S. Grachev, *Final Days: The Inside Story of the Collapse of the Soviet Union* (Boulder, Colo.: Westview Press, 1995), 82, and Pankin 1996, 246.

14. Grachev 1995, 71.

15. Matlock 1995, 623.

16. The extent to which other "Young Turks" fully shared his views on the need for the dissolution of the USSR is not clear.

17. Hough 1997, 467.

18. Feodor Burlatsky, "Who or What Broke Up the Soviet Union," in *Separatism: Democracy and Disintegration,* ed. Metta Spencer (Boulder, Colo.: Rowman and Littlefield Publishers, 1998), 144–48.

19. Brown 1996, 308.

20. Boris Yeltsin, *The Struggle for Russia,* trans. Catherine A. Fitzpatrick (New York: Times Books, 1994), 151.

21. Yeltsin 1994, 110–11. That Yeltsin was still very much opposed to the complete dissolution of the union as long as Ukraine remained a part of it was suggested by a statement he had made to President Bush just prior to the coup. In his memoirs, Bush recalls Yeltsin telling during their meeting in Moscow on 30 July that "Ukraine must not leave the Soviet Union" because without Ukraine the union would have a lopsided majority of non-Slavic constituent republics (Bush and Scowcroft 1998, 512). As Yakovlev argues in his memoirs, "Yeltsin and everyone around him at that time simply didn't know

what to do next. They were not prepared for the coup. They weren't ready for that turn of events," Aleksandr Yakovlev, *Omut Pamyati: Ot Stolypina do Putina,* vol. 2 (Moscow: Vargius, 2001), 145.

22. Grachev 1995, 95.

23. Grachev 1995, 91–92.

24. Matlock 1995, 624.

25. Pankin 1996, 262–63.

26. Grachev 1995, 95.

27. Grachev recalls that Yeltsin had been particularly irritated by Gorbachev's criticism of the Russian government for declaring a state of emergency at the time in Checheno-Ingushetia (see below) on 7 November and the dispatching of RSFSR interior ministry troops to the republic to "restore order." Yeltsin irately began his letter to Gorbachev, "Our new relations have lasted all of three months, and now they're over" (Grachev 1995, 116). Grachev also reports, however, that Gorbachev then managed to mollify the Russian president, at least temporarily.

28. Gorbachev 1995, 656. Again, what exactly this would have entailed is not made clear, although Gorbachev's language suggests that the new union would have had to give up its seat at the UN. Whether the other successor states would have easily accepted Russia taking the USSR's seat is, however, unclear.

29. Grachev 1995, 111.

30. During the discussion of the possibility of establishing a "confederative state," Switzerland and Canada were cited as possible models (Grachev 1995, 107). Arguably, Switzerland, with its very weak national government, would qualify as a "confederation," depending upon how one defined the term, but it is more difficult to argue that Canada is a "confederation." In practice, the terms "federation" and "confederation" tend to be used interchangeably in Canadian political discourse, although the latter is more frequently used to describe the act of forming the Canadian "federation." See, for example, Wolfgang Koerner, "The Foundations of Canadian Federalism" (Ottawa, Canada: Library of Parliament, Research Branch, BP-878E, October 1988).

31. Grachev 1995, 109.

32. Grachev 1995, 113.

33. The participants seem to have believed that this phrase had a precise and well-understood legal meaning, with obvious political implications. In fact, individuals, not only "states" or other political collectivities, can be "subjects" of international law, as the Nuremberg Trials and today's international human rights tribunals make clear. Moreover, the self-designation of the new union as a "subject of international law" would have had little impact on the decision by other states to afford it diplomatic recognition.

34. Grachev 1995, 108.

35. Gorbachev had apparently concluded that Kravchuk, who after all was a former Communist Party official and who was constantly blaming the Ukrainian parliament for tying his hands in regard to the union treaty negotiations, was simply grandstanding for political purposes and would eventually return to the Novo-Ogarevo process after putting an appropriate spin on the meaning of the referendum results (Grachev 1995, 8).

36. *Izvestiia,* 15 November 1991, *CDSP,* vol. 43, no. 46, 10.

37. Matlock 1995, 626.

38. *Izvestiia,* 15 November 1991, *CDSP,* vol. 43, no. 46, 10.

39. On 22 November, the RSFSR Supreme Soviet refused to grant Yeltsin the right to appoint the chairman of the central bank—instead, Russia's central banker would be appointed by the Supreme Soviet, which decided to retain the head of the USSR State

Bank, Viktor Gerashchenko. In early 1992, Gerashchenko would refuse to go along with Yeltsin's plans to lower inflation by limiting the money supply.

40. *Izvestiia,* 25 November 1991, 3.

41. Gorbachev 1995, 656.

42. Pankin 1996, 265.

43. Matlock 1995, 628.

44. Yeltsin 1994, 110.

45. Motyl and Krawchenko 1997, 250.

46. One Western specialist would later note that Kravchuk "never plunged into nationalism wholesale, and tacked and trimmed when necessary . . . until the botched assault on the Baltic republics in January 1991 allowed him to resume a course toward building Ukrainian sovereignty and promoting himself as its main guarantor" (Wilson 2000, 163).

47. Motyl and Krawchenko 1997, 252.

48. Grachev quotes Gorbachev as telling a delegation from Czechoslovakia in mid-November: "The situation there [in Ukraine] is complex and contradictory. At the top, you have a bunch of loudmouths who say they are in favor of separation. But at the grass roots, the popular mood is in favor of preserving a Union" (Grachev 1995, 105). According to Chernyaev, Gorbachev's assumptions about the weakness of the nationalist opposition in Ukraine apparently dated back to the early days of the USSR's "nationality crisis." Chernyaev quotes Gorbachev telling the Politburo after a trip to Ukraine in late February 1988, referring to both Ukrainians and Belarussians: "These are large nations. And since they belong to the same family as Russia, their languages are similar and their histories have been closely linked for so many centuries that sometimes it is difficult to tell a Russian from a Ukrainian or Belorussian. That is why it's complicated with the language [issue]. . . . But I have to say that among both cadres and the people, internationalist attachments are still very strong. That is why the heralds of 'separatism' have to import the virus from the Baltics" (Chernyaev 2000, 190–91). Chernyaev argues that Gorbachev continued to misread the situation in Ukraine after the coup: "[Gorbachev] underestimated the role of Ukraine in the process of disintegration. He didn't believe, didn't want to believe, that Ukraine could leave. He was too attached to it, he loved, knew Taras Shevchenko [the Ukrainian national poet] by heart, spoke Ukrainian" (Chernyaev 2000, 382). In fact, Gorbachev may have been generally correct about the lack of genuine popular enthusiasm for separation in Ukraine, and he was hardly alone in thinking this—some Ukrainian nationalist leaders even doubted that the referendum would receive majority support (Wilson 2000, 168).

49. Grachev 1995, 137.

50. Wilson 2000, 169.

51. Peter J. S. Duncan, "Ukraine and the Ukrainians," in *The Nationalities Question in the Post-Soviet States,* ed. Graham Smith (London: Longman, 1996), 199.

52. Grachev 1995, 20.

53. Grachev 1995, 53.

54. Pankin 1996, 265.

55. Beschloss and Talbott 1994, 448.

56. Beschloss and Talbott 1994, 449.

57. *Izvestiia,* 6 December 1991, *CDSP,* vol. 43, no. 49, 21.

58. *New York Times,* 5 December 1991.

59. Hough 1997, 478–79.

60. *New York Times,* 7 December 1991.

61. *New York Times,* 8 December 1991.

62. *New York Times,* 8 December 1991.

63. Matlock 1995, 635. Kravchuk's version of the events of 7–8 December 1991 generally confirmed those of Yeltsin and Grachev, particularly on the question of Yeltsin's willingness to discuss Gorbachev's draft treaty and Kravchuk's unequivocal refusal to do so (Wilson 2000, 169).

64. *New York Times,* 11 December 1991.

65. Burlatsky 1998, 150.

66. Yeltsin 1994, 112.

67. *Rossiiskaia gazeta,* 10 December 1991, 1–2.

68. *Izvestiia,* 9 December 1991.

69. *Izvestiia,* 9 December 1991.

70. Gorbachev 1995, 659.

71. *Izvestiia,* 10 December 1991.

72. Duncan 1996, 200.

73. *Izvestiia,* 11 December 1991, *CDSP,* vol. 43, no. 50, 14. Gorbachev may have explored the possibility of a military coup earlier, albeit obliquely, although the evidence in this regard is weak. The Soviet minister of defense, Yevgenii Shaposhnikov, later wrote that in mid-November, Gorbachev had asked him to come to the Kremlin to discuss various options for dealing with the USSR's crisis of statehood. One option mentioned by the Soviet president, according to Shaposhnikov, was a military takeover to stabilize the situation, after which the country would be returned to civilian rule. When Shaposhnikov pointed out that a coup had been tried already and that the outcome had been prison for its perpetrators, Gorbachev responded, "What are you talking about Zhenia? . . . I wasn't proposing anything to you, simply stating variants, thinking aloud," quoted in Hough 1997, 487, from Yevgenii Shaposhnikov, *Vybor,* 2d ed. (Moscow: Nezavisimoe Izdatel'stvo PIK, 1995), 138. The exchange, if true, is revealing. The August coup had clearly been illegal—the State Committee for the State of Emergency had usurped power by claiming that Gorbachev was too ill to carry out his duties. At the time of the Belovezhskaia meeting, however, Gorbachev was still the legally installed Soviet president and had Soviet law on his side. He could accordingly have declared presidential rule and ordered the military to fulfill its duty to protect the Soviet constitution and the Soviet state. That he did not do so suggests the extent to which Soviet law had lost virtually all legitimacy by late 1991.

74. *New York Times,* 10 December 1991.

75. *Rossisskaia gazeta,* 26 December 1991, *CDSP,* vol. 43, no. 54, 1.

76. Tatarstan was a special case that deserves mention. As we saw in chapter 4, Tatarstan, under the leadership of Mintimir Shaimiev, had been the most politically assertive of the RSFSR's autonomies as the "parade of sovereignties" had begun. Shaimiev made clear from the start, however, that his government would not demand full independence from Russia. Rather it would insist that as a "sovereign state" Tatarstan had a right to define its relationship with Russia on the basis of a bilateral treaty between formally equal partners (i.e., the Russian Federation and Tatarstan, not the Russian Federation and all the subjects of the federation). Tatarstan (along with Chechnya) would later refuse to sign a special federation treaty that Yeltsin sponsored in early 1992 in the hopes of formalizing the division of powers between Russia's newly independent federal government and the federation's constituent units. On March 20, 1992, less that two weeks before the federation treaty was scheduled for signing, Tatarstan conducted a referendum that asked, in artfully ambiguous language, "Do you agree that Tatarstan is a sovereign state and a subject of international law that is building relations with Russia and other republics and states on the basis of equal treaties?" The referendum was approved by

61.4 percent of the voters. Tatarstan never declared full independence, however, and in February 1994, after prolonged negotiations, it signed a bilateral treaty with Moscow that afforded the republic considerable autonomy. Tatarstan thereby managed to avoid a violent conflict with the Russian federal government over its status, unlike Chechnya, Edward W. Walker, "The Dog That Didn't Bark: Tatarstan and Asymmetrical Federalism in Russia," *Harriman Review* (Spring 1997).

77. Diane Curran, Fiona Hill, and Elena Kostritsyna, *The Search for Peace in Chechnya, A Sourcebook 1994–1996* (Cambridge, Mass.: Strengthening Democratic Institutions Project, John F. Kennedy School of Government, Harvard University, March 1997), 95.

78. Curran, Hill, and Kostritsyna 1997, 97.

79. For the sake of brevity, I will refer to the Crimean, Transdniestrian, and Gagauz republics as "autonomies" even though they had no legal status under Soviet law. Transdniestra and Gagauzia would eventually be afforded autonomous status under the Moldovan constitution adopted in July 1994. Crimea would likewise be designated an autonomy under Ukrainian law, but would later have that status rescinded (see below).

80. Furtado and Chandler 1992, 430. The declaration was in fact made at a joint session of the Karabakh legislature, the State Council, and the legislature of Shaumian district, which was located within Azerbaijan proper outside the borders of what had been Nagorno-Karabakh ASSR and which had a large Armenian population.

81. In fact, the April 1990 USSR law on secession gave autonomous areas a right not to independence but to remain a part of the USSR, and this only after a number of steps had been taken. Karabakh Armenians responded, however, that the USSR still formally existed at the time of its independence declaration, so it was a part of the USSR up until its dissolution, at which point it became independent by default.

82. Recall that the law required the union republics to take a number of steps before they could declare independence, including conducting two referendums (which the law on referendums had made illegal) and tallying the results of those referendums separately in the autonomies. Only then (presumably on the basis of a majority vote against secession, although this was not specified by the law) could the autonomies "decide independently the question of remaining in the USSR or within the seceding union republic, and also to raise the question of their own state-legal status." The claim of the Karabakh Armenians and the South Ossetians that Azerbaijan and Georgia did not have the right to nullify their status as autonomous districts (which they did) under Soviet law is more persuasive, although even here the Soviet constitution provided that only the status of autonomous republics, not autonomous oblasts, could not be changed without their approval—both Karabakh and South Ossetia were autonomous oblasts, not autonomous republics.

83. For example, neither Karabakh nor Armenia had the opportunity to carry out the two separate referendums on independence required by the April 1990 law. Azerbaijan made no pretense of even attempting to comply with the law, the necessary first step before Karabakh could exercise its right under the law to remain a part of the USSR.

84. The leaders of Abkhazia and South Ossetia publicly expressed their support for the coup. The Transdniestra Supreme Soviet was somewhat more equivocal, declaring that the legality of the Emergency Committee's declaration of emergency rule should be determined by the courts. The parliamentary leader of Checheno-Ingushetia, Doku Zavgaev, was in Moscow at the beginning of the coup and failed to condemn the putschists until it was clear that the coup was collapsing. The Presidium of the republic's Supreme Soviet also ordered the arrest of a leader of the nationalist forces in the republic, Zelimkhan Yandarbiev, while its Interior Ministry refused to carry out the orders of RSFSR

authorities. Mintimir Shaimiev, the influential leader of Tatarstan, flew to Moscow to confer with Gennadii Yanaev, one of the coup leaders, and then returned to his republic to make a radio address in which he asserted that the coup was justified and that the decrees of Yeltsin and the RSFSR had no legal force on Tatarstan territory.

85. *Izvestiia,* 10 December 1991, *CDSP,* vol. 43, no. 49, 7.
86. Brown 1996, 299.
87. Ericson 1995, 37.
88. Ericson 1995, 39, 49–50.

Chapter 7

Conclusion

There are two widespread but contradictory popular narratives of the Soviet dissolution. The first is particularly prevalent in the Soviet successor states and some parts of Eastern Europe. The second is particularly prevalent in the West and in the more successful post-Communist societies of Eastern Europe. The first is a story of historical tragedy, the second a heroic epic.

The essence of the first can be summarized as follows. The destruction of the "age-old," multinational, Tsarist/Soviet state was a historical crime carried out by a handful of willful politicians who brazenly ignored the objective interests of the Soviet peoples and their expressed preference for a preserved union. The perpetrators of the act—above all Yeltsin, but others as well—were motivated by a selfish desire to protect their positions and enhance their power at the expense of that hapless and ineffective defender of a renewed union, Mikhail Gorbachev. They were aided and abetted in their efforts by the West, the United States in particular, which very much favored the humbling and fragmentation of its principal strategic competitor. The consequence was a shattering of the complex web of social and economic linkages between myriad peoples and regions that had taken centuries to develop, followed by economic ruin, disorder, and conflict for the victims of the disaster—the beleaguered citizens of the former Soviet state.

The nostalgia this narrative suggests for the Soviet era is certainly understandable. The dissolution has indeed been followed by profound hardships for many, indeed most, citizens of the Soviet successor states—severe economic contractions, civil wars, violent ethnic conflicts, an explosive growth in crime, a collapse in social services, the undermining of traditional beliefs and mores, and the failure of new ideologies to persuade people that their future will be better than their miserable present. There is also a widespread sense of loss at no longer being citizens of a geographically enormous state and a global superpower. Even those former Soviet citizens who had no intention of ever leaving their union republics are today aware that they are no longer part "owners" of fourteen of the fifteen successor states—rather, they are foreigners in lands where they were once citizens, with all the symbolic and legal implications that alien status entails.

While understandable, this interpretation does not bear close scrutiny. It fails to acknowledge the genuine aspirations for independence in some of the union republics, above all in the Baltics. It underestimates the destabilizing role of the institutions and norms of Soviet federalism and the incoherence in the design of the "renewed union" championed by Gorbachev. It neglects the uncertainty and ambiguity that confronted key decision makers in 1990–1991, including Yeltsin and his colleagues at Belovezhskaia Pushcha. It exaggerates the extent to which Yeltsin in particular deliberately set about destroying the union. It misrepresents the position of Western governments and the international community, which overwhelmingly favored a reformed but preserved union. And above all, it exaggerates the economic and political benefits of a preserved union under the conditions prevailing in the USSR in the final years of its existence.

Indeed, the implication that the dissolution is responsible for the hardships the Soviet successor states have undergone since 1991 is a simplification of a complex reality. Economically, it is entirely unclear whether the successor states as a whole or individually would have been better off had the union remained intact. The USSR's economic difficulties long predated the "nationalities crisis" of the late 1980s and early 1990s, and reforming the USSR's centrally planned economy would have been a long and painful process under the best of circumstances. It is very unlikely that Gorbachev's "socialist market," even if implemented successfully, would have substantially improved performance, irrespective of the rise of antiunion sentiments in the union republics. Even less likely was a significant economic turnaround given the mounting political chaos in Moscow.

More broadly, the belief that there would have been great economic benefit to a preserved union rests on a common but erroneous assumption that there is a necessary and obvious economic advantage to larger national economies in terms of either territory or population. The claim, as we have seen, was asserted repeatedly by Gorbachev in advocating a preserved union. In fact, there is no such relationship. State size and economic performance vary independently, as numerous studies have shown.[1] Many small states—Luxembourg, Monaco, San Marino, Andora, Liechtenstein, and Singapore, to name but a few—are very prosperous. In contrast, the economic record of many of the world's largest countries—Congo, Nigeria, India, or indeed Russia itself—is poor in the extreme.[2] The postdissolution economic performance of the largest successor states—Russia, Ukraine, and Kazakhstan—has also been notably poorer than that of Estonia, Latvia, and Lithuania, despite dwarfing them in size.

Nor are the economic consequences of nonviolent secession or dissolution invariably negative. On the contrary, they are almost entirely a function of the policies adopted, and the institutions present, in the preexisting and succeeding states, policies, and institutions that can be infinitely varied. Certainly in some cases, economic costs can be considerable, especially if the governments involved adopt highly protectionist trade policies or otherwise mismanage the economy. But in other cases, particularly where there has been extreme economic mismanagement by an existing national government, the effect can be beneficial. Thus, it is not surprising that the economic record of the Czech Republic and Slovakia after their "velvet divorce" in 1993 has been better than that of many of the other post-Communist states of Eastern Europe, such as Romania or Bulgaria, that remained intact. Likewise, Slovenia, which unlike Croatia, Serbia, and Bosnia experienced very little violence during the fracturing of Yugoslavia, has had one of the better performing economies in the region in the 1990s.

In the Soviet case, it is impossible to estimate with any confidence the net costs and benefits of the dissolution over any particular time period for each successor state—there are too many variables and too much contingency, with indeterminacy growing the longer the time frame. For some republics, particularly those that were being subsidized by the center (notably, the Central Asian republics), doubtless short-term costs outweighed benefits. For others, however, the dissolution may have been a necessary, albeit not sufficient, condition for economic recovery. Certainly, there is little reason to believe that the Soviet government would have managed the national economy effectively. By 1991, its fiscal and monetary policies were entirely counterproductive, and it was clearly incapable of mustering the political will needed to reduce repressed inflation, free prices, create the legal and organizational infrastructure needed for a reasonably effective market economy, or begin the process of privatizing state industry. Union republics that managed to establish their own currencies and central banks were at least in a position to free themselves of monetary mismanagement by the center. Similarly, union republics that kept their own fiscal houses in order while ridding themselves of the burden of supporting an increasingly insolvent center were better off than those that remained tied to a debilitated and incoherent union government in Moscow.

Even the effect of the USSR's dissolution on interrepublic trade, and the relationship between interrepublic trade and economic performance, is unclear. Under most conditions, complex and long-distance trade is beneficial for national economies. However, marketizing an economy that has been centrally planned for over six decades necessarily entails the disruption of long-established production relations, which in the Soviet case included links between economic actors in different republics. Identifying, either a priori or ex post, which of these were sustainable under market conditions and which were not is impossible. Again, however, there is indirect evidence that the dissolution, and any disruption of interrepublic trade that it, rather than marketization, may have caused, was less costly than is often assumed. Those republics that were the most dependent upon interrepublic trade—Estonia, Latvia, and Lithuania—have fared much better than those that were less dependent, most notably Russia.

If the economic costs and benefits of the dissolution are impossible to assess with confidence, what of the political consequences? Again, it is a great oversimplification to conclude that elites gained but society lost. Rather, there were costs and benefits for both, and the balance was different for different republics (as it was for different individuals). The costs of no longer being a citizen of a vast state and a global superpower are balanced by the fact that those successor states with democratic or even semidemocratic regimes have governments that are less distant and alien from their citizenry than any all-union government, however democratic, could have possibly been. Titulars now have their "own" states, recognized as fully independent under international law and with the symbolic benefit of a seat alongside other "nation-states" in the UN General Assembly (and for Russia, on the Security Council as well). Titulars in the non-Russian republics are also free of the humiliation of being "lesser brothers" in the "brotherhood of peoples." The new states will also likely preserve titular languages and cultures more effectively, public goods that many consider of great value. Finally, for those who blame the dissolution for the former Soviet Union's ethnic and secessionist conflicts, most of those conflicts in fact predate the USSR's demise, and it is far from clear that a preserved union would have been any less susceptible to interethnic or secessionist violence.

The second interpretation of the Soviet dissolution contrasts dramatically with the first and is very widespread in the West. Here, the breakup, like decolonization before it, is viewed as an unambiguous triumph of justice. The "prison of nations" and the world's last great empire had met its inevitable fate, dispatched into history by the deeply rooted and hitherto repressed nationalist and separatist ambitions of the titular peoples of the USSR's union republics.

Again, this commonplace interpretation ignores the complexities and ambiguities of the USSR's demise. If the Soviet Union was indeed an "empire," it was certainly a peculiar one. For all its repressive character, the Soviet regime contributed to the entrenchment, and in some cases even the origin, of the national identities of its minority peoples. Particular nationalities were not denied citizenship, and neither did they suffer from legal discrimination (although some, particularly Jews, were discriminated against in practice). On the contrary, the great majority of nationalities were afforded cultural privileges and protections, while many benefited from preferential treatment within their "own" eponymous ethno-territorial homelands. These policies, along with threat of force and the repression of political nationalism, accounted for the interethnic peace that characterized most of the Soviet period. Even national minorities with histories of mutual enmity, such as the Azeris and Armenians, became habituated to treating each other with mutual respect, at least in public. If the USSR was a "prison of nations," by the late Soviet period it was a prison in which the inmates were not only safe from assault by their fellow prisoners but had collective privileges and protections unmatched in other imperial penitentiaries.

Nor was the breakup a triumph of "national self-determination" or "national liberation," at least in any obvious sense. Those titular "nations" that did not want independence—including at least the majority of titulars in the five Central Asian republics, Belarus, and (less clearly) Russia, who together constituted the great majority of the Soviet population—were hardly "liberated" by the Soviet Union's collapse. Nor was "self-determination" realized for those nationalities where separatist aspirations were high but that lacked their own union republics, such as the Chechens, the Abkhaz, the Karabakh Armenians, or (less clearly) the Volga Tatars.

Finally, one does not have to be an apologist for Soviet socialism, with its long record of violence against its citizenry and deepening systemic failures, to suggest that it might have been replaced by some kind of market democracy without fragmenting into fifteen successor states. Perhaps the secession of the Baltic republics, or of some of the other republics on the Soviet periphery, was inevitable with liberalization and democratization. But a different response from Gorbachev might well have led to the preservation of some kind of liberalized and democratized federated state.

If the dissolution was neither a capricious act of selfishness on the part of a subversive elite nor a triumph of national liberation, how best to characterize it? Normatively, the only defensible response is agnosticism. Large states are neither necessarily good nor necessarily bad, as suggested by the fact that normative political theory is virtually silent on the optimal boundaries of a political community. There is no objective formula for determining when a "people" becomes a "nation," when a "nation" deserves a state, or when a multicultural "nation" becomes an "empire." Neither does liberalism or democracy require that minorities be afforded a right of secession, despite the international community's ambivalent commitment to national self-determination. The only state today that provides for a constitutionally guaranteed right of secession is Ethiopia, and even there the mechanism for exercising that right is unspecified.[3] In short, the dissolution was not a Manichean struggle pitting good against evil—it had little to do with justice, one way or the other. For some individuals, and for some nationalities, it was doubtless objectively beneficial and subjectively desirable. For others, it was not.

If there is no obvious answer to the question of whether the dissolution was a net benefit to the USSR's former citizens, how then to explain it? As others have emphasized, preexisting antiunion sentiments and separatist aspirations certainly played a role, sentiments and aspirations that deepened and spread during perestroika, thanks in part to the USSR's mounting economic difficulties, policy errors by the central leadership, and demonstration effects whereby vanguard republics (Lithuania and Estonia especially) showed that antiunion mobilization was possible and consequential, as well as how best to effect it. Nevertheless, as the March 1991 referendum on the union showed conclusively, even at that late date the great majority of the Soviet electorate preferred a preserved union state.

The dissolution, in other words, was not simply demand driven. Equally important was the role played by the institutions and myths of Soviet federalism, institutions and myths that empowered the antiunion opposition, constrained the union's defenders, and induced Gorbachev to embrace a naive and highly ineffective program for preserving the USSR's territorial integrity. Likewise the form taken by the dissolution was intimately related to the institutions of Soviet federalism. Had Soviet ethnographers and constitutional drafters drawn the USSR's internal borders differently, today there might be an independent state of "Turkestan" in place of the five successor states of Central Asia; Karelia and Tatarstan might have seats at the United Nations; and Russia, Ukraine, Belarus, and northern Kazakhstan might have emerged as a single "Slavic" state. And certainly, the risk of bloodshed from any dissolution, had it occurred, would have been immeasurably greater in the absence of clearly delineated internal borders.

Less obvious is the way that Soviet myths and normative claims about the "friendship of peoples" influenced Gorbachev's response to the mounting nationality crisis. Like other Soviet leaders, Gorbachev attempted to represent his program as a return to traditional Soviet values and legitimizing myths, drawing in particular on the legacy of Lenin's advocacy of the moderate economic and social policies of the NEP (New Economic Policy) period.[4] He soon discovered, however, that antiunion challengers could do the same by stressing Lenin's advocacy of federalism, self-determination, and the right of secession for the union republics, all of which was effectively subsumed under the mobilizing slogan of "sovereignty."

The putative "sovereignty" of the union republics was in fact a formal attribute that remained uninterpreted by either judicial rulings or practice, and the term therefore entered the Gorbachev era trailing clouds of ambiguity. In but one of the many ironies of the dissolution, its very ambiguity helps account for its extraordinary efficacy as a political weapon in the hands of the antiunion opposition. Antiunion challengers could employ the slogan as a cover, arguing that it implied a unilateral right to full independence to one audience while posing as defenders of Leninist principles to another. Multiple meanings also made it particularly effective as a unifying slogan for an antiunion opposition that was in fact very diverse in its political preferences. The term was ideologically ambivalent, being neither overtly pro-Western, procapitalist, nor prodemocratic, and it could therefore be embraced simultaneously by liberal democrats, democratic socialists, and nationalists alike. Above all, it served as a mechanism for facilitating the transfer of loyalty of Party officials from the center to the republics. Communists could invoke Lenin's support for national self-determination and the right of secession to advocate genuine autonomy and eventually full independence for the union republics. This proved particularly important in the Baltic republics in the early stages of nationalist mobilization, facilitating the support given to the opposition by the local Party leadership. And it proved equally important in 1990–1991 in the RSFSR, where being pro-Western, pro-capitalist, or prodemocratic could be interpreted as anti-Russian because of the privileged position of Russians in the Soviet "union of nations." The slogan, "Sovereignty for the RSFSR!" in contrast, was almost as easy for Aleksandr Rutskoi and his allies in the moderate wing of the Communist Party of the Russian Federation to employ as it was for liberals and social democrats.

"Sovereignty" thus proved an explosive political weapon, wielded against the center by a broad coalition of political forces in the union republics. By early 1988, Gorbachev found himself confronting an ever-escalating set of claims associated with increasingly radical interpretations of the term's meaning. In effect, the "war of sovereignties" became a war of interpretation, with meaning becoming concretized, step by step, through practice.

As a champion of "socialist democratization" and a "socialist rule of law," and doubtless due to a personal aversion to violence as well, Gorbachev was extremely reluctant to respond to the "sovereignty campaign" with repression. He was also increasingly constrained from resorting to force by his desire to maintain a benign international atmosphere and his need for financial and political support from the West. But Gorbachev was deeply influenced by traditional Soviet propaganda about nationality policy and nationalism as well. He wanted above all to preserve the "friendship of peoples," and he concluded that the best way to do so was to return to what he understood to be the original principles of Leninist federalism (principles that he felt had been egregiously violated by Stalin)—the reaffirmation of the USSR as a voluntary union of equal and "sovereign" states, joined together in a single "union state" in which power would be delegated to an all-union government by means of a mutually agreed-upon treaty. Gorbachev, perhaps under the influence of his legal training, thus made the fateful mistake of taking literally language that, on the face of it at least, was couched in the legalistic and rationalist tradition of the enlightenment but that in fact had been adopted originally for narrow political reasons and that had long since been transformed into a sacralized origin myth for the Soviet state.

Gorbachev thus stubbornly adhered to the seemingly contradictory nationalities policy elaborated in the CPSU platform of 1989—implacable opposition to secession and the transformation of the USSR into a truly voluntary union. In doing so, he abandoned the one myth of Soviet federalism—the right of secession—that might have helped to preserve the union, while he embraced others that would have been far better ignored—above all, the voluntary delegation of powers by the union republics to the federal center through a union treaty. Had a reasonable law on secession provided its most recalcitrant members—particularly the Baltic states, but perhaps others as well—with a meaningful opportunity to opt out, the center could then have amended the national constitution to provide for a practicable division of powers between the center and the remaining republics. That arrangement could in turn have been legitimated through a clearly worded national referendum, which almost certainly would have been easily approved, as the results of the March 1991 referendum suggest. Defenders of the union would then have been able to draw on their ultimate trump card—the great reluctance of the international community to sanction the USSR's breakup or legitimate unilateral secession from a legally recognized state. Had a republic other than Estonia, Latvia, and Lithuania, whose incorporation had never been recognized as legal by Western governments, declared independence in violation of Soviet law, it would have met the same reception from the international community as Chechnya, Abkhazia, South Ossetia, Karabakh, and Transdniestra have today.

Instead, Gorbachev's strategy required that the executives and legislatures of all fifteen union republics—and to a degree those of all the autonomies as well—negotiate and approve a new foundational document. Each republic was thus effectively able to exercise veto power over the treaty's terms. By the time the federal government agreed to recognize the independence of the Baltic republics, it was too late. The center was by then hopelessly weak, the federal system provided for in Gorbachev's proposed union treaty entirely impractical. Like the United States under the Articles of Confederation, or like Yugoslavia under its constitution of 1974, the new union would have been highly unstable and in all likelihood short-lived had the coup not intervened to prevent its ratification. Even then, Gorbachev would spend his final months in office promoting a decidedly less practical version of his cherished union treaty.

There is another irony in the efficacy of "sovereignty" as a solvent to the USSR's territorial integrity. As discussed in chapter 2, it was a largely contingent phenomenon. The establishment of the USSR as a formally federal state was a political choice made by political actors making decisions in chaotic conditions and under considerable time pressure. These actors had only a very limited understanding of the long-term implications of their decisions. Certainly Lenin had no idea that his decision to equate self-determination with secession in 1913 would mean that a right of secession would be included in the first Soviet constitution—indeed, at the time he had no idea that a socialist revolution in Tsarist Russia was imminent. Nor could he or the other Bolshevik leaders have anticipated that his embrace of federalism for the RSFSR in 1917–1918 or for the USSR in 1921–1922 would lead to the particular federal structure or the internal borders that Gorbachev inherited in 1985. Least of all did they anticipate that the Soviet Union's federal system would facilitate the fragmentation of the USSR. Had Lenin taken different positions on the meaning of "self-determination" and "sovereignty" or on Soviet-style ethno-federalism and the formal right of secession, or had he been incapacitated in 1918 instead of 1922, Stalin's autonomization plan might well have been adopted. The Soviet state would then have been a collection of numerous "autonomies," none of which would have had a formal right of secession and all of which would have possessed effectively equal rights with the nonethnic oblasts and krais. Alternatively, the Bolsheviks might well have established a unitary state, like the great majority of Communist states established by Moscow in East Central Europe after World War II.

The breakup of the Soviet Union was thus a dramatic, and at the same time rather peculiar, case of institutional path dependency. Decisions about institutional design made with limited information and in the heat of political battle ended up having enormously important, but unforeseen and unforeseeable, consequences decades later. What was peculiar about the Soviet case was that many of its institutions, including many of its institutions of federalism, were through the great bulk of Soviet history principally symbolic in function and mythological in character, with little or no practical or legal meaning. Above all, the right of secession was understood to be no right at all. Nevertheless, it proved to be a "legal boomerang" that would play a crucial role in the breakup of the Soviet state. That part of the Soviet edifice that had rested originally on the legal-rationalist discourse of the enlightenment, with its faith in social progress through the scientific crafting of social institutions, came to life in a moment of crisis, a resurrection that would have fatal consequences for the state.

There is yet a final, less obvious irony to the role played by "sovereignty" in the USSR's dissolution. The adoption of the term as the central slogan of the antiunion opposition helped to obfuscate about what the different actors engaged in the negotiations over the union treaty actually wanted, and what, exactly, was at stake in the struggle over the design of the "renewed union." Endless debate about the meaning of "sovereignty," and about related terms such as "self-determination," "territorial integrity," "federalism," "confederation," "autonomy," "union," and "commonwealth," meant that even those directly involved in the negotiating process could not be sure what their interlocutors were striving for. This semantic confusion contributed at the same time to unrealistic expectations about the prospects and significance of the CIS on the part of some of its founders. The formation of the CIS was not, as we have seen, the product of carefully designed plans based on informed assessments of costs and benefits and a good understanding of the implications of alternative institutional arrangements. On the contrary, it was, like the formation of the USSR before it, a product of rapidly changing political exigencies and decisions made in a dense fog of political warfare. As it turned out, the CIS was not, as Yeltsin argued, the only way to preserve some kind of meaningful union. Instead, it would mean no union at all.

Notes

1. Alberto Alesina and Enrico Spolaore, "On the Number and Size of Nations," *Quarterly Journal of Economics* 112, no. 4 (1995): 1027–57; Peter J. Katzenstein, *Small States in World Markets: Industrial Policy in Europe* (Ithaca, N.Y.: Cornell University Press, 1985).

2. World Bank, *World Development Report 1997* (Washington, D.C.: World Bank, 1998).

3. The Canadian federal government's position on secession deserves a word of explanation here. Canada's Supreme Court issued a rather ambiguous "advisory opinion" to the federal government on 20 August 1998 in which it confirmed that Canada's provinces—notably Quebec—do not have a unilateral right of secession under either the Ca-

nadian constitution or international law. It went on, however, to assert that democratic principles would require the federal government to amend the constitution should a provincial majority vote for secession in a referendum (a position, it bears noting, that Abraham Lincoln did not share). The key passage in the ruling reads as follows: "A clear majority vote in Quebec on a clear question in favor of secession would confer democratic legitimacy on the secession initiative which all of the other participants in the Confederation would have to recognize" (*The National Law Journal,* The New York Law Publishing Company, 31 August 1998). What exactly "recognize" meant was left unclear.

4. George W. Breslauer, *Khrushchev and Brezhnev as Leaders: Building Authority in Soviet Politics* (Boston: George Allen & Unwin, 1982); and Breslauer 2002.

Suggested Additional Readings in English on Perestroika and the Breakup of the USSR

The best general treatments of the politics of the Gorbachev period in English are Dunlop 1993; Brown 1996; Hough 1997; McFaul 2001; and Breslauer 2002. There are also many good biographies of Gorbachev and Yeltsin, including Medvedev 1986; Doder and Branson 1990; and Kaiser 1991 on Gorbachev, and Morrison 1991 and Aron 2000 on Yeltsin. Memoirs of key figures include Yeltsin 1990, Ligachev 1993; Yeltsin 1994; Gorbachev 1995; Grachev 1995; Matlock 1995; Pankin 1996, Palazchenko 1997; Bush and Scowcroft 1998; and Chernyaev 2000. The best firsthand account of the perestroika period by a Western journalist is Remnick 1993. Three excellent books on the Soviet "nationality question" cover the Gorbachev period (Suny 1993; Kaiser 1994; Tishkov 1997), while three others compare the dissolution of Czechoslovakia, Yugoslavia, and/or the Soviet Union (Lukic and Lynch 1996; Janos 1997; and Bunce 1999). A very useful compilation of primary materials can be found in Furtado and Chandler 1992. The best analysis of the "demand side" of the Soviet dissolution is Beissinger 2002. Finally, many works focus on nationalist mobilization in individual union republics, including Senn 1990; Dunlop 1993; Karklins 1993; Leiven 1993; Kuzio and Wilson 1994; Fish 1995; Dawson 1996; and Szporluk 2000.

Aron, Leon. *Yeltsin: A Revolutionary Life*. New York: St. Martin's Press, 2000.

Beissinger, Mark R. *Nationalist Mobilization and the Collapse of the Soviet State*. New York: Cambridge University Press, 2002.

Beschloss, Michael R., and Strobe Talbott. *At the Highest Levels: The Inside Story of the End of the Cold War*. New York: Back Bay Books, 1994.

Breslauer, George W. *Gorbachev and Yeltsin As Leaders*. New York: Cambridge University Press, 2002.

Brown, Archie. *The Gorbachev Factor*. New York: Oxford University Press, 1996.

Bunce, Valerie. *Subversive Institutions: The Design and the Destruction of Socialism and the State*. New York: Cambridge University Press, 1999.

Bush, George, and Brent Scowcroft. *A World Transformed*. New York: Alfred A. Knopf, 1998.

Chernyaev, Anatoly S. *My Six Years with Gorbachev*. Translated by Robert D. English and Elizabeth Tucker. University Park: Pennsylvania State University Press, 2000.

Dawson, Jane I. *Eco-Nationalism: Anti-Nuclear Activism and National Identity in Russia, Lithuania, and Ukraine*. Durham, N.C.: Duke University Press, 1996.

Doder, Dusko, and Louise Branson. *Gorbachev: Heretic in the Kremlin*. New York: Viking Press, 1990.

Dunlop, John B. *The Rise of Russia and the Fall of the Soviet Empire*. Princeton, N.J.: Princeton University Press, 1993.

Fish, M. Steven. *Democracy from Scratch: Opposition and Regime in the New Russian Revolution*. Princeton, N.J.: Princeton University Press, 1995.

Fowkes, Ben. *The Disintegration of the Soviet Union: A Study in the Rise and Triumph of Nationalism*. New York: St. Martin's Press, 1997.

Furtado, Charles F., Jr., and Andrea Chandler, eds. *Perestroika in the Soviet Republics: Documents on the National Question*. Boulder, Colo.: Westview Press, 1992.

Gorbachev, Mikhail. *Memoirs*. Translated by Georges Peronansky and Tatjana Varsavsky. New York: Doubleday, 1995.

Grachev, Andrei S. *Final Days: The Inside Story of the Collapse of the Soviet Union*. Translated by Margo Milne. Boulder, Colo.: Westview Press, 1995.

Hough, Jerry F. *Democratization and Revolution in the USSR 1985–1991*. Washington, D.C.: Brookings, 1997.

Janos, Andrew C. *Czechoslovakia and Yugoslavia: Ethnic Conflict and the Dissolution of Multinational States*. Berkeley: International and Area Studies, University of California, Berkeley, 1997.

Kaiser, Robert G. *Why Gorbachev Happened: His Triumphs and Failures*. New York: Simon & Schuster, 1991.

Kaiser, Robert J. *The Geography of Nationalism in Russia and the USSR*. Princeton, N.J.: Princeton University Press, 1994.

Karklins, Rasma. *Ethnopolitics and Transition to Democracy: The USSR and Latvia*. Baltimore: Johns Hopkins University Press, 1993.

Kuzio, Taras, and Andrew Wilson. *Ukraine: Perestroika to Independence*. New York: St. Martin's Press, 1994.

Leiven, Anatol. *The Baltic Revolution*. New Haven, Conn.: Yale University Press, 1993.

Ligachev, Yegor. *Inside Gorbachev's Kremlin: The Memoirs of Yegor Ligachev*. Translated by Catherine A. Fitzpatrick, Michele A. Berdy, and Dobrochna Cyrcz-Freeman. New York: Random House, 1993.

Lukic, Reneo, and Allen Lynch. *Europe from the Balkans to the Urals: The Disintegration of Yugoslavia and the Soviet Union*. New York: Oxford University Press, 1996.

Matlock, Jack F., Jr. *Autopsy on an Empire: The American Ambassador's Account of the Collapse of the Soviet Union*. New York: Random House, 1995.

McFaul, Michael. *Russia's Unfinished Revolution: Political Change from Gorbachev to Putin*. Ithaca, N.Y.: Cornell University Press, 2001.

Medvedev, Zhores A. *Gorbachev*. New York: W. W. Norton & Co., 1986.

Morrison, John. *Boris Yeltsin: From Bolshevik to Democrat*. New York: Dutton, 1991.

Musil, Jiri, ed. *The End of Czechoslovakia*. Budapest: Central European Press, 1995.

Palazchenko, Pavel. *My Years with Gorbachev and Shevardnadze: The Memoir of a Soviet Interpreter*. University Park: Pennsylvania State University Press, 1997.

Pankin, Boris. *The Last Hundred Days of the Soviet Union.* Translated by Alexei Pankin. London: I. B. Tauris, 1996.

Remnick, David. *Lenin's Tomb: The Last Days of the Soviet Empire*. New York: Random House, 1993.

Senn, Alfred Erich. *Gorbachev's Failure in Lithuania*. New York: St. Martin's Press, 1995.

———. *Lithuania Awakening*. Berkeley: University of California Press, 1990.

Silber, Laura, and Allen Little. *Yugoslavia: Death of a Nation*. New York: Penguin USA (TV Books), 1996.

Solnick, Steven. *Stealing the State: Control and Collapse of Soviet Institutions*. Cambridge, Mass.: Harvard University Press, 1996.

Stein, Eric, and Lloyd Cutler. *Czecho/Slovakia: Ethnic Conflict, Constitutional Fissure, Negotiated Breakup*. Ann Arbor: University of Michigan Press, 2000.

Strayer, Robert W. *Why Did the Soviet Union Collapse? Understanding Historical Change*. Armonk, N.Y.: M. E. Sharpe, 1998.

Suny, Ronald Grigor. *The Revenge of the Past: Nationalism, Revolution, and the Collapse of the Soviet Union*. Stanford, Calif.: Stanford University Press, 1993.

Szporluk, Roman. *Russia, Ukraine, and the Breakup of the Soviet Union*. Stanford, Calif.: Hoover Institution Press, 2000.

Tishkov, Valeriei A. *Ethnicity, Nationalism, and Conflict in and after the Soviet Union: The Mind Aflame*. Thousand Oaks, Calif.: Sage, 1997.

Woodward, Susan L. *Balkan Tragedy: Chaos and Dissolution after the Cold War*. Washington, D.C.: Brookings, 1995.

Yeltsin, Boris. *Against the Grain: An Autobiography*. Translated by Michael Glenny. New York: Summit Books, 1990.

———. *The Struggle for Russia*. Translated by Catherine A. Fitzpatrick. New York: Times Books, 1994.

Index

Abdulatipov, Ramazan, 95, 100
Abkhazia, 12, 36, 39, 67, 74, 88-89, 92, 96, 130, 164, 165-66, 167, 168, 177n84, 186
Adygeia, 96
Allison, Graham, 122
Alma Ata Accord, 162-63
Alma Ata riots, 56, 58, 70, 82n3
Andropov, Yurii, 44, 56
Armenia, 27, 32, 39, 57, 64, 103, 110, 115, 129, 135n67, 139, 140, 141, 147, 166; earthquake in, 66-67; sovereignty declaration, 63-64, 83n22, 99n27, 105
autonomies (ASSRs, AOs, okrugs), 2-3, 29, 31, 49n27, 88, 117, 123, 166, 177n79; delineation of powers and, 5, 12-13, 33, 37, 73-74, 90-91, 97n10, 115, 120-21, 133n11, 166-67; independence declarations, 165; international community and, 12-13, 167; Law on Secession (USSR) and, 74, 91, 165-66, 177n82; mobilization against union republics, 71-72, 75, 81, 88-89, 92, 94-97, 102; sovereignty and, 5-6, 91, 93-95, 176n76; sovereignty declarations, 96; support for attempted coup, 166, 177n84; union treaty and, 105, 115, 116, 119-21, 130, 135n68, 150, 166. *See also individual autonomies*
autonomous district (okrug). *See* autonomies
autonomous oblast (AO). *See* autonomies
Autonomous Soviet Socialist Republic (ASSR). *See* autonomies
autonomy, concept of, 7, 24, 94, 98
Azerbaijan, 27, 32, 38, 42, 57, 64, 92, 109-10, 115, 118, 129, 140, 141, 144, 177n83

Baltic republics: demonstrations in, 57; economic autonomy, 43-44, 58, 72-73, 170; ethnic violence in, 56-57; incorporation into USSR, 32,

About the Author

Edward W. Walker is executive director of the Berkeley Program in Soviet and Post-Soviet Studies and adjunct associate professor in the Department of Political Science at the University of California, Berkeley.